LATER CRIMINAL CAREERS

Later Criminal Careers

SHELDON/and ELEANOR) GLUECK *1896-*

NEW YORK

1937

Reprinted with the permission of
Sheldon and Eleanor T. Glueck

KRAUS REPRINT CORPORATION
New York
1966

Printed in U.S.A.

AUTHORS' PREFACE

IT was not until some years after *500 Criminal Careers** had been published, that the wisdom of continuing follow-up studies of this and other groups of criminals over successive five-year periods became evident. This volume comprises the first of these further follow-up investigations, which we hope to be able to continue, in order to complete the life cycle of a group of criminals.

With the generous financial aid of the Milton Fund of Harvard University and, later, the Commonwealth Fund of New York, we have been able to restudy the five hundred former inmates of the Massachusetts Reformatory (originally reported in *500 Criminal Careers*) over a second five-year period that has elapsed since the expiration of their sentences from the Reformatory.

In the course of this research, which has taken four years to complete, we have had to depend on the cooperation and good will of hundreds of officials of public and private agencies throughout Massachusetts and other states. Without their sincere interest in the purpose of our investigations, it would have been quite impossible to amass and verify the necessary materials. We are particularly indebted to the Massachusetts Department of Correction, the Massachusetts Board of Probation, the Massachusetts Department of Mental Diseases, the Massachusetts Department of Public Safety, and the Boston Social Service Index. Although we cannot thank personally all the members of these organizations, we should like particularly to express our appreciation to Commissioner Arthur Lyman, Miss Florence King, Mr. Seymour Stone, and Mr. Richard Winslow of the Department of Correction; to Commissioner Albert Carter and Miss Mary Sweeney of the Board of Probation; to Dr. Winfred Overholser, until recently Commissioner of Mental Diseases; to Mr. Roscoe Hill and Miss Carrie V. Moyer of the Fingerprint Division of the Department of Public Safety;

---

* New York, Alfred A. Knopf, 1930.

and to Miss Laura G. Woodberry of the Boston Social Service Index.

To the many court, police, and probation officers throughout Massachusetts and other states, to social workers in and outside of Massachusetts who have in one way or another assisted us in our investigations, and to the many unnamed private individuals who have been kind enough to respond to our requests for information, we are sincerely grateful.

As in our previous investigations, our thanks are due to Professor Earnest Hooton of the Anthropology Department of Harvard University for his generously given advice during the progress of the research; and to Mrs. Sarah Cotton, a member of Professor Hooton's statistical staff, for doing many of the machine tabulations.

We wish also to express our gratitude to Dr. Carl Doering of the Harvard School of Public Health for his very able assistance to us in connection with the handling of certain statistical problems encountered in this research.

To the members of our research staff, Mrs. Mildred P. Cunningham and Mr. Samuel C. Lawrence, and to our secretaries, Mrs. Miriam B. Sachs, and Mrs. Beatrice C. Scheff, we owe much for their enthusiastic participation in the various aspects of this investigation. We want also to thank Mr. Benedict Alper and Mrs. Henry Feild for part-time work on certain details of this study.

To former Dean Roscoe Pound of the Harvard Law School and to Acting Dean Edmund Morgan, we wish to express our appreciation for their continued facilitation of our work.

Our thanks are due to Alfred A. Knopf for permission to use those findings of the prior research published in *500 Criminal Careers* which are relevant to the present study, as well as the definitions of certain terms in Appendix B which originally appeared in *500 Criminal Careers* and *500 Delinquent Women*.

It would take very many pages to acknowledge fully our indebtedness to all those who have in one way or another contributed to the gathering of the detailed data upon which this work is based. We want them to know how truly grateful we are, and hope that we may count on their continuing interest in our researches.

E. T. G.
S. G.

Harvard Law School
January, 1937

CONTENTS

Chapter I

INTRODUCTION

IN 1930 we presented the results of an investigation into the careers of 510 young-adult male offenders who had been incarcerated in the Massachusetts Reformatory.[1] That study embraced the activities of the offenders before their sentence to the Reformatory, during their incarceration, while on supervised liberty under parole, and, most significant, during a five-year period following the completion of their sentences.[2] The offenders in question were of a median age of somewhat over twenty years on entering the institution. The majority of the young men (61 per cent) had entered the Reformatory in the years 1916–1917, and the sentences of the entire group expired during the years 1921–1922. However, half the men had left the institution in the years 1917–1918 and 17 per cent more during 1919–1920.

By the close of the five-year post-parole period, a total of 55 of the original army of 510 men had been claimed by death, 11 having passed away in the Reformatory, 22 during parole, and 22 during the five-year period. One man died only two days after the end of the post-parole period, making a total of 56 men no longer alive at the beginning of the second five-year period. They are therefore not the concern of the present work.

When the original investigation was undertaken in 1925,[3] there was no plan for a *continuous* tracing of the careers of the 510 former inmates of the Massachusetts Reformatory. This was suggested later after the completion of another follow-up study, *One Thousand Juvenile Delinquents*,[4] in which it was discovered that

---

[1] *500 Criminal Careers*, New York, Alfred A. Knopf, 1930.

[2] All but thirty-six of the 510 offenders embraced in *500 Criminal Careers* were released on parole for varying periods. The thirty-six were compelled to serve the entire sentence in the Reformatory.

[3] Under the sponsorship of the Department of Social Ethics, Harvard University, and financed by the Milton Fund of Harvard University.

[4] Cambridge, Harvard University Press, 1934. (Harvard Law School Survey of Crime and Criminal Justice in Boston, Volume I.)

the rate of recidivism of the more youthful offenders embraced in that study was somewhat greater than in the older group of offenders previously investigated. This finding, together with reflection upon other suggestive evidence, led us to the decision to pursue, for as long as possible, further investigations into the later careers of the ex-inmates of the Reformatory (and of other groups of criminals) to determine what changes occur in their criminal and other behavior with the passing of the years. This project should be of value both as a contribution to knowledge and as a basis for improving correctional policies and practices.

In the present volume is reported the first of these continuing re-studies of offenders. It embraces their activities during the second five-year period following the expiration of their sentence from the Reformatory. Although the research was originally concerned with 510 men, it is perforce now narrowed to the 454 surviving at the beginning of the second five-year period. The reader interested in a detailed analysis of the previous histories of these men is invited to consult the prior work, *500 Criminal Careers,* as well as Appendix C of the present volume, in which latter appear in conveniently summarized form the tables on which the first follow-up study was based.

In the present volume we shall only briefly review the status of the group as a whole up to the end of the first five-year period; and from Chapter II on our interest will center upon the 454 men who were living at the beginning of the second period.

Relevant Findings of 500 Criminal Careers

The salient findings of the prior research that are more or less relevant to the present study may be summarized as follows:

FAMILY BACKGROUND

(a) Fifteen per cent of the families of the ex-prisoners were dependent on social agencies or on relatives for support; almost 60 per cent more were in marginal circumstances, i.e., living on their daily earnings and saving little or nothing—and this in a non-depression period. In 28 per cent of the cases the mother worked outside the home, to supplement the family income. Almost 60 per cent of the families had been dealt with by some 600 social welfare agencies (largely relief organizations). As might be expected, almost 65 per cent of the fathers of the men were either unskilled or semi-skilled laborers.

(b) In only 13 per cent of instances did one or both parents of our men have even a common school education.

(c) In 60 per cent of the cases an abnormal, frequently unhealthy, home situation existed by reason of the prolonged or complete absence from the household of one or both parents; in 70 per cent of these cases the rift in the home occurred when our youths were at the impressionable and formative ages of fourteen or less.

(d) The Reformatory inmates came from families appreciably larger than the average.

(e) Over half the families of the offenders had an official record of arrest or commitment for various offenses prior to the sentence of our young men; and 30 per cent more contained members who were delinquent and criminal, but who for some reason had not been arrested.

(f) While complete and reliable data regarding the mental condition of the parents or other near blood relatives of the offenders were impossible to obtain, in at least 17 per cent of the families a condition of mental disease or defect was noted.

PRE-REFORMATORY HISTORY OF THE OFFENDERS

(a) The group contained two and a half times the number of native-born sons of foreign or mixed parentage than was found in the general population. This raises the question of the difficulty of adjustment between parents with Old World ideals and customs and children of the New World. On the other hand, there were two and a half times as many foreign-born of foreign parentage in the general male adult population as in the Reformatory group, indicating that it is not foreign birth *per se* that is associated with criminality.

(b) Four-fifths of the group had left the family roof at a very early age and for unusual reasons.

(c) The young men had been characterized by a widespread prevalence of various demoralizing habits and vices before entering the Reformatory. Thus 40 per cent had markedly vicious habits (drinking, gambling, and the like) and 95 per cent had demoralizing associates. At least 85 per cent had never been absorbed into organizations for the wholesome use of leisure. Poor church attendance characterized the group.

(d) To a far greater extent than the normal youth population, these young men were retarded educationally.

(e) They entered early in life into industrial competition, acquired poor work habits, and were largely unskilled workers.

(f) They manifested delinquent or criminalistic trends at very early ages, these resulting in arrests and imprisonments for various offenses (in many instances on more than one occasion) preceding their sentence to the Reformatory.

(g) In substantial measure, they had an abnormal mental make-up, as evidenced by a considerable incidence of mental defect and other forms of pathology; that is, a fifth were feebleminded, a fifth were psychopathic personalities (3 per cent with definite psychoses), and a high proportion had notable temperamental-emotional handicaps.

REFORMATORY HISTORY

(a) While 17 per cent of the men committed no offenses in the Reformatory, an average of more than six violations of the rules was chargeable to the group as a whole, there having been more than 3,200 breaches of institutional rules, half of them of a serious nature.

(b) Almost 70 per cent of the men attending school in the Reformatory did not advance beyond the sixth grade.

(c) Although 80 per cent of the men were occupied at one or more institutional trades long enough to acquire a rudimentary knowledge of them, only 17 per cent (in the opinion of the trade school teachers themselves) were sufficiently equipped upon their release to earn a good living in these trades. However, in more than 70 per cent of the cases their occupational status had been more or less improved.

PAROLE HISTORY

Of special significance, both in the investigation previously reported upon and in that which forms the basis of the present volume, is the parole history of these men. The theory of parole is that most prisoners ordinarily arrive at a stage in their incarceration when further stay in the institution will be of less value both to them and the public than a period spent in supervised freedom in the community.[5] The intermediate stage of limited oversight between absolute control in a peno-correctional institution and absolute freedom in the community is thus, in a sense, a testing-ground of the prisoner's capacity ultimately to stand on his own feet after all restraint is removed. It also affords an opportunity to aid the offender in making the always difficult adjustment of the transitional period between prison life and life on the outside. Consequently, adequate supervision of the parolee is of the utmost significance in the administration of such a service.

The major findings in respect to the parole of 474 of the 510 men who were released for community oversight may be summarized as follows:

(a) In about half the cases the period of oversight of the parolees by the parole agents fell short of the theoretical length of the parole period. The discrepancy was in fact so marked that while the average theoretical parole period was about forty months, the average *actual* span of supervision was but eighteen. As further indicating the imperfection of parole supervision, it was found that

[5] Prison Association of New York, *Prison Progress in 1916: 72d Annual Report,* New York, the Association, 1917, p. 72.

over half the parolees were not once visited personally on the initiative of the parole agent himself; and in another third the parolees were not personally seen oftener than on an average of once in six or more months. Finally, in only 12 per cent of the cases was the employment required by the parole board as a condition precedent to the prisoner's release secured by the parole agents.

From these and other findings, it was established that the parole supervision of the ex-prisoners fell below, not only the ideal, but the standard.[6]

(b) Doubtless the very imperfect parole oversight had something to do with, although it was not completely to blame for, the poor behavior of the parolees in supervised freedom. Two-fifths (43 per cent) of the 474 men who were released on parole had their permits to be at liberty officially revoked by the parole board either because of violation of the conditions (some of them on more than one occasion), or because of resentence to the Reformatory for new crimes.[7] And even among the 271 men whose parole permits were not revoked by the parole board, or who were not returned to the Reformatory, over 7 per cent were arrested or were wanted on a warrant issued by the police; 5 per cent were arrested and sentenced to other institutions; and 8 per cent failed to make their whereabouts known to the parole board (thereby violating an obviously important condition of parole). If to the number whose permits were officially revoked, are added the 59 men who had grossly misbehaved with knowledge of the parole board (but who for some reason did not have their permits revoked), and the 25 parolees who misconducted themselves without knowledge of the officials, the number of failures on parole mounts to 287 of the 474 parolees, or 61 per cent.

(c) Violations of parole conditions were generally most frequent within a short time after the prisoners' release on parole—a finding

---

[6] Parole administration in Massachusetts has been improved in recent years.

[7] About 70 per cent of the revocations were ordered because the parolees had committed new crimes.

indicating the great importance of careful, intensive supervision of ex-prisoners during the hazardous transitional stage between incarceration and complete freedom.

(d) The industrial instability of the men and the obtaining of jobs merely to satisfy one of the technical conditions precedent to parole are illustrated by the fact that 59 per cent of the parolees held their first job following release from the Reformatory for a month or less if at all, and by the further finding that at least a fifth of all jobs of the parole period were abandoned by the parolees for reasons not reflecting credit upon them.

CRIMINAL CONDUCT DURING FIRST FIVE-YEAR FOLLOW-UP PERIOD

We come now to the crucial matter of the criminal careers of these young ex-inmates of the Reformatory during the first five-year period following completion of their sentences.[8]

(a) First and foremost, a total of 333 men, or almost 80 per cent of the 422 men whose conduct beyond the parole period could be ascertained, committed offenses during the five-year period following the expiration of their sentences. This dismal record contrasts sharply with the optimistic estimates previously made, and since reiterated in certain quarters, that some 75 per cent to 95 per cent of parolees are "successes" on parole and, by implication, are successes thereafter. As was stressed in *500 Criminal Careers,* the significance of this fundamental and irrefutable finding can hardly be overestimated. At least it shows that nothing less than a painstaking and unbiased search for the post-parole histories of former inmates of peno-correctional institutions can answer the crucial question: What happens to ex-prisoners?

[8] This period was of course of equal length for all the offenders investigated, but it should be borne in mind that: (a) in the case of thirty-six of the men who were kept incarcerated throughout their sentences the five-year follow-up period was not preceded by a parole period, and (b) in the case of the others, the parole periods preceding the five-year follow-up period were of varying lengths, depending upon the size of the original sentences and upon the differing proportions of such sentences that were served on parole as opposed to imprisonment.

The 307 men whose criminal conduct was officially recorded[9] committed at least 1,014 known offenses during the post-parole period,[10] in addition to which there were 49 sentences to penal institutions for crimes committed before the technical expiration of the parole period and served for part or all of the post-parole period. The average frequency with which these men committed officially recognized offenses was once every 24.2 months; but there was much variation in frequency, so that at one end of the scale 55 (20 per cent) of the men committed offenses as frequently as once every six months while at the other end 40 (14.6 per cent) were arrested only once during the entire five-year period.[11] The intensity of their recidivism may be inferred from the further finding that 111 of 260 arrested men,[12] or 43 per cent, had been apprehended three or more times—many of them seven or more times—during the five-year post-parole period.

A third of the offenses committed by the 307 men during the period following expiration of sentence were classifiable as major; two-thirds as minor.[13] Property crimes comprised 70 per cent of the

[9] The figure of 333 mentioned above includes offenders whose misconduct had not been officially recorded.

[10] There were 938 arrests (about 92 per cent of the 1,014 infractions involved), of which 811 (86.5 per cent) resulted in convictions; 17 warrants for arrest were issued; there were 7 escapes from penal institutions, following which apparently no warrants had been issued; there were 23 dishonorable discharges from the army or navy, of which 12 were due to desertions; and there were 29 more desertions.

[11] This computation is based on a total of 275 men. The difference between the 307 men who committed officially recorded offenses and the 275 comprised cases in which for one reason or another the average number of arrests could not be calculated, as for example because the offender had been in penal institutions throughout the period.

[12] Forty-seven of the 307 post-parole offenders were not included in the above tabulation for reasons given in the preceding note.

[13] The "major" or serious offense category comprises: (a) property crimes, such as burglary and possessing burglar's tools, larceny and receiving stolen goods, robbery, arson, embezzlement, obtaining property by false pretenses, and the like; (b) sex offenses of a serious nature, such as rape and pathologic sex behavior (e.g., homosexuality, incest); and (c) such other offenses as homicide, escape, or rescue; being a fugitive from justice; serious automobile offenses; and dishonorable discharge from army or navy.

The "minor" or "less serious offense" group includes: (a) offenses involving habit-forming drugs or stimulants (e.g., possessing or dealing in drugs, drunkenness, violations of liquor laws); (b) vagrancy, begging, living on the proceeds of prostitution; (c) such

serious offenses; crimes associated with use of stimulants and habit-forming drugs (particularly drunkenness) comprised two-thirds of the minor offenses.

Nine-tenths of the 938 arrests which occurred in the first five-year follow-up period resulted in convictions. Almost 40 per cent of these were followed by sentence to penal or correctional institutions, 16 per cent by probation, the balance by various other dispositions, such as fines, files, and the like. Of the 307 offenders who committed officially recognized crimes during the five-year period, over 61 per cent served new prison terms as the result of such offenses, the imprisonments totalling 397. The seriousness of this situation may be inferred from the further finding that half the prisoners spent 21 or more months of the five-year period in penal institutions, and a fourth were incarcerated between 41 and 60 months.

(b) In order to gauge the progress or retrogression of the men, a comparison was made of their criminal conduct during three periods; that preceding their sentence to the Massachusetts Reformatory, the parole period, and the five-year post-parole period. This comparison could not be made on the basis of the offenses committed, because these varied from period to period. It therefore became necessary to transpose the specific offenses of the men into the categories of "success," "partial failure," and "total failure." For this purpose, the following definitions were adopted:

Success: No police, court, or prison record, except for occasional tech-

---

sex offenses as adultery, lewd and lascivious cohabitation, technical rape, accosting females, fornication; (d) offenses involving domestic relations (e.g., non-support, desertion, bastardy, cruelty to children, and the like); (e) simple assaults (assault and battery, except with intent to kill, rape, or rob); (f) disturbing the peace, including "idle and disorderly" conduct; (g) malicious mischief; (h) offenses involving merely technical violations of automobile regulations (such as speeding, violating parking rules, operating without a license, and the like). A third category, in which there were relatively few cases, was "juvenile offenses" (e.g., being a stubborn child, a delinquent child, etc.).

There may of course be some differences of opinion in respect to the classification of a few of the above offenses as "serious" or "minor." For further details, see *500 Criminal Careers.*

nical automobile offenses;[14] no dishonorable discharge or desertion from the army or navy,[15] no commission of criminal acts,[16] even though no arrest or prosecution actually followed such commission.

Partial failure: Conviction on two minor offenses, or arrest for not more than three minor offenses. In the case of petty automobile offenses or drunkenness as many as five arrests were allowed in the partial-failure class. (There was not one case, however, in which assignment of a man to a particular category depended *solely* upon an automobile or drunkenness record; other types of offenses had also been committed.) Cases in which there had been arrests for not more than two serious offenses not followed by conviction were also considered partial failures. So also were those in which there had been an arrest for one serious offense not followed by conviction and for not more than two minor offenses for which the violator of the law was neither arrested nor prosecuted (that is, cases of sporadic, rather than continual, misconduct definitely known to have occurred, but as to which no official action was for various reasons taken).[17]

[14] These comprise any automobile offenses except operating recklessly, or under the influence of liquor, or to endanger life and safety; or going away after an accident. The exceptions here noted were rated as serious offenses.

[15] A soldier or sailor dishonorably discharged, or one who has deserted, is customarily regarded as a serious offender by the army and navy. However, some may prefer to class such conduct among "minor" offenses and thereby to put such offenders in the partial-failure group. In the pre-Reformatory period, 8 men were classified as *total failures* because of such misconduct, in the parole period 25, in the post-parole period 22. However, it should be pointed out that among these were some men who had committed minor offenses in addition to the military violations.

[16] This includes any misconduct for which the person might have been arrested, including such authenticated offenses as bootlegging, possession of drugs, non-support, adultery, vagrancy, etc. However, it should be pointed out that there were very few men who could not be put into the "success" class solely because the only offenses committed by them were petty ones for which they had not been arrested. See *500 Criminal Careers,* Appendix E, which gives details and figures of the components of the above judgments of criminal conduct, so that the reader may know exactly on what elements they are based.

[17] Wherever there had been an arrest for not more than two serious offenses or for three or more minor offenses, without conviction, the cases were rated *partial failures.* While it is true that under the American system a person is presumed to be innocent until he is found guilty, in the case of persons with consistent past criminal records the probabilities of their actual guilt on the new charge reasonably outweigh the possibilities of their innocence. On the other hand, it would not be fair to place them in the total-failure group, because of the bare possibility of their innocence; for we must take into account the fact that the police not infrequently make arrests of persons with prior criminal records on

Total failure: Cases in which there had been arrests for three or more serious offenses not followed by conviction (there was in fact but one such instance), or arrests for more than three minor offenses (excepting drunkenness) not followed by conviction (actually, it turned out that there were no such instances); or convictions for one or more serious offenses; or convictions for more than five charges of drunkenness (comprising but a very few cases); or desertion or dishonorable discharge from the army or navy; or the known commission of serious offenses, or a continual course of minor offenses, for which the men were somehow not arrested or prosecuted.[18]

There may very legitimately be a difference of opinion in respect to the constituents of the above categories, although the internal evidence of the study strongly supports the usefulness of this categorization of offenders. Classifying the 422 men whose post-parole conduct was ascertainable, it was found that 89 (21.1 per cent) were *successes;* 71 (16.8 per cent) were *partial failures;* 262 (62.1 per cent) were *total failures.*[19]

slight provocation or suspicion. However, there was but one case of arrests for minor offenses not followed by conviction and there were but four of arrests for serious offenses not followed by conviction. Every possibility had of course to be taken into account in making the categories, even though some of the possible combinations actually turned out to be applicable to but a few cases.

[18] It should be pointed out that sentences for offenses committed after discharge from the Reformatory but before the expiration of the parole period, and served during part or all of the post-parole period, were also taken into account in determining the post-parole criminal status of the men in accordance with the above-described categories. These comprised 25 instances. If the sentence was for a minor offense, the person was classified as a partial failure; if for a serious one, as a total failure.

[19] Of the 333 men who comprised the post-parole failures (partial and total), 144 (43.3 per cent) were convicted of one or more serious offenses during the post-parole period; 5 (1.5 per cent) were arrested for serious offenses, although not convicted; one man was arrested for minor offenses but not convicted; 69 (20.7 per cent) were convicted of minor offenses. In one instance there were serious offenses not officially known; in 25 (7.5 per cent) minor offenses not officially known. In 15 instances (4.5 per cent) warrants were outstanding for the commission of serious offenses; in 25 (7.5 per cent) a sentence for a serious offense had been imposed during parole and was served for part or all of the post-parole period; in 26 (7.8 per cent) there had been conviction for minor offenses, together with the continual commission of other minor crimes which were not officially known. In 22 cases (6.6 per cent) there had been dishonorable discharge or desertion from the army or navy. If one combines cases in which the judgment of partial or total failure was based on serious offenses officially recorded with those in which the criminal activity had not re-

(c) Comparing the status of the men in the three periods analyzed in *500 Criminal Careers,* it was found that 6.6 per cent[20] were *successes* in the pre-Reformatory period, 30.4 per cent in the parole period,[21] and 21.1 per cent in the five-year post-parole period.[22] The *partial failures* were 5.7 per cent in the pre-Reformatory period, 13.5 per cent in the parole period, and 16.8 per cent during the follow-up period. The *total failures* comprised 87.7 per cent in the pre-Reformatory period, 56.1 per cent during parole, and 62.1 per cent in the post-parole period. In other words, the percentage of *total failures* in the supervised parole period—even with the imperfect oversight already noted—was measurably less than in either the pre-Reformatory or the post-parole periods. This probably reflects the effect of supervision (with its threat of return to the Reformatory) and, in some instances, the influence of the institutional régime. Despite the improvement over the pre-Reformatory period, however, the offenders as a group showed little benefit from either incarceration or parole supervision.

NON-CRIMINAL BEHAVIOR DURING FIRST FOLLOW-UP PERIOD

Not only was the criminal conduct of these men in the three periods examined, but other aspects of their lives were studied— their occupational adjustments, their assumption of economic responsibilities, their family relationships, and their use of leisure time.

(a) Although there was an appreciable improvement over the pre-Reformatory period in the work habits of the men, in 42 per cent of the cases these remained poor during the five-year follow-up period. Almost half the men had to be adjudged industrial failures during the post-parole period—laziness, continual drunkenness, and *Wanderlust* comprising two-thirds of the ascertainable

---

sulted in arrest or other official recognition, then 190 (57.1 per cent) of the men are classifiable as partial or total failures. In 121 instances (36.3 per cent) the judgment of partial or total failure was based on the commission of minor offenses, and in 22 (6.6 per cent) on dishonorable discharge or desertion from the army or navy.

[20] Based on 510 cases.   [21] Based on 413 known cases.

[22] Based on 422 known cases.

reasons for occupational failure. Nor was there any marked improvement in the types of work done by the men during the five-year follow-up period. Lack of skill persisted to such an extent that during this period over two-fifths of the group about whom this information was obtainable were unskilled workers and less than a fifth skilled.

(b) Associated with the foregoing was a slight decrease in economic dependency during the five-year follow-up period. There was also a considerable decrease in the proportion of those in comfortable circumstances with a compensating increase of those in "marginal" circumstances. A substantial improvement was, however, noted in respect to the meeting of economic obligations, the proportion of those classifiable as fulfilling their responsibilities very well (*good*)[23] rising in the five-year follow-up period and those classified as not meeting their economic obligations (*poor*) dropping markedly. Nevertheless, there were still 34 per cent who failed to meet their economic obligations, and 55 per cent who did so in only minimal fashion (*fair*).

Associated factors, such as the physical condition of the home and neighborhood, need not for the present purpose be considered.[24]

(c) Summarizing, now, the changes in the family relationships of the men, it was found that according to carefully defined criteria of success and failure[25] there was an appreciable increase during

---

[23] These judgments were obtained as follows: A person who was supporting himself or dependents comfortably was placed in the "good" group; one who was maintaining himself in marginal economic circumstances if single, or his wife if married, or other near dependents, to the best of his ability without more than occasional public or private charitable aid (including sporadic assistance from relatives when he should have been absolutely self-supporting), was placed in the "fair" group; one who failed to support himself or dependents, or who was contracting avoidable debts or receiving frequent aid from social agencies or from his family when he should have been self-supporting, was placed in the "poor" class. It should be recalled that the behavior in question pertains to a period of normal employment, before the depression.

[24] See *500 Criminal Careers*, pp. 201–202.

[25] The judgments were based on the following definitions, each case being separately scrutinized before it was classified:

The *standard* of socially acceptable conduct in regard to family relationships was defined as follows: The man must not be harming his family in any way deemed injurious

the five-year period in the proportion of men whose family relationships were good, none having been so classifiable in the pre-
Reformatory period and 20 per cent in the post-parole period.

(d) Improvement was also noted in respect to use of leisure.
Thus, in the pre-Reformatory period none of the men could legitimately be regarded as using their spare time constructively[26] and
the high proportion of 97 per cent spent their leisure harmfully;
while during the five-year period, 4 per cent were using their spare
time constructively and 62 per cent were using their leisure harmfully.

PREDICTING RECIDIVISM

Before stating some of the problems raised by *500 Criminal
Careers*, the partial answers to which are sought in the present
follow-up study, it is pertinent to mention another feature of the
first research.

In order to obtain a basis for the construction of a prognostic

to the institution of the family; that is, if married, he must not neglect or desert his wife
or children and must not be separated or divorced from his wife, not have illicit relations
with other women, nor be abusive to his wife or children, nor be continually away from
home in the evening. If single and living away from home, he must be in touch with his
parents or nearest relatives. If single and living at home, he must have given evidence that
he considers it more than merely a convenient place to sleep and eat in; for example, he
must not be continually out in the evening, or living at home only when he is in need of
funds.

If a man's relationship with his family in the respects noted in the standard was especially wholesome, he was classified as *good*. If he met the above standard, he was classified
as *fair*. If he failed to meet the above standard, he was classified as *poor*.

[26] For a man to be classified as using his leisure *constructively*, he had to be a member of a well-supervised social group, such as the Y.M.C.A.; he had to utilize his leisure to
further himself culturally or vocationally (as by attendance at high school); and he had
to be free from bad habits of the kind indicated below. To be placed in the *negative*
group he must at least not have been engaged in harmful activities, even though not
utilizing his time constructively. Further, he must have had no marked bad habits. This
category includes also persons who otherwise met the conditions, but who were known
occasionally to gamble at cards or dice at home, or to drink at home to a degree rarely or
never resulting in intoxication. Those who were using their spare time harmfully, who had
pronounced bad habits and associations, who were indulging in forms of recreation which
might lead to criminal conduct (such as membership in gangs, association with bootleggers, prostitutes, and loafers; drug addiction, excessive drinking or gambling, sex immorality) were classified in the *harmful* group.

instrumentality with which to determine the future behavior of ex-prisoners, individual correlations were made between more than fifty factors in the pre-Reformatory, Reformatory, and parole careers of the men, and their success or failure in criminal conduct during the five-year follow-up period. This procedure indicated that the following factors were *considerably* associated with behavior during the five-year period: pre-Reformatory work habits, the seriousness and frequency of pre-Reformatory criminality, arrests prior to commitment to the Reformatory, penal experience preceding Reformatory incarceration, economic responsibility preceding the Reformatory sentence, mental abnormality at the time of commitment to the Reformatory, frequency of offenses in the Reformatory, criminal conduct during parole.

On the basis of these factors, prognostic tables for consultation by judges and parole boards were constructed, and illustrations of their practicality were presented.

Some Aims and Inquiries of the Present Research

This briefly summarizes the findings of *500 Criminal Careers.* The distinctive feature of that work was the intensive tracking down of the behavior of the graduates of a well-known American reformatory, not only during the parole period but during a five-year span following the expiration of sentence (which in all but a few cases meant following the end of parole). It was found, as we have indicated, that with the passage of time, certain improvements occurred in the behavior of the men. Among the salient questions raised by that work, therefore, are these:

Does the added passage of time bring about still further improvement in the conduct of the ex-inmates of the Reformatory?

What are the influences exerted by Father Time, with the inevitable effect upon the biologic and psychologic processes?

What are the effects of the social transformations which come with the passage of time?

Answers to these and related questions should be of significance not only theoretically but in the solution of such practical problems as the desirable length of the "indeterminate sentence," and the amount of time during which offenders of different types should be removed from the community in order that the best results may be obtained in terms of benefit to them and to society. Perhaps further study will also suggest needed modifications in correctional programs.

Certainly analysis of the data obtained in a further follow-up investigation of our ex-prisoners will at least partially answer these questions and perhaps suggest other fruitful hypotheses and theories. Let us therefore reexamine the ex-inmates of the Reformatory to whom we bade farewell in *500 Criminal Careers,* and see what the Ancient Man with the scythe and the hour-glass has done to them during the second five years which have elapsed since the expiration of their sentences to the Massachusetts Reformatory.

Chapter II

ENVIRONMENTAL CIRCUMSTANCES

BEFORE proceeding to the analysis of the findings of the present inquiry, a word of explanation is necessary regarding the method of presenting the material.

From this point on we shall fix our attention upon the 454 ex-inmates of the Massachusetts Reformatory who were living at the beginning of the second five-year follow-up period, since it is they with whom this study is concerned. A basic aim of the present research is to compare the status of the ex-prisoners at several measurable stages in their careers, emphasizing the comparison between their status during the first five years following completion of their sentences and the second five-year period. In this connection, two forms of comparison are employed—the case-by-case method and the group method. Each is useful for particular purposes. In the former, however, only those cases are included in the text for which reliable information about the particular factor under comparison is known and applicable in respect to both the first and second periods. In making mass comparisons, however, such a consideration does not apply, since the status of the group *as a whole* is now being compared to determine changes in the incidence of the particular factors, and therefore changes with respect to the status of *individuals* do not affect the group comparison.

It should also be pointed out that occasionally data about some item were not available for the first five-year period, in which event no comparison was of course possible. Such data have been reserved for footnotes. This was done in order to leave the text free for strictly comparable information relative to the two five-year periods.[1]

In the body of this book only the most significant data are

[1] See Appendix A, *Note on Method.*

presented. For details the reader can conveniently refer to Appendices C, D, E, and F.

A word as to the tables and computations. All percentages are based on the number of cases in which the particular bit of information involved was both known and applicable. Consequently, the base figure on which the percentages have been computed changes somewhat from table to table. For the sake of smoother reading the number of "unknowns" in each factor will not be stated in the text, unless it is so excessive as to necessitate unusual caution in interpreting the data. The exact number of unknowns for each factor discussed is of course indicated in the appendices. The subcategories of each factor which are designated "inapplicable" pertain to men who spent most of one or both of the five-year periods in institutions and as to whom, therefore, certain data (such as character of home or neighborhood) are not relevant. These also are not recorded in the text, unless the number involved in some particular item is unusually large.

In connection with the case-by-case comparisons, attention is called to Appendix E in which will be found the number of cases that were *unknown* or *inapplicable* in one period but known and applicable in the other.

It should also be pointed out that certain tables which appear in Appendix C have been entirely omitted from discussion in the text because of the high proportion of unknown cases or because for one reason or another the factor in question was not found to be significant to the discussion, although the data had originally been gathered. Finally, it should be stated that in addition to the comparisons most frequently made in the following pages, that is, those between the first and second five-year follow-up periods (frequently designated as Period I and Period II), we have occasionally compared the status of the men in one or both of these follow-up periods with their status prior to their commitment to the Massachusetts Reformatory. But this was done only where such a comparison is deemed significant to the point under discussion.

For other comparisons of this nature the reader is referred to Appendix D in which likenesses and differences are recorded in respect to all factors about which comparable information exists.

Findings

INTERVIEWS WITH EX-PRISONERS

During the course of this investigation, the ex-prisoners were themselves personally interviewed by our field investigator in 49.6 per cent of the cases; in an additional 32.4 per cent, although the men themselves could for some reason not be seen, their close relatives were interviewed. In 2.6 per cent of the 454 cases it was for one reason or another not feasible to see either the ex-prisoner himself or his relatives; and in these few instances other persons in a position to know of the activities of the men (such as police or probation officers, employers, social service workers) were interviewed. Finally, in 15.4 per cent of the cases it was not necessary to conduct any personal interviews in connection with the follow-up investigations, since all the necessary data were available either through already recorded and reliable sources of information or by correspondence.[2]

It should be noted that in 90.2 per cent of the cases the attitude of the ex-prisoners personally interviewed was entirely friendly to this continuing follow-up of their careers; it was indifferent in 4.9 per cent, and somewhat hostile in only 4.9 per cent. In most of this latter group, the field investigator ultimately succeeded in breaking down any unfriendliness and was able to arrive at an entirely satisfactory basis for the interviews and other aspects of the necessary investigations.[3]

We are now ready to turn to a consideration of the environmen-

[2] Appendix C, 2–H81a. In the investigation of the status of the men during the first five-year period (*500 Criminal Careers*), 37.8 per cent of the men were personally interviewed, in 35.1 per cent of the cases the relatives were interviewed, in 20.6 per cent other persons were seen. The remaining 6.5 per cent (33 men) died before the beginning of the post-parole period.

[3] See Appendix A, *Note on Method*, pp. 213 *et seq.*, for further details.

tal circumstances of the 454 ex-inmates of the Massachusetts Reformatory who were living at the beginning of the second five-year follow-up period.

AGE AT END OF SECOND PERIOD

The limits of the second five-year period fell in the years 1931 and 1932—in 46.5 per cent of the cases in 1931, and in 53.5 per cent in 1932.[4] By the end of Period II, the mean age of the 454 men was 35.2 years (±.16), 13.6 per cent being between 26 and 30 years old, 46.9 per cent between 31 and 35, 25.6 per cent between 36 and 40, 9.9 per cent between 41 and 45, while 4 per cent were 46 or over.[5]

WITH WHOM LIVING AT BEGINNING AND END OF PERIOD

At the time of their commitment to the Massachusetts Reformatory, 357 (80.8 per cent) of the 454 men with whom we are concerned had been making their homes with their parents, siblings, or other close relatives; 60 (13.6 per cent) were living alone; 24 (5.4 per cent) with wives and children. The close of Period I found only 72 (17.8 per cent) making their homes with their parents, siblings, or near relatives; a like proportion were living alone; and 156 (38.6 per cent) were residing with wives and children. In addition, 13 (3.3 per cent) were living with women to whom they were not married, 3 were residing in the homes of their employers, and 87 (21.5 per cent) were in penal or non-penal institutions. By the end of Period II, 71 (17.7 per cent) were making their homes with their parents, siblings, or other relatives; 64 (16 per cent) were living alone; 168 (41.9 per cent) were living with wives and children; 7 were residing in the homes of employers; 7 were living with women to whom they were not married; and 70 (17.5 per cent) were in institutions of one kind or another.[6] By that time 14 (3.5 per cent) of the men had died (5 accidentally, one by suicide, 6 from pulmonary diseases, one from malaria, and one from nephritis).[7]

[4] Appendix C, 2–1b.　　　　　[5] Appendix C, 2–2.
[6] Appendix D, 1.　　　　　[7] Appendix C, 2–H105.

The considerable reduction in the proportion of men who in both periods were living in the homes of parents, siblings, or close relatives is to a large extent accounted for by the rise in the percentage of those living with wives and children.

The changes occurring in Period II as contrasted with Period I may be seen more specifically by noting the shift of status in each group:

(a) Of 72 men who at the end of Period I were making their homes with parents, siblings, or other relatives, 43 (61.4 per cent) were still living with their relatives at the end of Period II; 14 (20 per cent) were then making their homes with wives or children; one was living in the home of an employer; 7 were living alone; 4 were in institutions; one was dead, and information about the remaining 2 was not available.

(b) Of 156 men who at the end of the first period were living with their wives and children, 131 (85.1 per cent) were still living with them at the close of Period II; 4 had returned to their parental homes or were living with close relatives; one was living with a woman to whom he was not married; 6 were living alone; 7 were in institutions; 5 were dead, and the information in respect to 2 of this group was not available.

(c) Of 13 men who at the end of Period I were living with women to whom they were not married or with whom they had contracted an unlawful marriage, 3 were still making their homes with these women at the close of the second period; 2 were then living with their lawful wives; 4 had returned to the parental roof; one was living in the home of an employer, one was in an institution, one had died, and the whereabouts of one was unknown.

(d) The 3 men who at the close of Period I were living in the homes of employers were still doing so at the close of Period II.

(e) Of 72 men who were living alone at the end of the first five-year period, only 30 (42.9 per cent) were still living alone at the end of Period II; 17 (24.3 per cent) were then making their homes with wives and children; 8 were living in the households of their parents or siblings; 2 were living with women not their wives; 2 were making their homes with employers; 7 were in institutions, 4 were dead, and the whereabouts of 2 were unknown.

(f) Of 87 men who at the close of Period I were in institutions, only 49 (57.6 per cent) were still in institutions at the end of Period II; 3 were making their homes with wives and children; 12 were living with their parents or siblings; one was living with a "sweetheart"; 18 were making their homes alone; 2 had died, and the whereabouts of 2 were unknown.[8]

From this analysis it appears that the changes in place of residence were not marked except in the cases of the 72 men who were in the first period living alone, and in the 87 who were in institutions. It is also clear that the group who at the close of the first five years were living with their wives and children showed the greatest degree of stability, as only 15 per cent were no longer making their homes with their families at the end of Period II.

WHEREABOUTS AT END OF FIRST AND SECOND PERIODS

Turning now to the whereabouts of the men at the close of the respective periods, we find that at the end of the first five years, 179 (39.5 per cent) of them were living in various cities in Massachusetts, and at the end of the second five-year period, 191 men (42.1 per cent) were residing in Massachusetts.[9] At the close of the first period, 80 men (17.6 per cent) were living in other states; at the end of the second, 108 (23.8 per cent).[10] At the conclusion of Period I, 7 men were residing in foreign countries; at the end of the second period, 6.[11]

A more significant shift occurred in respect to incarceration in

[8] Appendix E, 1.

[9] At the close of the second period, 92 men were living in Boston or its suburbs, the remainder in various cities or towns throughout the state.

[10] Various cities or towns in Maine, Vermont, New Hampshire, Rhode Island, Connecticut, New York, New Jersey, Pennsylvania, Maryland, Ohio, Michigan, Wisconsin, Illinois, Louisiana, Tennessee, Florida, Mississippi, North Carolina, Texas, California, and the District of Columbia.

[11] Italy, Poland, Greece, Syria, Mexico.

penal institutions at the close of each period. The number of men imprisoned at the end of the first period was 85 (18.8 per cent); at the end of the second, 55 (12.1 per cent).[12] Another striking shift occurred in the proportion who were fugitives from justice. At the end of Period I there were 31 (6.9 per cent); at the close of the second period only 3. The remaining cases were distributed as follows: at the end of the first period, 7 men were in non-penal institutions, usually mental hospitals, 6 were drifting about the country, 6 were in the army or navy, 6 were at sea; the whereabouts of 20 (4.4 per cent), though unknown at the end of the first period were determined for part of it, while the location of 27 (5.9 per cent) was completely unknown both during and at the close of the first five-year period. At the end of Period II, 14 men were in hospitals of various kinds, 12 were drifting around the country, 3 were in the army or navy, one at sea; the whereabouts of 15 were unknown, although they were ascertained for part of this second period, and the whereabouts of 33 (7.3 per cent) were completely unknown.[13]

INSTITUTIONAL EXPERIENCES

During the first period, the 454 men had a total of 361 institutional incarcerations (penal and non-penal); during the second, 421. Analysis of these institutional experiences reveals the following: During Period I, 10.5 per cent of the 361 institutional experiences occurred in reformatories, 26.3 per cent in prisons, 60.1 per cent in jails, houses of correction, or state farms, and 3.1 per cent in non-penal institutions (mostly state hospitals). During Period II, only 1.7 per cent of the 421 institutional experiences occurred in reformatories, 23.3 per cent in prisons, and 67.7 per cent in in-

---

[12] Outside of those incarcerated in various penal institutions in Massachusetts, there were men in Folsom Prison and McNeil Island Prison (California); State Penitentiaries of Virginia, Kansas, Ohio, Montana, Michigan, Connecticut; Kennebec County Jail (Maine); Great Meadow Prison (New York), Erie County Penitentiary (New York), Auburn Prison and Sing Sing (New York); penitentiary in Montreal, Canada; U.S. Penitentiary at Atlanta (Georgia); Eastern Penitentiary (Pennsylvania); Jail in Dayton (Ohio).

[13] Appendix D, 2.

stitutions for short-term offenders; while 7.3 per cent were in non-penal institutions.[14] The sharp decline in the proportion of reformatory experiences is of course explained by the advancing years of the group, which legally disqualifies them for sentence to "young men's" reformatories.

An equal proportion of the institutional experiences in Periods I and II were spent in prisons, reformatories, and jails in Massachusetts (73.1 per cent during the first span, 71.3 per cent during the second).[15]

The shift in the status of the men with reference to institutional experiences was not very marked. Thus, of 188 men who had lived in institutions of one kind or another during Period I, 54 (28.7 per cent) had not done so during Period II; and of the 204 men who had had no institutional experiences during the first five years, 31 (15.2 per cent) had been institutionalized during the second.[16]

By combining institutional experiences (penal and non-penal), a slight decrease in the proportion of men who were subjected to such experiences becomes evident. Thus, in the period prior to their commitment to the Reformatory, 49.6 per cent had been in institutions, during the first follow-up period 48.6 per cent, and during the second 42.4 per cent.[17]

LENGTH OF TIME IN COMMUNITY

Closely related to the institutional experiences of the men is the question of the length of time, during each of the periods under review, that the 454 men were at liberty in the community.[18] During Period I, the average time spent in the community by those men who were at liberty at all in these five years was 45.74 months (±.50). However, 10 men were not in the community at all during the sixty months comprising Period I. During Period II, the average

---

[14] Appendix D, 47.   [15] Appendix D, 48.
[16] Appendix E, 3.   [17] Appendix D, 4.

[18] This pertains to the time not spent as patients in hospitals for the mentally ill or the chronic physically ill, or under restraint of the army and navy, or in imprisonment—largely the latter.

number of months in the community of those of the group who spent any time at all in freedom was 47.06 months ($\pm$.50)—a slightly longer span than in the preceding period. During the second follow-up period 30 men (7.5 per cent), thrice the number of those in Period I, spent no time whatsoever in the community.

The decrease in the proportion of men living in the community in the second five-year period as compared with the first is partially explained by the fact that by now their mental or physical disorders were so marked that long incarceration was indicated for certain of them.[19]

Detailed analysis of the time during which the men were living in the community shows that: during Period I, 29 (6.9 per cent) were in the community less than a year, 26 (6.2 per cent) from one to two years, 36 (8.7 per cent) from two to three years; 108 men (25.9 per cent) were unconfined from three to five years; while 208 men (45.9 per cent) were at liberty throughout the sixty-month span. During Period II, 22 men (5.5 per cent) were in the community for less than 12 months, 25 (6.3 per cent) from one to two years, 22 (5.5 per cent) from two to three years; 80 of the men (20.0 per cent) resided in the community from three to five years; and 221 (55.2 per cent), a higher proportion than in the preceding period, were at liberty throughout Period II.[20]

The changes that occurred in respect to the time spent in the community are more specifically shown in the following analysis:

(a) Of 10 men who throughout the first period were in institutions or in the army or navy, 6 remained there throughout the second, and 4 spent part but not all of the second period in the community.

(b) Of 199 men who spent only part of the first period in the community, 24 (13 per cent) were not at liberty at all during the second period, 109 (59.2 per cent) spent part of the time in the com-

---

[19] Of 179 men who were known not to have been in the community throughout the sixty-month period, 147 had been incarcerated in penal institutions, 20 had been in hospitals for chronic physical diseases, and 10 had been in the army and navy. Appendix C, 2–7.

[20] Appendix D, 3.

munity, while 51 (27.8 per cent) were unconfined throughout the second period.[21]

(c) Of 208 men who lived in the community throughout the first period, 167 (83.1 per cent) continued to do so throughout the second; that is, they were not incarcerated in penal institutions, were not patients in hospitals for mental diseases or for chronic physical diseases, and were not in the army or navy at any time during the second period. Thirty-three (16.4 per cent) of the men who had lived in the community throughout the first period did so for but part of the second, while one man was in institutions throughout the second period.[22] In 37 cases no information was available regarding the length of time spent in the community either in the first or second period.[23] In brief, the change of status in respect to length of time spent in the community was not marked, except in the case of those who, having spent but part of the first sixty-month period in the community, were entirely at liberty throughout Period II.

MOBILITY

Partially related to the foregoing is the information in respect to mobility, which discloses a slight falling off in the incidence of excessive moving about. Thus, in Period I, 54.8 per cent of the men either moved about so much in one city, or from one city to another, as not to strike root in any one region; in Period II, 46.9 per cent moved about excessively. Of 179 men who had previously moved about considerably, only 37 (20.7 per cent) settled down during the second period; of 166 who had not circulated a great deal during the first period, only 18 (10.8 per cent) did so in the second.[24] Here again, therefore, the changes were not great, although there is a slight trend toward increasing stability in the group as a whole.

This trend toward greater stability is further manifested by less shifting about of the men from one household to another. A word

---

21 Information in this regard concerning the remaining 15 men was lacking.
22 Information on the status of 7 of the men in this group was unavailable.
23 Appendix E, 2.   24 Appendix E, 4.

of explanation is necessary as to what may be regarded a change of household. For example, if a man had been living with his parents and then went away to live alone, this is considered a change in his household; if he then married and made a new home with his wife, this is a second change in the household; if thereafter he left his wife to go to a mistress, this is counted as a third change; if, finally, he left the mistress and returned to his parental home, this comprised a total of four changes in his household during the period under consideration.

During the course of Period I, 36.7 per cent of our ex-prisoners shifted from one household to another three or more times; 24.3 per cent once or twice; while in 39 per cent of the cases the household relationship remained stable throughout the five years. In the second period, 32.8 per cent of the men shifted three or more times; 12.8 per cent once or twice; and 54.4 per cent remained in one household throughout the five years, indicating, on the whole, an appreciably increased stability in their household relationships.[25] This improvement is seen more clearly in the following analysis:

(a) Of 110 men who shifted from one household to another three or more times during the first period, 32 (29.1 per cent) no longer continued to change homes so excessively. (b) Of 75 men whose household arrangements were modified once or twice during Period I, 52 (69.3 per cent) remained in a single household throughout Period II. (c) Of 131 men who were attached to but one household throughout the first five years, 102 (77.9 per cent) maintained a like status throughout the second period; 17 (13 per cent) shifted households once or twice during Period II, while 12 (9.1 per cent) made three or more changes.[26]

HOME CONDITIONS

Comparison of the home conditions of the ex-inmates of the Reformatory during Periods I and II again indicates some, though

[25] Appendix D, 6.   [26] Appendix E, 5.

not a marked, improvement. Thus, during Period I, only 26.2 per cent of the homes could be characterized as *good,* by which is meant a place of living in which there is adequate space (not more than two persons, excluding an infant, to a bedroom), plenty of light, good ventilation, and sufficient furniture to meet minimal requirements. During the second period, this proportion rose to 33.5 per cent. Again, in Period I, 36.3 per cent of the homes had to be designated *poor,* so far as physical condition is concerned, in that they were overcrowded, badly ventilated, dirty, and (or) shabbily furnished. In Period II, the proportion of poor homes was reduced to 30.8 per cent.[27] The slight improvement is further indicated by the finding that (a) of 102 homes previously characterized as *poor,* 23 (22.6 per cent) were in the second period at least *fair;* (b) of 113 homes previously deemed *fair* in their physical conveniences, 19 (16.8 per cent) were now *good;* (c) and only one of the homes of 81 men previously rated as *good* was later classifiable as *poor,* 8 (9.9 per cent) as *fair.*

NEIGHBORHOOD CONDITIONS

In what kind of neighborhoods did our 454 men make their homes during the second period, and what changes occurred as compared with the first? Before considering this question, it should be noted that during Period I, 78 per cent of the men were urbanites, during the second period 81.7 per cent; in Period I, 6.9 per cent lived in very small towns or rural regions, in Period II, 9.8 per cent. During the first five years, 15.1 per cent of the men moved back and forth between city and country, during the second only 8.5 per cent did so, this last being the most notable change. Analyzing this in greater detail we find that, of the 255 men who resided in urban communities in Period I, 95.3 per cent continued to do so in Period II; of 24 men who lived in rural regions in the first period, 20 (83.4

---

[27] In the first period, 37.5 per cent of the homes were *fair* (that is, they had more than one of the characteristics of good homes but also some traits of the poor homes); in the second period, 35.7 per cent of the homes were *fair* (Appendix D, 7).

per cent) continued to do so in the second, the remaining 4 being equally divided among urban residents and those who shifted back and forth from city to country. Of 43 men who had moved back and forth during the first five years, only 17 (39.5 per cent) continued to do so later; 18 (41.9 per cent) became urban dwellers; and 8 (18.6 per cent) remained in the country.[28]

Turning now to the character of the neighborhoods from the point of view of favorable and unfavorable influences, relatively little improvement is noted. Thus, in Period I, 15.3 per cent of the men lived in regions that could legitimately be called favorable in that they contained no street gangs or centers of vice or crime within the immediate district and at the same time had organized facilities for wholesome recreation, such as school and community centers, settlements, decent club houses, parks, and the like. This proportion remained practically unchanged in Period II, when 14.2 per cent lived in favorable neighborhoods. During the first five years, 43.9 per cent of the men resided in fair neighborhoods, that is, regions not having really vicious influences but which lacked in opportunities for constructive recreation. In the second five years, this proportion was increased to 50.6 per cent. In Period I, 40.8 per cent resided in definitely poor neighborhoods, that is, regions containing vicious influences such as houses of prostitution, gambling dens, cheap cafés, commercial dance halls, shady poolrooms. In these areas gangs were very much in evidence.[29] The 40.8 per cent incidence of bad neighborhoods was reduced to 35.2 per cent in the second period.

Considering now the changes that occurred case by case we see that: Of 117 instances in which the men had previously lived in

[28] Appendix E, 7. During the second period, 36.1 per cent of the men made their homes in urban districts that were rapidly changing from residential to business areas; 36.7 per cent lived usually in residential areas of cities not far removed from business or factory districts; 7.7 per cent lived in residential suburbs of large cities. Like data were unfortunately not available for the first five-year period.

[29] In some of these neighborhoods there were facilities for constructive recreation but the vicious influences far outweighed the constructive facilities.

poor neighborhoods, 29 (24.8 per cent) now lived in fair or good regions; of 133 men residing in fair neighborhoods in Period I, 15 (12 per cent) later moved into poor neighborhoods and only 9 (6.8 per cent) had moved to good ones. Finally, of 46 men previously living in good neighborhoods, 18 (39.1 per cent) were in the second period making their homes in regions not as favorable.[30] A partial explanation for the fact that some who previously had lived in fair or good neighborhoods later resided in poor ones may be found in the industrial depression years 1929 to 1933, which began in the midst of the second five-year period.

MORAL ATMOSPHERE OF HOME

Less tangible, though probably more significant, is the moral atmosphere of the homes of these men. Data regarding this feature of our inquiry had unfortunately not been obtained for Period I, hence a definite conclusion in respect to improvement or deterioration cannot be arrived at. However, the moral atmosphere of the men's homes during the second five years is of interest in itself. In 40.1 per cent of the cases, the moral tone of the household could legitimately be designated as good; that is, there was definite evidence of thrift, of wholesome ideals, and of conformity to the requirements of the law on the part of the members of the ex-prisoner's immediate family. In 23.8 per cent of the cases, the moral atmosphere was only fair, because though there was conformity to law among the members of the household, there was also an absence of thrift and wholesome ideals. In 37.1 per cent of the cases the moral atmosphere was poor, as evidenced by delinquency of one kind or another among the members of the household or, where there was no actual delinquency, by light regard for, and even encouragement of violations of, the law.[31]

[30] Appendix E, 8.

[31] In cases where the man was living by himself and was not a member of any household, the atmosphere of his immediate physical environment was taken into account. If a man was living in a rooming house by himself, for example, the general moral tone of the rooming house was considered in determining the standards by which the man was surrounded (Appendix C, 2–16a).

Trend of Environmental Conditions

A composite picture of the situation in Period II, embracing the physical characteristics of the homes, the neighborhood surroundings, and the moral atmosphere of the households shows that in 24.8 per cent of the 454 cases the environing circumstances of the men could rightly be designated as *good,* meaning by this that (a) their homes were adequate from a physical point of view to insure a minimum of comfort, (b) the neighborhood conditions were wholesome, and (c) the moral standards of the households were high. In 42.8 per cent of the cases, the environing circumstances were only *fair,* a designation applied to cases in which one or two of the constituents entering into the situation were not entirely favorable. Finally, in 32.4 per cent of the cases the conditions surrounding the men were *poor,* which means that at least two of the three component elements were entirely unfavorable, the third only fair.[32] Although comparison of this composite picture of environmental conditions in the two periods is impossible because of the absence of information about the moral atmosphere of the households of the 454 men during the first five-year period, the upward trend is definitely revealed in the fact that in the fifth year of the second follow-up span the environmental conditions of the group were good in 31 per cent of the cases as compared with 24.8 per cent by the end of the fourth year of the second follow-up period.[33]

[32] Appendix C, 2–15b.
[33] Appendix C, 2–65a.

Chapter III

FAMILY RELATIONSHIPS AND ASSUMPTION
OF ECONOMIC RESPONSIBILITIES

WE are next concerned to see whether the general trend of
improvement which has occurred in the environmental circumstances of our 454 men is also evidenced in their family relationships and the assumption of their economic responsibilities.

Findings Regarding Family Relationships

MARITAL STATUS

It has already been noted in the previous chapter that a far lower
proportion of men than formerly were living in their parental
homes during Period II. It was suggested that this is due to the fact
that a considerable proportion of these men had married during
the ten years following parole and are now living with their wives
and children. At the time of their commitment to the Reformatory,
411 (90.9 per cent) of the 454 men were single; at the end of the
first five years only 187 (45.2 per cent) were single; while by the
end of the second period the number of unmarried men had been
reduced to 157 (38.2 per cent) of those whose status was known.[1]

The changes which have taken place in the marital status of the
men are evident in the following analysis:

(a) Of the 187 men who were single at the end of Period I, 156
(84.3 per cent) were still single at the close of Period II, and 22
(11.9 per cent) were by then married and living with their wives,
while 7 (3.8 per cent) who had married during the second five-year
span, were already separated or divorced by the close of that period.

Of 159 men who at the end of the first five-year period were
married and living with their wives, 16 (10.4 per cent) were separated or divorced by the close of Period II; one man though not
living with his own wife had illicitly married another and was

[1] Appendix D, 10.

making his home with her, and another had left his wife, married another woman illicitly, and was already separated from her. Three of the men were widowed by the end of Period II.

(b) Of the 52 men who at the end of the first period were already separated or divorced from their wives, 5 (9.6 per cent) had remarried during the second period and were at the end of that time living with their new wives; 2 men, though not actually divorced, married illicitly and were living with these "wives."[2]

It is evident, therefore, that there has been an increase in the proportion of married men, and some shifting about in the marital relationships.[3]

NUMBER OF CHILDREN

The average number of children of these marriages has remained fairly constant throughout the years. At the time that our men were committed to the Reformatory, those who were married had on an average of 2.2 children ($\pm$.27); by the end of the first five-year period there were 2.0 children per married man ($\pm$.07);[4] and by the end of the second five-year period 2.46 children per married man ($\pm$.11).[5]

[2] Appendix E, 9.

[3] During the second five-year period 45 men married once and one man was married twice (Appendix C, 2–21).

[4] One hundred and two of our men became fathers during this second five-year period (not necessarily for the first time). In 87 of these cases they became the fathers of legitimate children; in 3 cases, of children conceived out of wedlock but whose mothers they married before the birth of the children; in 3 cases they were single men who became the fathers of illegitimate children; in 9 cases they were married men but had illegitimate children (Appendix C, 2–27).

The attitude of our men toward their children (legitimate, illegitimate, or stepchildren) might be considered *good* in 59.7 per cent of the cases, as indicated by the fact that they were fond of these children and did all within their limited means to look after them or, if they were for one reason or another living away from the children, they were at least maintaining an active interest in them; in 18.1 per cent their attitude might be deemed *fair* in that they were rather casual toward their children or, though really fond of them, were neglectful of the children's interests or, if living away from them, were at least keeping in touch with them even though not maintaining an active interest in them; and in 22.2 per cent of cases the attitude of our men toward their children was *poor,* in that they showed no affection for or were really abusive of them and if living away from them were entirely out of touch with them (Appendix C, 2–29a).

[5] Appendix D, 11.

CONJUGAL RELATIONS

During the second five-year period the conjugal relationships of 60.7 per cent of the men were *good,* by which is meant that husband and wife were living together compatibly; in 14.9 per cent of the cases the marital relationships were *fair,* in that although the couples were indifferent or hostile to each other no open breach occurred; while in 24.4 per cent of the cases the conjugal relations were *poor,* as reflected in actual separation, desertion, or divorce. The marital relationships of the married men prior to their commitment to the Reformatory and during the first and second five-year periods show substantially little change.[6]

The constituent modifications in conjugal relationships among those who were married during the first and second follow-up periods are more readily seen from the following analysis:

(a) Of 109 men whose conjugal relationships were *good* in the first period and who continued to live with their wives for all or part of the second period (that is, those who themselves, or whose wives, were not living in institutions for most or all of the second period), the conjugal relationships of 4 (3.7 per cent) were only *fair* in Period II, while in 9 cases (8.2 per cent) separation, desertion, or divorce occurred during this second period.

(b) Of 29 men whose conjugal relationships were *fair* in Period I, two had so improved as to be later characterized as *good,* while in 10 cases (34.5 per cent) the precarious marital relationship previously manifest later terminated in desertion, separation, or divorce.

(c) In 27 cases in which the men had deserted or were separated from their wives before the end of the first five years, 2 had returned to the fold but their relationships were none too good, while in 3 cases a compatible association was established.[7]

[6] Appendix D, 12.

[7] Appendix E, 11. As data comparable with the first five-year period are not available, the following information regarding the marital situation of our men during the second five years is here given in the footnote: In 89.7 per cent of the cases the wives of our men may be said to have assumed their marital responsibilities during the second period, in that they did not neglect or desert their husbands or children, were not unfaithful and not physi-

RELATIONSHIP TO NEAREST RELATIVES

What were the ties existing between our men and their nearest relatives, or between them and their siblings if the parents were not living? During the second period it was found that in a little over half the cases (52.5 per cent), our men had an entirely friendly feeling toward their near relatives, and in one-fifth of the cases (19.5 per cent) our men were in touch with their relatives only because or when they were in real need of assistance or shelter; while in 28.3 per cent of the cases they were rarely if ever in contact with their relatives. The group as a whole shows little change in this regard from the first five-year period.[8]

The changes in attitude are more clearly seen in the following analysis:

(a) Of 181 men who were entirely friendly toward their relatives during the first five-year period, 9 (5 per cent) maintained contact with them during the second only when they needed assistance, and 5 (2.7 per cent) rarely if ever communicated with their relatives.

cally or mentally abusive to their husbands or children. These wives were carrying all their household duties and assisting in the burden of support of the family when necessary. In 10.3 per cent of the cases the wives of our men were neglecting their marital responsibilities during this period (Appendix C, 2–24).

Seven out of ten of these wives were systematic, economical, clean, and neat in their housekeeping; 22.4 per cent were only fair housekeepers, in that they were at times entirely competent and at other times very erratic in their housekeeping due either to low morality or temperamental difficulties; while 7.7 per cent of the wives were wasteful, indifferent, or careless (Appendix C, 2–26).

Although the information is quite incomplete because it was not possible carefully to pursue in any detail the behavior of the wives of our men, we do know that fully one-fifth of them (20.9 per cent) were themselves delinquents during the second five-year period (Appendix C, 2–30).

We have noted that 89.7 per cent of the wives actually assumed their marital responsibilities during this period. Only 62.2 per cent of the men themselves assumed their responsibilities, however (Appendix C, 2–23).

Taking into account both the men and women, we find that in 60.4 per cent of the cases both husband and wife were assuming their marital responsibilities while in the remainder of the cases one or both did not do so during the second five-year period (Appendix C, 2–25).

[8] Appendix D, 13.

(b) Of 75 men who, during Period I, had been in touch with their relatives only when they were in need of aid, 13 (17.3 per cent) had drifted completely away from their relatives and rarely communicated with them during Period II, while the ties in 12 cases (16 per cent) were strengthened to the point of real friendliness.

(c) In 78 cases in which the men had previously been rarely if ever in touch with their relatives, 4 men (5.1 per cent) later made themselves sufficiently known to their relations to ask assistance from them even though they did not maintain a friendly association; while in 4 more cases an attitude of friendliness on the part of the men toward their relatives developed during this second period.[9]

In only 7.3 per cent of the cases may it be said that during Period II parents or siblings showed definite disgust for or hostility or disapproval of the ex-prisoners. In almost a third of the cases (30.9 per cent) their attitude was one of indifference, while in 61.8 per cent it was entirely friendly.[10]

Trend of Family Relationships

Has there been any improvement in the family relationships of our men?

Having reviewed the conjugal relationships of those of the 454 men who were married, and indicated something of the relationship of the entire group to their relatives, it will be helpful, before answering this question, to summarize the family relationships of the 454 men. If a man is married, his family relationships embrace his attitude to his wife and children; if he is separated, divorced, or widowed during a particular period but has children, his relationship to the latter forms the basis for a consideration of his family relationships. If, however, he has no children or is single, an estimate is made of his relationships to his parents or siblings. In the case of a married man, his family relationships therefore are con-

---

[9] Appendix E, 12.   [10] Appendix C, 2–18b.

sidered successful if he does not neglect or desert his wife or children or is not separated or divorced, does not have illicit relationships with other women, is not abusive to his wife or children. A single man or one who is separated, divorced, or widowed before the beginning of the particular period under investigation, and has no children, is considered successful in his family relationships if he at least keeps in touch with his parents or other near relatives. If, however, he is living with relatives he must give some evidence that he considers his home more than merely a convenient place to sleep and eat in. Men who do not meet the above standards are classified as failures.

By these criteria, half of the group can be considered *successful* in their family relationships during the second five-year period, and half *failures*. Although little change is evident in this regard as compared with the family relationships during the first five years, there is, nevertheless, a considerable improvement over the period prior to the commitment of the men to the Reformatory when 67.6 per cent of those about whom the information was available had to be regarded as failures in their family association.[11]

It should be said, also, that the trend is in the direction of a slight improvement in family relationships, for in the fifth year of the second period the proportion of the group who were maintaining successful family relations rose to 56.1 per cent.[12]

The internal change which has occurred in the group in this regard is slight, as is evident from the following analysis:

(a) Of 183 men who were successful in their family relationships during the first period, 29 or 15.8 per cent were later failures.

(b) Of 156 men who had failed in their family relationships during the first five years, 23 or 14.7 per cent were later successful.[13]

Findings Regarding Economic Responsibility

DISPOSITION OF EARNINGS

We next turn our attention to the question of what changes if

[11] Appendix D, 14. [12] Appendix C, 2–63a. [13] Appendix E, 13.

any have taken place in the manner in which our men disposed of their earnings. Were they assuming their responsibilities in the support of those dependent upon them? During the second period 69.1 per cent of the men had persons dependent upon them—wives and children if they were married men or aged parents if they were single.[14] This marks practically no change from the situation during the first five-year period, when 67.3 per cent of the group had dependents.[15]

The constituent changes which have taken place are seen from the following analysis:

(a) Of 108 men who had no persons dependent upon them during the first five-year period, 23 (21.3 per cent) later had dependents. (This refers mostly to wives and children.) (b) Of 240 men who had dependents during the first period, 18 (7.5 per cent) later had no dependents either because they were widowed or the parents previously dependent upon them had died.[16]

It has just been pointed out that almost one-third of the group had no dependents during either the first or second five-year follow-up period. However, only slightly over half the men (53.4 per cent in the second period and 54.3 per cent in the first) were mostly supporting themselves—a fact which in itself indicates that quite a few were not meeting their economic obligations either in the first or second period.[17] In fact, of 246 men who had dependents during the first period and about whom information was available concerning the disposition of their earnings, 80 (32.5 per cent) were utilizing their earnings for themselves and not in anyway aiding dependents. Little change occurred during the second period when, of 236 men who had dependents, 75 (31.8 per cent) were not contributing to their support.

ECONOMIC CONDITION

What alterations, if any, took place in the economic condition of

---

[14] It has been noted that by the end of the second five-year period but 38.2 per cent of our men were single, as compared with 45.2 per cent at the close of Period I.

[15] Appendix D, 15.　　　　　　　[16] Appendix E, 14.

[17] Appendix D, 16.

the men in the second, as compared with the first five-year period? Here it should be noted that the industrial depression following 1929 entered into the middle of Period II which terminated either in 1931 or 1932. In order that the picture of the economic condition of these men should not be completely distorted by the depression years, their circumstances only up to the beginning of the depression were taken into account, unless of course it was obvious that their situation was in no way or only slightly affected by the industrial decline. Fifty-eight (17.2 per cent) actually were victims of the depression.[18]

On this basis, we see comparatively little difference in the economic condition of the group in the second five-year period as compared with the first. In Period II, 10 per cent of the men were in comfortable economic circumstances (i.e., they had accumulated resources sufficient to maintain themselves and their families for at least four months in case of unemployment), while during the first five years 8.4 per cent of the men had been in comfortable circumstances. During Period II, 72.1 per cent were in marginal circumstances (i.e., they were living on their daily earnings, accumulating practically no reserves, and being constantly on the borderline between self-support and dependency). This proportion compares closely with the 79.2 per cent who were in marginal circumstances during Period I. However, there is evident a slight increase in the proportion of men who were largely dependent either on relatives or on social agencies for support (17.9 per cent as compared with 12.4 per cent).[19]

The case-by-case changes which took place within the group in the two follow-up periods are as follows:

(a) Of 31 men who in Period I were in comfortable economic circumstances, 10 (32.2 per cent) were in marginal circumstances in Period II. This change in status may largely be accounted for by the fact that their families had grown in size and what was previously sufficient to maintain them comfortably was later not quite enough to do so.

[18] Appendix C, 2–H116.   [19] Appendix D, 17.

(b) Of 253 men who were previously in marginal economic circumstances, 12 (4.7 per cent) later became comfortably situated, while 28 (11.1 per cent) dropped back into the ranks of dependency. This last is accounted for largely by a slow process of deterioration which has taken place in certain of our men, notably in those who drank excessively. (It has already been pointed out that the economic condition of our men only up to the point of the financial depression in 1929 was considered.)

(c) Of 39 men who during the first five-year period were dependent economically, 8 (20.5 per cent) later moved up into the group who were able to get along with only occasional, if any, aid from relatives or social agencies.[20]

AID BY SOCIAL SERVICE AGENCIES

With added problems presented by growing families, it is to be expected that our men were needing more assistance in the management of their personal affairs in Period II than in the preceding five years. This is evidenced by the fact that during the second follow-up period, 41 per cent of the group were being assisted by social service agencies in one way or another, as compared to but 24.3 per cent during the first.[21] In 90 (61.6 per cent) of the 146 cases dealt with by social agencies during this second period, relief agencies were involved; in 88 (60.3 per cent) the aid given had to do with problems of physical or mental health; in 29 (19.9 per cent) vocational assistance was asked for; in 20 cases (13.7 per cent) questions of welfare of the children of our men were involved; and in 11 cases (7.5 per cent), general problems of family welfare, mainly dealing with matters pertaining to domestic relations, had to be

---

[20] Appendix E, 16. It is worthy of note that almost one-fourth of the men (23.8 per cent) had some savings, only 34 of them, however, having enough laid by to maintain their economic responsibilities for at least four months in case of unemployment. The precarious economic situation of many of these men is evidenced in the fact that half of them (51.1 per cent) had no insurance of any kind (Appendix D, 18); and that one-fifth of those who had insurance did not pay the premiums thereon themselves; these were paid by their relatives (Appendix D, 19).

[21] Appendix D, 20.

dealt with.[22] The mean number of agencies dealing with this group of 146 men was 2.12 ($\pm$.08).[23]

The changes which took place within the group in regard to assistance by social service agencies are seen from the following analysis: (a) Of 255 men previously not dealt with by social service agencies, 80 (31.4 per cent) later became clients of one or more welfare organizations. (b) Of 79 men previously known to social agencies, 20 (25.3 per cent) were later not being dealt with by such organizations.[24]

Despite the high proportion of men receiving assistance of one kind or another in the management of their affairs from social agencies during the second period, many obvious needs were not looked after. In fact, in only 77 (22 per cent) of the 350 cases in regard to which this factor was pertinent were there no conditions present requiring the ministrations of social service organizations. In 30 cases (8.6 per cent) all the needs were met by agencies, in 108 cases (30.9 per cent) some were met, while in 135 cases (38.6 per cent) obvious requirements were not met at all. It will be seen, therefore, that needs of one kind or another were present in 243 of the 350 cases. Moreover, necessities indicated in these cases are only the glaring ones. For instance, the men mentioned as requiring vocational guidance are only those who in this second period were very poor and irregular workers; the cases in which recreational supervision was obviously needed were those in which leisure time was being spent harmfully and not merely wastefully; the cases in which family guidance was indicated are the ones in which there were serious marital difficulties, and so forth.

The various needs not met by agencies have been analyzed case by case as follows:

(a) In 189 cases (77.8 per cent) the obvious requirement was organized recreational outlets either for the men themselves or for members of their immediate families.

[22] Appendix C, 2–36.
[24] Appendix E, 17.

[23] Appendix C, 2–35.

(b) 182 cases (74.9 per cent) called for the friendly supervision which a social worker might give to the men or their families who very clearly needed that kind of propping up in the conduct of their affairs; in 121 (49.8 per cent) vocational guidance was necessary; in 81 cases (33.3 per cent) attention to some problem of mental health was indicated; in 68 cases (28.0 per cent) there were clearly problems of family welfare, usually those involving domestic relations, which remained uncared for. In 7 cases the welfare of the children of our men was at stake and not attended to; in 5 cases there were problems of physical health which were not receiving attention. As against these lacks, however, there was but one case in which financial relief was needed and not given by a social agency.[25]

The high incidence of social, economic, and medical problems which were not coped with by the communities' existing facilities throws into bold relief a major obstacle to rehabilitation of ex-offenders. If it be true that physical, mental, and social handicaps contribute to the origins of delinquent and criminal careers, it is no less true that society's failure to extend a practical helping hand to the former prisoner who returns to its midst, contributes to recidivism and delays reformation. The process of rehabilitation does not end either at the gates of the Reformatory or at the close of a brief period of supervision on parole. It ought to be a continuing task entailing both recognition of social duty and social insurance against further criminalistic aggressions on the part of ex-prisoners.

Trend in Meeting Economic Responsibilities

Was there any improvement in the meeting of their economic obligations by our group of men?

In order to be adjudged as *meeting his economic responsibilities,* a man, if single, separated, widowed, or divorced, and without legal dependents (wife, children, or parents), has to be supporting himself (even if by illegitimate employment) at least in

[25] Appendix C, 2–60.

marginal circumstances and with only occasional assistance from agencies or relatives. If he has dependents, he has to make every reasonable effort to support them at least in marginal circumstances or he cannot be considered as meeting his economic obligations.

By this standard 60.8 per cent of our men were meeting their economic responsibilities during the second five-year period, as compared with 66 per cent during the first.

Those men were regarded as *not meeting their economic obligations* who, through their own fault, were not achieving the standard above described, as evidenced by the contraction of avoidable debts or obtaining unwarranted assistance from social agencies or relatives.[26]

The changes that have taken place within the group in the assumption of their economic responsibilities are more clearly seen in the following analysis:

(a) Of 215 men who were meeting their economic responsibilities during the first five-year period, 27 (12.6 per cent) were not doing so during the second. (b) Of 109 men who, during the first period, were not meeting their economic obligations, 17 (15.6 per cent) were assuming them during the second.[27]

On the whole, therefore, there has been no improvement in the economic conditions and in the assumption of their economic responsibilities by our group of 454 men in Period II as compared with Period I. The former may be attributed to several causes among which should be mentioned the difficulty of making progress industrially if men have little in the way of a skilled trade and desirable work habits to build on; the general hardship encountered by ex-prisoners in making a "come-back" in society; the added difficulty of obtaining employment during a period of industrial decline.

The lack of improvement in the meeting of economic obligations is partially related to the foregoing reasons and partially dependent, perhaps, on long-standing habits of irresponsibility.

[26] Appendix D, 21.
[27] Appendix E, 18.

Chapter IV

INDUSTRIAL ADJUSTMENT

IT has already been pointed out that the marked industrial depression beginning in 1929 intervened in the middle of the second follow-up period and somewhat complicated the determination of whether or not our men were industrially successful during that time. As was pointed out, 58 (17.2 per cent) of 337 men about whom this information was clear from a detailed study of the industrial history of the individual cases, and to whom it was entirely applicable because they were for the most part not confined in institutions, were actually victims of the depression in that they either lost their work completely or were reduced to part-time employment directly because of the industrial crisis and not because some of them were and always had been irregular and sporadic workers.[1] Therefore, in order to make as fair a presentation as possible not only of the economic but of the industrial status of our 454 men during this second period, the situation of these 58 men only up to the beginning of the depression years was determined. In the other cases, their status throughout the five-year period was examined because they were little if at all affected by the depression, largely because of the fact that so many of them always were and now continued to be irregular workers. In other words, it would not be sound to lay the recidivism of most of these men at the door of the industrial depression since even in more favorable economic times they were largely irregular and incompetent workers—many of them unemployable and not merely unemployed.

Findings

NATURE OF OCCUPATIONS

With these preliminaries we may look into the occupations in

[1] Appendix C, 2–H116.

which our men were engaged during Period II as compared with Period I; determine the number of different occupations at which they tried their hands; ascertain whether as many of them were engaged in illegitimate occupations as before; learn whether there has been any improvement in their industrial skill; discover if any of them continued to utilize the occupation in which they were trained in the Reformatory.

During the second five-year period, 21.3 per cent of our men were largely occupied at rough labor as compared with 22.3 per cent during the first; 10.8 per cent were usually engaged as trucksters or teamsters throughout Period II as compared with 13.5 per cent so occupied in the first period; 11.3 per cent were usually employed in factories, as compared with 15.9 per cent during the first period; 7.9 per cent were salesmen or store clerks and a like proportion (8 per cent) had been so engaged in the first period. Almost a fifth (17.2 per cent) of the men were engaged in skilled trades (carpentry, electrical work, bricklaying, plumbing, painting) while slightly over a fifth (22.5 per cent) had been so occupied in the first follow-up period; 5.4 per cent of the men worked in restaurants or hotels during the second period as compared with 4.5 per cent during the first; 3.3 per cent were farm hands during Period II while 2.9 per cent had been so employed during Period I; 6.4 per cent of the men were almost entirely engaged in some illegitimate employment in Period II as compared with 7.2 per cent during the first five years.[2] There was thus very little change in the character of the occupations usually engaged in by our men as a group during the second period.

A case-by-case analysis more clearly shows the changes that have taken place in the type of the usual occupations engaged in by our men during both periods:

(a) Of 20 men who had previously been engaged throughout the period in illegitimate occupations, 15 (75 per cent) were still so employed, one was idle throughout the second period, one was

[2] Appendix D, 22.

occupied in rough work of the day laborer type, one had become a restaurant worker, and two were now trucksters.

(b) Of 72 men who had previously engaged in rough labor, 49 (68.1 per cent) continued to be so engaged, 6 (8.3 per cent) were now idle even though they were fully able to work, 5 (6.9 per cent) now had a trade, 4 (5.6 per cent) had turned to illegitimate employment, 3 had become trucksters, 2 now worked in restaurants, one became a factory hand, one a farm hand, one a store clerk.

(c) Of 46 men who previously had been usually occupied in trucking, teaming, or chauffeuring, 30 (65.3 per cent) were still so occupied, 10 (21.7 per cent) were now day laborers, 2 had turned to illicit employment, 2 were now store clerks, one was idle practically throughout the period although he was fully able to work and was not a depression victim, and one was now a restaurant employee.

(d) Of 52 men who had usually been factory hands during the first period, 39 (75 per cent) continued to work in factories during the second period, 5 (9.6 per cent) became day laborers, 3 worked in restaurants, 3 were idle practically throughout the second five-year period although they were fully able to get work, one was now a truckster, and one had acquired a skilled trade.

(e) All 10 men who previously were farm hands continued to be so engaged in the second five-year period.

(f) Of 27 men who were salesmen or store clerks, 25 (92.6 per cent) continued to be so occupied. The other two men were now mostly idle.

(g) Of 64 men who were plying skilled trades during the first period, 57 (77 per cent) continued to do so, 5 (6.8 per cent) had turned to rough labor to earn a living, 3 had become trucksters, 3 factory hands, 2 farm hands, 2 were earning their livings illicitly, one was now a store clerk, and one was mostly idle.

(h) Of 17 men who had previously been employed in restaurants or hotels (mostly as waiters or short-order cooks), 10 (58.8 per cent) continued to be so employed, 5 (29.4 per cent) had shifted to rough day labor and 2 now engaged in skilled trades.[3]

[3] Appendix E, 19.

The average number of different occupations engaged in by our men in Period II was 1.77 (±.05). This information was not available for Period I.[4]

It might be expected that because of the industrial depression a considerably higher proportion of our men than previously would in Period II have turned to illegitimate employment. This is not the case, however. In the second period, 23 or 7.4 per cent of the men were engaged in illegitimate occupations throughout and a like number were so engaged during the first five-year period; while 50 or 16.1 per cent of the group were for part of the time engaged in illegitimate occupations during the second five-year period and 51 men had been so engaged during the first.[5]

These changes are more clearly seen from the following analysis:

(a) Of 19 men who were engaged in illicit employment throughout Period I and about whom the information for Period II was known, 15 (78.9 per cent) continued to earn their livings illicitly during the second period; while 3 (15.8 per cent) were then only partly earning their livings in illicit enterprises, and one man was entirely engaged in legitimate employment.

(b) Of 35 men who had been partially occupied in illicit employment during the first period, 24 (68.6 per cent) continued to earn their livings partly in illicit occupations during the second period; while 4 (11.4 per cent) had turned completely to illicit employment; but 7 (20 per cent) had entirely given up an illegitimate occupation during the second period.

(c) Finally, of 226 men who previously had had no illegitimate employment, 9 (4 per cent) later turned to some unlawful occupation.[6]

SKILL

In the light of these slight shifts in the usual occupation in the second period, as compared with the first, it is well to see whether there really has been any change in the degree of skill of the group in the two periods. During the second five years 11.4 per cent of

[4] Appendix C, 2–40a. [5] Appendix D, 23. [6] Appendix E, 20.

our men were skilled workmen as compared with 9.8 per cent during the first; 50.9 per cent were semi-skilled workers as compared with 51.5 per cent previously; and 37.7 per cent were unskilled workers as compared with 38.7 per cent in the first period.[7]

Thus, there has been very little change in the industrial skill of the group.

A case-by-case analysis shows what changes have taken place in the skills of the men:

(a) Of 120 men who were unskilled workers during Period I, 20 (16.7 per cent) later became semi-skilled and one had become a skilled worker.

(b) Of 159 men who previously were semi-skilled workers, 6 (3.8 per cent) had now become entirely skilled while 17 (10.7 per cent) had turned to unskilled work for the making of a living. The depression does not entirely account for this. In many of the cases deterioration due to alcoholism or mental disease explains the change in industrial status from more to less skilled work.

(c) Of 33 men who were previously skilled workers, 3 (9.1 per cent) were now finding employment in semi-skilled occupations.[8]

USE OF REFORMATORY OCCUPATION

Did many of the men continue to utilize the training which they had received in the Reformatory? Of our 454 men, 81.7 per cent had not done so during the first five-year period, 18.3 per cent had taken advantage of the training which they received in the institution. During the second period little change occurred since 83.7 per cent were then not utilizing the occupations in which they had been trained in the Reformatory.[9]

A case-by-case analysis shows that:

(a) Of 259 men who had not during the first period utilized the vocational training which they had received in the Reformatory, 97 per cent continued not to do so. (b) Of 59 men who had used the Reformatory occupation during the first period, 17 (28.8 per cent) did not do so during the second. It is evident, therefore, that

---

[7] Appendix D, 24.   [8] Appendix E, 21.   [9] Appendix D, 25.

although there has actually been a falling off in the utilization of the training gained in the Reformatory, the status of the group as a whole had not changed in this regard.[10]

EARNINGS

The average weekly earnings of our men during the first five-year period were $26.45 ($\pm$.42) and during the second, $25.25 ($\pm$.44). Thus there was practically no change in earning capacity, except for that very small group of men who were really direct victims of the depression and they, as already explained, are not included in this estimate.[11]

The changes which have taken place are more clearly seen in this analysis:

(a) Of 78 men who were earning less than $25 weekly during the first period, 30 (38.5 per cent) were later earning between $25 and $35 a week, and 5 (6.4 per cent) were earning on the average of $35 or more.

(b) Of 58 men who had earned between $25 and $35 a week in the first period, 29 (50 per cent) were still receiving the same average salary, 8 (13.8 per cent) were earning less than $25 a week, and 21 (36.2 per cent) were earning $35 or more a week.

(c) Of 32 men who had previously earned $35 or more, 28 (87.5 per cent) were continuing to earn such a salary, while 4 (12.5 per cent) had been reduced to weekly average earnings of between $25 and $35.[12] These internal changes are considerable, even though the earnings of the group as a whole remained practically unaffected.

An examination of the highest wage earned by our men during this period shows comparatively little change. The average of the highest wage during the first five-year period was $30.75 ($\pm$.36); while in the second period it was $32 ($\pm$.47).[13] A case-by-case analysis shows, however, that:

(a) Of 71 men whose highest earnings had previously amounted to less than $25 a week, 12 (16.9 per cent) now achieved a top salary

[10] Appendix E, 22. [11] Appendix D, 26.
[12] Appendix E, 23. [13] Appendix D, 27.

ranging between $25 and $35 a week, and 7 (9.9 per cent) were earning $35 and more.

(b) Of 74 men who had previously earned between $25 and $35 a week, 18 (24.4 per cent) had now earned a larger wage; while 22 (29.7 per cent) were reduced to less than $25 a week. The general effects of the industrial depression of course had something to do with this, even though these men could not be considered serious depression victims.[14]

(c) Of 83 men whose highest salary had previously been $35 or over, 64 (77.1 per cent) were still maintaining this high level, 16 (19.3 per cent) were earning no more than between $25 and $35 a week, while 3 were now reduced to less than $25 a week as their highest salary.[15]

WORK HABITS

What kind of work habits did these men have during the second period? Were they on the whole reliable, industrious workers who were an asset to their employers, or were they lazy, dishonest, unstable? During the second five-year period 41.2 per cent of our men were good workers, by which is meant that they were reliable, honest, industrious, as compared with 33.6 per cent who could be so classified in the first period. As against 30.3 per cent who were fair workers during the first period, 22.9 per cent were such during the second. This designation means that they had the qualifications of good workers but permitted their work to be interrupted by periodic drinking, by the drug habit, by occasional vagabondage, or by the deliberate choice of irregular occupations, such as longshoring, for the chief purpose of having leisure time. Only one-fourth (25.9 per cent) of our men, however, were now poor workers as compared with 36.1 per cent who had to be so classified during the first period. This designation pertains to those who were

---

14 The salaries of the 58 men who had been markedly affected by the depression are considered only through 1929.

15 Appendix E, 24.

unreliable, loafed a good deal, were dishonest or unstable or engaged in illegitimate occupations.[16]

A case-by-case analysis shows the internal changes in the group more clearly:

(a) Of 116 men who were regarded as good workers during the first period, 13 (11.2 per cent) had later to be categorized as fair, and one as poor. (b) Of 100 men who previously were fair workers, 22 (22 per cent) later became good workers, while 10 (10 per cent) had deteriorated into poor workers. (c) Of 107 men who in Period I had been poor workers, 26 (24.3 per cent) later became only fair workers and 11 (10.3 per cent) had become sufficiently reliable and industrious to be classified as good workers.[17]

Clearly, then, a definite improvement occurred in the work habits of the group.

The work habits of the men are somewhat more clearly reflected in the reasons why they left their employment. During the first period, of 262 men who left their work frequently, 169 (64.5 per cent) did so through their own fault; that is, they had been arrested and had to leave a job, or had been discharged for inefficiency, dishonesty, drinking, unreasonable disagreement with an employer, causing disturbance, and so on. This proportion was cut to 54.2 per cent (129 out of 238 men) during the second period.[18]

The changes which occurred within the group in this regard are as follows:

(a) Of 122 men who lost jobs during the first period entirely through their own fault, 101 or 82.8 per cent continued to do so in the second, while the remainder achieved a certain degree of industrial stability and were not losing their jobs so readily through any fault of their own.

(b) Of 84 men who previously did not lose jobs through their own fault, or who changed from one job to another to better their condition, 11 (13.1 per cent) had deteriorated industrially to the

---

[16] Appendix D, 28.   [17] Appendix E, 25.   [18] Appendix D, 29.

extent of losing jobs in the second period largely because of their own shortcomings.

(c) Of 51 men who had worked steadily throughout the first period and rarely changed jobs, 4 (7.8 per cent) were shifting from job to job during the second period mostly through their own fault.[19]

STEADINESS OF EMPLOYMENT

We have compared the work habits of our men during the first and second periods. What now of the steadiness of their employment? During the first five years, 21.8 per cent of the men were regular workers as compared with 28.2 per cent during the second. These men suffered very few breaks in their work at least up to the point in 1929, when the industrial depression began. A third of our men were fairly steadily employed during both periods (33.1 per cent in Period I, 34 per cent in Period II). These men were at times unemployed in excess of two months a year but had long periods of continuous employment at least up to 1929. Irregular employment (that is, frequent or long protracted periods of unemployment instead of sustained work up to 1929, if they were really victims of the depression thereafter) was the lot of 45.1 per cent of our men during the first period, the proportion being reduced to 37.8 per cent during the second. Hence there was an increased steadiness of employment during the second period.[20]

The changes which have taken place within the group, case by case, are brought out in the following analysis:

(a) Of 136 men who in the first period were irregular workers or engaged entirely in illegitimate occupations, 25 (18.4 per cent) later became fairly regular workers and 6 were steadily employed during Period II. (b) Of 112 men who previously had been fairly steady workers, 20 (17.8 per cent) later became regular workers while 17 (15.2 per cent) deteriorated into irregular workers. (c) Of

---

[19] Appendix E, 26.   [20] Appendix D, 30.

77 men who previously had been regular workers 9 (11.7 per cent) later worked only fairly regularly and one became an irregular worker.[21]

The average time that our men held jobs varied little from the first to the second period. During Period I they held their jobs on an average of 21.86 (±.93) months, while during Period II the average was 19.7 months (±.80). There was, however, a considerable increase in the proportion of men who held positions for two years and over during the second period as compared with the first. In Period II, 31.1 per cent of the men held their jobs on an average of two years or longer, while during Period I, only 17.5 per cent of our men held their jobs for so long. Therefore, despite the general effects of the industrial depression on all employment (omitting of course consideration of the group of 58 cases beyond the year 1929), it did not impede the progress of certain of the men toward steadier employment. This is seen more clearly in the following analysis:

(a) Of 94 men who held a job on an average of less than 3 months during Period I, 16 (17.1 per cent) were later employed for longer stretches of time. (b) Of 39 men who were formerly employed on the average of from three months to a year in their various jobs, 12 men (30.8 per cent) later held jobs for longer periods, while 7 men (17.9 per cent) retained them for less than 3 months. (c) Of 74 men who previously held their jobs from one to three years, 35 or 47.3 per cent retained them for three years or longer during the second period, while 9 of the men (12.2 per cent) now held their jobs on the average of less than a year.[22]

The increased steadiness of employment is further reflected in the *longest* period of time that our men held a job during the second five-year period as compared with the first: 23.3 (±.77) months in Period II as compared with only 17.88 (±.64) months in Period I.[23]

[21] Appendix E, 27.   [22] Appendix E, 28.   [23] Appendix D, 32.

Trend of Industrial Adjustment

A slight trend has been noted toward greater industrial stability in our men during the second period as compared with the first, and this despite the general effects of the industrial depression. It may well be, of course, that this improvement in the group would have been greater had not the depression intervened. However, it has already been pointed out that to a large extent this effect has been taken into account by not considering beyond the year 1929 the status of the 58 men who were really affected by the depression, and basing the judgment of the industrial adjustment, about to be made, upon the situation only up to that time.

For the purpose of describing the industrial adjustment of our 454 men, they were deemed *industrially successful* if their work habits were good and they were steadily employed; as *partial successes* if their work habits were good but they worked irregularly, or though they worked only fairly regularly their work habits were fair or poor, or they worked regularly but their habits of work were fair or poor. They were rated as *failures industrially* if they were irregular workers with poor work habits.

By these criteria, 24.8 per cent of our men were successful industrially during the second period as compared with 21.3 per cent in the first; 37.9 per cent were partially successful, as compared with 33.8 per cent during the first; and 37.3 per cent were now failures industrially as compared with 44.9 per cent in the first five-year period.[24] The changes occurring within the group are reflected in the following analysis:

(a) Of 74 men who were industrial successes in Period I, 9 (12.2 per cent) later had to be rated as only partial successes, one as a failure. (b) Of 115 men who previously were partial successes, 12 (10.4 per cent) were later entirely successful industrially, while 13 (11.3 per cent) had deteriorated into failures in the second period. (c) Of 132 men who previously were industrial failures, 22 (16.7

---

[24] Appendix D, 33.

per cent) later became fairly successful industrially, while 5 were entirely successful.[25]

That the trend of industrial adjustment is slightly upward is seen in the fact that during the fifth year of the second period, with the exception of those men who were by then definitely and directly victims of the depression (that is, who had lost good jobs or were reduced to occasional work), 28.7 per cent were industrial successes, 35.3 per cent were partially successful, and 36 per cent were failures.[26]

[25] Appendix E, 30.
[26] Appendix C, 2–63b.

Chapter V

USE OF LEISURE TIME

BEFORE turning to the crucial question of the extent to which our men continued to be recidivists during the second follow-up period, it will be helpful to consider the character of their companionships, of the places where they typically spent their leisure, and of their spare-time activities. It is well known that these matters have a vital bearing on both the origins of delinquent conduct and on recidivism.

Findings

COMPANIONS AND HAUNTS

During the first five-year period, 68.6 per cent of our men had questionable companions, association with whom actually did lead or might well have led to delinquency. These included street-corner loafers, habitués of poolrooms, chronic drinkers, gamblers, men and women who lived by their wits, and the like. In the second five-year period this proportion was reduced to 63 per cent.[1] Detailed analysis shows how slight has been the change in this regard in the second five-year follow-up period:

(a) Of 200 men whose companionships were harmful during the first period, 22 (11 per cent) were later consorting with men and women whose influence, though not necessarily wholesome, was at least not detrimental. (b) Of 102 men whose companionships were harmless during the first period, 12 (11.8 per cent) were later associating with very questionable companions.[2]

In Period II, half the men (48.7 per cent) were meeting their "pals" very frequently on street corners and in corner stores and spending most of their leisure time loafing about in the streets[3] with their "gang" or "crowd." In this connection, it is to be noted

---

[1] Appendix D, 34.   [2] Appendix E, 31.   [3] Appendix C, 2–50b.

that even during the second follow-up period only 8 per cent of the men were members of gangs (that is, gangs organized for definite anti-social purposes such as theft); 45.8 per cent tended to hang about with several other men, but in such association there was evidently no particular purpose, social or anti-social, other than mere idling.[4]

During Period I over three-fifths of our men (68 per cent) frequented places of recreation that were distinctly harmful in character such as gambling dens, bootlegging joints, houses of ill fame, cheap cafés where hangers-on, drunkards, thieves, and prostitutes gathered. During the second five years 61.5 per cent of the men frequented similar places. A very slight improvement is thus evident.[5]

The changes which occurred in the utilization of their leisure time by each of our 454 men are clarified in the following analysis:

(a) Of 189 men who during the first period spent their leisure time in disreputable places, 22 (11.6 per cent) were no longer doing so. (b) Of 102 men who previously were finding recreational outlets in places which though not necessarily wholesome were at least not too disreputable (such as cheap political clubs, bowling alleys, public dance halls, skating rinks), 12 (11.8 per cent) later turned to definitely disreputable resorts for the enjoyment of their leisure time.[6]

Indicating serious social negligence is the fact that very few of these men held membership in organizations for the constructive use of leisure time, such as the Y.M.C.A., church societies, and so on. Actually only 4 per cent of our men were members of such organizations during the first period. A like low proportion (4.7 per cent) belonged to such organizations or societies during the second period. Almost a tenth (8.2 per cent) were members of other clubs of one kind or another during the first period, mostly political in character but not of a particularly wholesome nature. During the second five-year period 9.1 per cent of our men belonged to clubs of this kind. The men went to these places some-

---

[4] Appendix C, 2–50a.   [5] Appendix D, 35.   [6] Appendix E, 32.

times just to sit around idly or play cards and fritter away time without any constructive supervision. But the great majority of the group (87.8 per cent in the first period and 86.2 per cent in the second) were at no time members of clubs, societies, or organizations for the constructive, or at least harmless, use of their leisure hours.[7]

Here is a point of attack that calls urgently for action on the part of social planners. Unless organized society can offer wholesome substitutes for the expenditure of leisure time that will successfully compete with demoralizing attractions, one channel to the rehabilitation of ex-prisoners must remain blocked.

The changes which had occurred within the group in this aspect of the use of their leisure time are more clearly seen from the following:

(a) Of 264 men who during the first five-year period did not belong to any clubs or organizations, 5 later became members of agencies like the Y.M.C.A., where they utilized their spare hours constructively, while 10 joined political clubs or other organizations where much of their time was wasted and little of the remainder was occupied constructively. The great majority of the men (94.3 per cent) did not belong to any organizations for the use of leisure.

(b) Of 13 men who in Period I frequented places for the constructive employment of spare time, 10 continued to do so, 2 had given up this membership, and one later became a member of a political club.

(c) Of 28 men who previously belonged to societies or clubs in which membership did not imply the wholesome use of leisure, 12 (42.9 per cent) later dropped their membership in these clubs and did not join any others.[8]

RELIGIOUS ACTIVITIES

Was any of the leisure time of our men being absorbed in regular church attendance or associations? As a matter of fact only a

[7] Appendix D, 36.   [8] Appendix E, 33.

little over a tenth (12 per cent) of the men attended church regularly in Period II; 40.4 per cent, although members, went to church only very occasionally; while 47.6 per cent did not attend church at all during this period. This marks very little if any change between the first and second period. During Period I, 12.6 per cent of the men were regular church attenders, 43.5 per cent went irregularly, while 43.9 per cent neither attended nor belonged to church.[9]

The changes which took place within the group in this regard are seen from the following analysis:

(a) Of 31 men who attended church regularly in the first period, 8 (25.8 per cent) later became irregular attendants, while 3 (9.7 per cent) no longer went to church. (b) Of 102 men who formerly had attended church off and on, 7 (6.9 per cent) later became regular church-goers while 17 (16.6 per cent) stopped attending altogether. (c) Of 107 men who previously did not attend church at all, 9 (8.4 per cent) subsequently went to church occasionally, and one became a regular church-goer.[10]

EDUCATIONAL ACTIVITIES

In the light of the picture already drawn of the use of leisure time by our men, it is not surprising to find that only 5.6 per cent of them engaged in any educational or vocational training during Period II, such as attendance at evening school or the taking of a correspondence course to improve their vocational status. In this regard, the situation is little better than it was during the first period, when only 4 per cent of the men pursued such activities.[11] Here, again, a great opportunity is being missed for supplying attractive adult educational and vocational services as part of a rehabilitative program.

The slight change within the group in respect to educational activity is seen from the following:

(a) Of 291 men who had not pursued any educational or voca-

[9] Appendix D, 37.   [10] Appendix E, 34.   [11] Appendix D, 38.

tional training during the first period, only 6 (2.1 per cent) did so
during the second. (b) Of 12 men who previously had some educational or vocational training, 5 (41.7 per cent) were no longer
taking advantage of such opportunities.[12]

Trend in Use of Leisure

How marked was the improvement in use of leisure?

Considering the foregoing findings in a composite picture, by
and large only 4.3 per cent of our men could be said to have utilized
their leisure time *constructively* during the second five-year period
—a designation which implies either that they were members of
well-supervised organizations for the use of leisure or were spending most of their spare time to further themselves culturally or vocationally by taking courses, attending night school, and the like.
This does not differ from the first period, when 4.7 per cent of the
men utilized their leisure time constructively.

Almost a third of the men (29.9 per cent) may be said to have
employed their spare time *indifferently* during the second period,
—a characterization which implies that although constructive activities were not carried on in their spare time, there was at least
no indulgence in harmful activities. During the first period, 26 per
cent of the men fell into this class.

But the large proportion of two-thirds of our men (69.3 per
cent during Period I and 65.8 per cent during Period II) very definitely utilized their leisure *harmfully,* in that they indulged in the
kind of spare time activity which might lead to conflict with the
law, such as membership in gangs, association with bootleggers,
prostitutes, loafers, drug addicts, gamblers.[13]

The changes that took place within the group in the utilization
of leisure time are seen in the following analysis:

(a) Of 17 men who in Period I employed their leisure constructively, 10 (58.8 per cent) continued to do so in Period II, while 5

[12] Appendix E, 35.   [13] Appendix D, 39.

men (29.4 per cent) were then making indifferent use of their spare time, and 2 had definitely turned to harmful outlets for their free hours.

(b) Of 89 men who previously utilized their leisure time indifferently only 5 (5.6 per cent) were later using it constructively, while 13 (14.6 per cent) were using it harmfully.

(c) Of 215 men who during the first period spent their spare time harmfully, 19 (8.8 per cent) were no longer doing so in the second, but at the same time had not found constructive outlets for their leisure.[14]

That the trend in the use of leisure continues upward is seen in the fact that during the fifth year of the second period, but 56.5 per cent of our men were utilizing their spare time harmfully, as compared with 65.8 per cent who had so misspent their leisure during all or part of the first four years of the second five-year period.[15]

[14] Appendix E, 36.   [15] Appendix C, 2–65b.

Chapter VI

CRIMINAL CONDUCT

THE chief point of interest in an investigation of this kind is of course the criminal history of the ex-prisoners. Have they, during the past five years, continued to recidivate to the same extent as in the first follow-up period? Has there been any change in the frequency of their arrests, in the kinds of offenses which they have committed, in the character of their offenses? Have they been more or less frequently convicted than heretofore? Have they spent as much time as previously in penal institutions? To these and other crucial questions concerning the delinquency and criminality of our men we now turn our attention.

Findings

NUMBER AND NATURE OF ARRESTS

During the second period our 454 men were arrested 955 times, while during the first this same group of men had been arrested 938 times. The average number of arrests among those arrested during the second period was 3.71 ($\pm$.12)[1] as compared with 3.3 ($\pm$.11) in the first five-year period. Of the 955 arrests which occurred during the second period, half (51.3 per cent) were for drunkenness,[2] an increase in the proportion of arrests for drunkenness as compared with the first period when 41.4 per cent of all arrests were for this offense. Almost one-fifth of the arrests in the second period (17.2 per cent) were for offenses against the public health, safety, and policy, such as vagrancy, violation of license laws, disturbing the peace, gaming, profanity, being idle and disorderly, and the like. During the first five-year period a like proportion of arrests (17.9 per cent) had been for similar offenses. In Period II offenses against property amounted to only 17.3 per cent of the total num-

---

[1] Appendix C, 2–53. [2] Appendix C, 1–9.

ber, as compared with 26 per cent during the first five-year period. This designation refers largely to larcenies, burglaries, pickpocketing, receiving stolen goods, possessing burglar's tools, robbery, and similar offenses. In Period II 4.1 per cent of the arrests were for offenses against family and children, a category which usually refers to arrests for non-support, desertion, bastardy, cruelty to children, and so on. During the first five-year period 3.7 per cent of arrests had been for such offenses. In the second period 4.3 per cent of arrests were for offenses against the person, a designation referring largely to cases of assault and battery without intent to kill, rape, or rob. During the first five-year period, only 1.5 per cent of arrests had been for this cause. There has occurred a dropping off in arrests for offenses against chastity (adultery, lewd and lascivious cohabitation, fornication, rape, and the like): only 1.8 per cent of arrests were for such offenses during the second period as compared with 6.3 per cent during the first. Arrests for drug addiction have, however, remained stationary—1.2 per cent in the second period as compared with 1.3 per cent in the first. In the second period 2.8 per cent of the arrests were for other offenses, such as arson, escape or rescue, being a fugitive from justice, and the like. During the first five years 1.9 per cent of all the arrests had been for such offenses.[3]

Of the 200 men represented by the 955 arrests during the second period, 86 (43 per cent) had been arrested for drunkenness one or more times; 88 (44 per cent) for offenses against the public health, safety, and policy; 86 (43 per cent) for property crimes; 22 (11 per cent) for offenses against the person; 21 (10.5 per cent) for offenses against family and children; 16 (8 per cent) for offenses against chastity, 11 (5.5 per cent) for drug selling, and a like number for other offenses. Unfortunately comparable data for the first five-year period are not available.[4] A total of 163 men were not arrested at all during the second period although 2 of these were dishonorably discharged from the army. It was unknown whether 57 had been

[3] Appendix D, 40.   [4] Appendix C, 2–58.

arrested, and 34 of the men were in institutions practically throughout the period and therefore could not have been arrested.

From the above analysis, it is evident that there has been rather a substantial change in the character of the arrests of the group. This is shown mainly by an increase in the proportion of arrests for drunkenness and a falling off in arrests for offenses against property. The change becomes more striking when comparison is made between the arrests occurring during the first and second periods with those which took place prior to the commitment of the men to the Reformatory. At that time 14.4 per cent of 1944 arrests were for drunkenness (as compared with 41.4 per cent during the first five-year period and 51.3 per cent during the second). Prior to commitment, 49.1 per cent of all the arrests were for offenses against property, as compared with 26 per cent during the first five-year period, and 17.3 per cent during the second.[5]

FREQUENCY OF ARRESTS

Has there been any change in the frequency of arrests among those men who were arrested more than once during the period? In Period II the average frequency of arrests was one in 12.5 months ($\pm$.45); while during Period I the average frequency had been one arrest in 13.52 months ($\pm$.40). The decrease in the frequency of arrests is therefore slight.[6] The internal changes which occurred in the group are more clearly evident, however, from the following analysis of the sub-classes:

(a) Of 57 men who, in Period I, had been arrested more often than once a year, 10 (17.5 per cent) were during the second five-year period being less frequently arrested.

(b) Of 40 men who previously had been arrested once in one or two years, 17 (42.5 per cent) were later being arrested more frequently, and 9 (22.5 per cent) less frequently.

(c) Of 11 men who previously had been arrested no oftener than

---

[5] Appendix D, 40.

[6] Appendix D, 41. For method of calculating frequency of arrests, see Appendix B, *Frequency of Arrests.*

once in two or more years, 8 (72.8 per cent) were later being arrested more frequently.[7] This comparison of course does not take account of those men who during the second period had not been arrested at all or only once, even though they had been arrested more than once during the first.

NUMBER AND NATURE OF DISPOSITIONS OF ARRESTS

What changes took place in the nature of the dispositions of the arrests of our men as they grew older? During the second period, 30.7 per cent of all the arrests resulted in commitments to peno-correctional institutions, as compared with 33.3 per cent during the first; while 13.6 per cent resulted, in both the second and first periods, in the offenders being placed on probation. In Period II, our men were fined following 16.7 per cent of all their arrests, as compared with fines imposed in 22.8 per cent of the cases during the first period. Commitment for non-payment of fine occurred as a result of 3.9 per cent of all the arrests in Period II as compared with 3.8 per cent in the first period. Cases were filed following 14.8 per cent of all the arrests which occurred during Period II as compared with 12.6 per cent in Period I. Finally, one-fifth (20.3 per cent) of all the arrests occurring in the second period resulted in nol prossing, a finding of "No bill," or "Not guilty," or were released by the probation officer without formal court appearance (in case of drunkenness), as compared with 13.9 per cent of similar dispositions during the first five-year period.

Essentially, therefore, there was very little change in the nature of the dispositions of offenses, except for the slight decrease in the proportion of offenses which were followed by fine; and the increase in releases, nol prosses, and like dispositions. A comparison of the outcomes of arrests in the first and second periods with that preceding the commitment of our men to the Reformatory indicates, as might be expected, a decided falling off in the incidence of probation; for prior to commitment, 28.4 per cent of the arrests

[7] Appendix E, 37.

were disposed of in this way as compared with 13.6 per cent in both the first and second periods. The decrease in the use of probation appears in general to have been largely absorbed by the greater use of fines.[8]

Of the 200 men who were arrested during the second five-year period 55.5 per cent were committed to peno-correctional institutions, 32.5 per cent were placed on probation, 38 per cent were fined, 9 per cent were committed for non-payment of fine, 35 per cent had charges against them filed, 15.5 per cent were released by probation officers following charges of drunkenness, 4.5 per cent had cases against them nol prossed, and in 42.5 per cent of the cases there was a finding of "No bill" or "Not guilty."[9] Unfortunately comparable data for the first follow-up period had not been obtained.

NUMBER OF CONVICTIONS

The mean number of convictions following arrests in these 200 cases was 1.69 ($\pm$.09),[10] this being considerably lower than during the first five-year period when the average number of convictions was 3.14 ($\pm$.10).[11] It will be recalled that in Period II, the average number of arrests was 3.71 ($\pm$.12); hence there were obviously far fewer convictions than arrests during the second period. This may suggest a greater skill in avoiding proof of guilt and in manipulating the processes of justice; for during the first period convictions had been almost as frequent as arrests (3.14:3.22).

FREQUENCY OF CONVICTIONS

Was there any decrease in the frequency of convictions in Period II? During that span the 200 men who were arrested received a conviction once in 15.65 months ($\pm$.48) which is nearly similar to the frequency of convictions of those arrested during the first period—one in 15.05 months ($\pm$.46). It will be recalled that during the second period, the average frequency of arrests was one in

---

[8] Appendix D, 44.
[9] Appendix C, 2-59.
[10] Appendix C, 2-54.
[11] Appendix C, 1-10.

13.52 months (±.40) and during the first it had been one in 12.5 months (±.45). The frequency of convictions was no greater even in the period prior to commitment to the Reformatory—one in 15.14 months (±.37). In this regard, therefore, little change has occurred.[12] However, a case-by-case analysis indicates considerable shift among the constituents of the group:

(a) Of 47 men who during the first period had been convicted as often as once in less than a year, 14 (29.8 per cent) were convicted less frequently during the second. (b) Of 31 men who previously had been convicted once in one to two years, 15 (48.4 per cent) were later being convicted more frequently, and 8 (25.8 per cent) less frequently. (c) Of 24 men who previously had been convicted no more than once in two or more years, 13 (54.2 per cent) were later being convicted more frequently.[13]

NUMBER AND NATURE OF PENO-CORRECTIONAL EXPERIENCES

In 111 of the cases of the 200 men who were arrested during the second period, conviction was followed by commitment to a peno-correctional institution. However, in addition to these 111 men who were committed directly during the second period 36 men had peno-correctional experiences which had been imposed during the previous period but continued in force for part or all of the second five years, making a total of 147 men (36.8 per cent of the known and applicable total) who had peno-correctional experiences of one kind or another during Period II. Of these 147, 95 (64.6 per cent) had one or two such experiences, and 52 (35.4 per cent) had three or more. During the first five-year period 177 of our men (43 per cent of the known and applicable total) had had penal experiences of one kind or another, 130 (88.4 per cent) of them having had one or two such experiences and 47 (32 per cent) three or more. Actually there has been a falling off in the number of penal experiences among that group of men who underwent peno-correctional treatment both in the first and second periods. The

[12] Appendix D, 45. [13] Appendix E, 39.

average number during the second period was 2.72 ($\pm$.12) as compared with 3.44 ($\pm$.08) during the first.

The decline in the proportion of men having penal experiences is further indicated by a comparison with the period prior to their commitment to the Reformatory, when 57.9 per cent of the men served sentences in peno-correctional institutions as compared with 43 per cent in the first post-parole period and 36.8 per cent in the second.[14]

A case-by-case comparison of our men in this regard shows that: (a) Of 164 men who had had one or more penal experiences in the first period, 51 (31.1 per cent) did not serve any time in penal institutions during the second. (b) Of 225 men who had not been imprisoned during the first period, only 30 (13.3 per cent) served one or more sentences in penal institutions during the second.[15] The general decline in imprisonments is of course consistent with the falling off in delinquency already noted.

Of the total number of peno-correctional experiences of our men during the second follow-up period, 1.8 per cent, as compared with 10.9 per cent in the first period, were spent in reformatories. This is of course largely due to the passing of the age limit set on those committable to such institutions. During Period II, 26.4 per cent of the incarcerations were in prisons,[16] as compared with 27.1 per cent during Period I. Finally, in the second five years, 71.8 per cent of the incarcerations were in institutions for short-term offenders, such as jails, houses of correction, or state farms, as compared with 62 per cent during the first period.[17]

TIME SPENT IN PENAL INSTITUTIONS

The 147 men who were in penal institutions at one time or another during the second period served on an average of 24.26 months each ($\pm$.05); while the 177 men who were incarcerated

---

[14] Appendix D, 46.   [15] Appendix E, 40.

[16] Seven of these at the Department for Defective Delinquents at Bridgewater, Massachusetts.

[17] For further details, see Appendix D, 47, from which these data have been extracted.

in penal institutions during the first period had been incarcerated on an average of 22.30 months ($\pm$.85) each.[18]

A case-by-case comparison indicates that:

(a) Of 225 men who in Period I had not been in penal institutions at all, 24 (10.7 per cent) were incarcerated for less than 20 months during Period II, while 6 (2.6 per cent) served for 20 or more months during this period.

(b) Of 89 men who had previously been in penal institutions for less than 20 months, 35 (39.3 per cent) later spent no time at all in penal institutions, while 20 (22.5 per cent) were under such restraint for longer than 20 months during the second period.

(c) Of 79 men who served for 20 or more months in Period I, 17 (21.5 per cent) were not incarcerated at all during Period II, while 10 (12.7 per cent) were in penal institutions for less than 20 months.

This falling off in penal servitude is in line with the general picture already presented of a reduction in the delinquency of the men.[19]

OFFICIAL AND UNOFFICIAL DELINQUENCY

Having reviewed the arrests, convictions, and penal experiences of our group as a whole during the first and second periods, we shall turn our attention to our 454 men as individual delinquents. In the above description of their offenses we obtained a picture of those delinquencies of 200 men which had been officially recognized by arrests during the periods in question. These men we can label "official" delinquents in that their misconduct was formally recognized by agencies of the law. To this group may be added two more men who might also be regarded as "official" delinquents because they were dishonorably discharged from the army during the period. In addition, however, to this total of 202 men who are designated "official" delinquents during the second period, there are 48 who actually committed offenses of one kind or another for

18 Appendix D, 49.   19 Appendix E, 41.

which they might have been arrested but were not, such as stealing, drunkenness, pathological sex offenses and others. This makes a total of 250 men who were known to be delinquents or criminals during the second five-year period.[20] In addition to these 250 men there were 24 who were in penal institutions for at least 55 months of Period II or were for part of this 55-month span in mental hospitals to which they had been transferred from penal institutions. The original sentences had been imposed during Period I, so that this group of men could not rightly be considered delinquents in the second five years. For present purposes they are therefore placed in a special group designated "inapplicable."

In 62 cases over and above those already noted, either the delinquencies of the men were entirely unknown or the men had been in the community for so brief a time during Period II that their misconduct could not fairly be judged. This applies either to men who died soon after the beginning of the period or who were in mental hospitals for a good part of the time. Deducting the various groups already accounted for from the 454 men involved, there remain *118 men (or 32.1 per cent) who were definitely non-delinquent during the second five-year period.*

It is significant to compare the situation in Period I. During the first period there were 325 men who had to be designated delinquents, of whom 36 were "unofficial" delinquents; 7 men, though they had spent at least 55 months of the first period in penal institutions or mental hospitals, were placed in a special group and not considered delinquents because the sentences had been imposed prior to the beginning of that period. The delinquencies of 33 men were either unknown or the men lived in the community for so brief a period that their delinquencies could not be determined. Deducting these, leaves a total of *only 89 men (or 21.5 per cent) who were non-delinquent during the first five-year period.*[21] *Thus there was an appreciable increase in the proportion*

---

[20] Appendix C, 2–51b.   [21] Appendix D, 50.

of rehabilitated ex-prisoners during Period II as compared with the first period (32.1 per cent: 21.5 per cent).

Omitting, now, those men in both periods whose delinquencies were unknown or who were in the community so brief a time that their delinquencies could not be fairly determined, and those who were in penal and other institutions on sentences imposed in the previous period, we next turn our attention to a more intensive comparison of the criminal activities of the 250 men who were actively delinquent or criminal during the second period and the 325 men who were delinquent or criminal during the first.

PREDOMINANT OFFENSE

Considering the delinquencies of these men from the viewpoint of the offenses which they most characteristically committed (regardless of whether they were always arrested for such offenses or not), we find that 37.2 per cent of this group during the second period as compared with 25.9 per cent during the first, were most characteristically drunkards; while only a fifth (20.7 per cent) in Period II as compared with a third (33.1 per cent) in Period I most typically committed offenses against property; and an eighth of the offenders in both the first and second periods usually committed offenses against public health, safety, and policy. Only 5.8 per cent of the men in the second period and 5.1 per cent in the first most typically committed offenses against chastity, while 3.3 per cent and 4.1 per cent, respectively, usually committed offenses against family and children. In the two periods in question, 2.5 per cent and 1.7 per cent, respectively, were most characteristically drug addicts, and .4 per cent and 1.7 per cent usually committed offenses against the person. Designation of the typical pattern of misbehavior of course does not mean that most of these men did not commit other kinds of offenses, in addition to the one indicated as predominant. In this connection, 17.3 per cent of the entire group of delinquents in Period II and 15.4 per cent in Period I could not be classified as characteristically committing any one type of offense, for their criminalistic activities shifted from one form of delinquency to another and they committed so many different kinds of crimes during the period that it was impossible, by case analysis, to determine any consistency in the pattern of their misconduct.[22]

The most important facts emerging from the above analysis are the increase in the proportion of men whose most characteristic offense was now drunkenness (37.2 per cent in Period II as compared with 25.9 per cent in the preceding period); and the decrease in the proportion of men now most typically committing property crimes (20.7 per cent as compared with 33.1 per cent). The trends here manifest are further accentuated by a comparison between the predominant offenses of our men in the first and second periods with their typical offenses during the time prior to their commitment to the Reformatory, when only 8.1 per cent of the men were characteristically drunkards, while 61.7 per cent had usually committed property crimes.[23]

The changes which have taken place in the character of the predominant offenses are more clearly seen from the following analysis:

(a) Of 59 men who in Period I typically committed property crimes, 44 (74.6 per cent) continued such offenses as the major form of criminal activity in Period II, 6 (10.2 per cent) were then usually committing offenses against the public health, 4 (6.8 per cent) had become chronic drunkards, a like number were committing a variety of offenses no single one being typical, and one man was characteristically committing offenses against chastity.

(b) Of 10 men who as a rule had previously committed offenses against chastity, 8 continued to do so while 2 men were later committing such a variety of offenses that it was impossible to place them in any one category.

(c) Of 8 men who during the first period were usually committing offenses against family and children, 6 continued to do so, one

---

[22] Appendix D, 42.   [23] Appendix D, 42, for further details.

was later characteristically a drunkard, and one was committing a variety of offenses.

(d) Of 28 men who had previously committed offenses against the public health, safety, and policy, 19 (67.9 per cent) continued to do so during Period II, 6 (21.4 per cent) became typically drunkards, 2 committed offenses against the family, and one committed a variety of offenses.

(e) Of 69 men who previously were mainly drunkards, 66 (95.7 per cent) continued so, while 3 men were later committing a variety of offenses.

(f) Of 5 who previously were rated as drug addicts, all continued to be mainly drug addicts.

(g) Of 2 men who previously were classified as usually committing offenses against the person, one later became an offender against public health.

(h) Of 39 men who during the first period were classified as committing a variety of offenses no one of which appeared predominant, 29 (74.3 per cent) continued to do so during the second period, 5 (12.8 per cent) were then characteristically drunkards, 3 (7.7 per cent) were chiefly committing offenses against property, one was committing offenses against chastity, and one had clearly evolved into a drug addict.[24]

PRINCIPAL COMPONENT OF MISCONDUCT

In Chapter I we pointed out the usefulness of classifying offenders into "serious" and "minor." The particular crimes so designated have already been indicated. The basis for the judgment of delinquency in each one of the cases of those who misbehaved during the first and second five-year periods was established as follows: If a man had actually been convicted of felonious or other serious crimes, he was classified as a serious offender. Somewhat over a third of our men (38.4 per cent) were so designated during the second period as compared with 45.5 per cent during

[24] Appendix E, 38.

the first. Next in line were those who had actually committed serious offenses and for whose arrest there were warrants out. These comprised 1.6 per cent during the second period and 4 per cent during the first. Next were classified those who had not been convicted for serious offenses and for whom there were no warrants outstanding for felonies but who were dishonorably discharged or had deserted from the army or navy, even though they might have committed "unofficial" serious offenses or had been arrested but not convicted for serious offenses, or were arrested or convicted for minor offenses, or had committed minor offenses not officially known. These constituted but 1.2 per cent during the second period and 2.8 per cent during the first. Then followed the group who had definitely committed serious offenses for which they had for some reason not been arrested. These amounted to 6 per cent during the second period and 3.4 per cent during the first. There followed a group of men regarding whom the chief component of misconduct consisted of arrests for serious offenses not followed by convictions, even though they might have been arrested or convicted for minor offenses. These amounted to but 2 per cent in the second five-year period as compared with 4 per cent in the first. So much for the serious offenders. A large group were adjudged delinquent chiefly because of their conviction for minor offenses. These comprised 30 per cent in the second period as compared with 23.4 per cent in the first. In addition there were 16 per cent of men in the second period, and 12.3 per cent in the first, who committed minor offenses for which they were for some reason not arrested; and finally a group of 4.8 per cent in the second period and 4.6 per cent in the first were arrested for minor offenses for which they were not convicted.[25]

Considering these designations now from the point of view of the commission of serious and minor offenses, we find that during the second five-year period a total of 50 per cent of the delinquents were serious offenders while during the first 59.7 per cent had been

[25] Appendix D, 50.

so designated. Obviously, therefore, there has been a falling off in the porportion of delinquents committing serious offenses.[26]

USE OF ALIASES; ASSOCIATES IN CRIME

During the second period, 39.9 per cent of the official delinquents about whom this information was known used aliases either occasionally or throughout the five years, as compared with 38 per cent of the men who had done so during the first follow-up period.[27] This would seem to indicate that at least the respective proportions of the official delinquents were in a sense "professional" criminals in that they were deliberately hiding their identity in an attempt to escape the attention of the police.

Of those men who were actually arrested during the second period and about whom the information was available, 57.3 per cent were committing their offenses alone. Although like data had not been gathered for the first five years, we know that 42.6 per cent of our men committed without accomplices the offense which resulted in their sentence to the Reformatory. A tendency to a greater commission of offenses by the man himself therefore appears. This can perhaps be accounted for, when considered in connection with the general drop in criminality during the second five-year period, by the fact that those who commit their offenses alone are the ones who are most likely to continue in criminality, because their behavior is not so dependent upon the influence of others.[28]

Trend of Delinquency

Omitting from consideration those men whose delinquencies were unknown or who lived in the community for so brief a period that their delinquent behavior could not be fairly estimated, and those who were in institutions on sentences imposed in a previous period, we have, then, a *total of 118 of the 368 men (32.1 per cent) who were clearly non-delinquents during the second five-year pe-*

[26] Appendix D, 54.   [27] Appendix D, 52.   [28] Appendix D, 53.

riod, as compared with 89 of the 414 men (21.5 per cent) during the first. This is an appreciable decrease in the proportion of delinquents and criminals during the second five years as compared with the first.[29] That the trend away from criminality is definitely upward is indicated by the fact that by the fifth year of the second period 42.7 per cent of 321 men then involved had become non-delinquent.[30] A case-by-case analysis reveals the upward trend more clearly:

(a) Of 157 men who had to be designated serious delinquents during the first period, 33 (21 per cent) were committing only minor offenses during the second, while 16 (10.2 per cent) had become non-delinquent.

(b) Of 115 men who previously were designated minor delinquents, only 11 (9.6 per cent) later reverted to serious delinquency, while 22 (19.1 per cent) were no longer delinquent in Period II.

(c) Of 88 men who during the first period were non-delinquents, 7 (7.9 per cent) were committing minor delinquencies in the second, while 3 (3.5 per cent) were then serious delinquents and the remainder continued to be non-delinquents.[31]

o   o   o

The crucial inquiry of this entire research is therefore concerned with determining the reasons for the improvement in criminal behavior. To this and related questions the next few chapters are devoted.

[29] Appendix D, 54.
[31] Appendix E, 45.
[30] See Appendix C, 2–57b for details.

Chapter VII

RELATIONSHIP OF CRIMINAL CONDUCT TO
OTHER BEHAVIOR

THE prior chapters have been concerned with describing the similarities and differences in the behavior of our men as a group during the two five-year periods which have elapsed since the expiration of their sentences to the Massachusetts Reformatory. Although general improvement has been noted in all the major aspects of the lives of these men—in their family relationships, in the assumption of their economic responsibilities, in their industrial adjustments, in their use of leisure, and, most important, in the character and extent of their delinquent behavior—we have not yet considered what may be the reasons for this general improvement. Before attempting this, however, we ought to determine whether any relationship exists between criminality and these other major aspects of the life activities of our men.

Findings

FAMILY RELATIONSHIPS AND DELINQUENCY

Is there any association between the attitude of our men toward their family responsibilities during the ten-year span and their criminal conduct? An examination of Table I indicates that a considerable relationship exists.

From this table we see that there is a substantial overlapping between success and failure in respect to family relationships and success and failure in regard to criminality. This is shown in a general way by the high coefficient of mean square contingency (.62) which is a convenient statistical device for summarizing the degree of relationship between two qualitative factors.[1] More spe-

---

[1] For details regarding the significance and use of the mean square contingency coefficient, see G. Udny Yule, *An Introduction to the Theory of Statistics,* London, Griffin and Company, Ltd., 8th ed. rev., 1927, pp. 64–67.

TABLE I. FAMILY RELATIONSHIPS IN TEN-YEAR SPAN CORRELATED WITH DELINQUENCY IN TEN-YEAR SPAN

DELINQUENCY IN TEN-YEAR SPAN	FAMILY RELATIONSHIPS IN TEN-YEAR SPAN								Total	
	Succeeded throughout		Failed throughout		Failed in I, succeeded in II		Succeeded in I, failed in II			
	Number	Per cent	Number	Per cent	Number	Per cent	Number	Per cent	Number	Per cent
Non-delinquent throughout	73	96.1	2	2.6	0	–	1	1.3	76	100
Minor in Period I, non-delinquent in Period II	16	72.7	1	4.5	5	22.8	0	–	22	100
Serious in Period I, non-delinquent in Period II	9	69.2	0	–	4	30.8	0	–	13	100
Serious in Period I, minor in Period II	7	25.9	14	51.9	2	7.4	4	14.8	27	100
Minor throughout	26	34.2	36	47.4	7	9.2	7	9.2	76	100
Serious throughout	8	9.6	62	74.7	3	3.6	10	12.1	83	100
Non-delinquent in Period I, delinquent in Period II	6	60.0	0	–	0	–	4	40.0	10	100
Minor in Period I, serious in Period II	3	27.3	5	45.5	0	–	3	27.2	11	100
Total	148	46.5	120	37.7	21	6.6	29	9.2	318	100

$C = .62$

cifically, the high association between the two factors in question is shown by the fact that while the incidence of successful family relationships over the ten-year span for the entire group was only 46.5 per cent, it was 96.1 per cent in the case of those men who were non-delinquent. Detailed analysis makes the significant relationship between non-delinquency and successful family relationships clearer:

(a) Of 76 men who were non-delinquent during the ten-year span, 73 (96.1 per cent) were successful in their family life during this time.

(b) Of 22 men who were minor delinquents in the first five-year period and non-delinquent in the second, 16 (72.7 per cent) were successful in their family relationships throughout both periods, while 5 (22.8 per cent) were unsuccessful during the first five years but not during the second, and only one man in this group failed throughout the ten years in his family relationships.

(c) Of 13 men who were serious offenders in the first five years and non-delinquent in the second, 9 (69.2 per cent) were successful in their family relationships throughout the ten-year period; while 4 (30.8 per cent), though failing in the first five years, improved during the second.

(d) Of 27 men who were serious delinquents in the first five-year period and minor delinquents in the second, 7 (25.9 per cent) were successful in their family relationships throughout the ten-year span; 14 (51.9 per cent) were failures in this respect during the ten-year period; 4 (14.8 per cent) though successful in the first five-year period failed in the second, while 2 who failed in their family relationships in the first period were successful in the second.

(e) Of 76 men who were minor offenders throughout the ten years, 26 (34.2 per cent) were successful in their family relationships during this time; 36 (47.4 per cent) were unsuccessful; 7 (9.2 per cent) failed in this regard in the first five-year period but improved in the second; and another 7 were successful in their family relationships in the first five years but not in the second.

(f) Of 83 men who were serious offenders throughout the ten years, only 8 (9.6 per cent) were successful in their family relationships throughout; 62 (74.7 per cent) were unsuccessful in their relations with the family throughout. Ten men (12.1 per cent), though successful in the first five-year period, were failures in the second; and 3, though failing in the first five years, succeeded in the second.

ECONOMIC RESPONSIBILITY AND DELINQUENCY

Did most of the men who were non-delinquent throughout the ten-year span likewise meet their economic responsibilities throughout? And, contrariwise, did those who were delinquent throughout the ten years fail to meet their economic responsibilities during that time? Table 2 contains the answers to these questions.

Again, a comparison of the incidence of the assumption of economic responsibilities by the entire group of men (50.6 per cent) with its incidence among those who were both non-delinquent and met their economic responsibilities throughout the two periods (95.9 per cent), indicates that there is a considerable degree of relationship between the assumption of economic responsibility and non-delinquency. Here again, the coefficient of mean square contingency (.72) confirms this high degree of relationship. The details of the table bring out more vividly the high associations between the factors in question:

(a) Of 73 men who were non-delinquent throughout the ten years, 70 (95.9 per cent) met their economic responsibilities during the entire time.

(b) Of 19 men who were minor offenders in the first five-year period and non-delinquent in the second, 17 (89.5 per cent) also met their economic responsibilities throughout the ten-year span.

(c) Of 16 men who were serious offenders in the first five years and non-delinquent in the second, 9 (56.3 per cent) met their economic responsibilities in both periods; 4 (25 per cent) did not do so in the first period but assumed their economic obligations in

TABLE 2. ECONOMIC RESPONSIBILITY IN TEN-YEAR SPAN CORRELATED WITH DELINQUENCY IN TEN-YEAR SPAN*

DELINQUENCY IN TEN-YEAR SPAN	ECONOMIC RESPONSIBILITY IN TEN-YEAR SPAN									
	Met throughout		Failed to meet throughout		Failed to meet in I, met in II		Met in I, failed to meet in II		Total	
	Number	Per cent	Number	Per cent	Number	Per cent	Number	Per cent	Number	Per cent
Non-delinquent throughout	70	95.9	2	2.7	1	1.4	0	–	73	100
Minor in Period I, non-delinquent in Period II	17	89.5	0	–	2	10.5	0	–	19	100
Serious in Period I, non-delinquent in Period II	9	56.3	3	18.7	4	25.0	0	–	16	100
Serious in Period I, minor in Period II	9	36.0	10	40.0	1	4.0	5	20.0	25	100
Minor throughout	0	–	5	16.7	25	83.3	0	–	30	100
Serious throughout	15	21.1	43	60.6	2	2.8	11	15.5	71	100
Non-delinquent in Period I, delinquent in Period II	6	66.7	0	–	0	–	3	33.3	9	100
Minor in Period I, serious in Period II	2	20.0	6	60.0	0	–	2	20.0	10	100
Total	128	50.6	69	27.3	35	13.8	21	8.3	253	100

$$C = .72$$

* There have been omitted from the correlation a few men who were unable to meet their economic responsibilities because of illness or the industrial depression.

81

the second; and 3 men in this group (18.7 per cent) failed to meet their economic obligations throughout the ten years.

(d) Of 25 men who were serious offenders during the first five years and minor offenders during the second, 10 (40 per cent) did not meet their economic responsibilities in either period, while 9 (36 per cent) assumed them in both periods, 5 accepted their economic obligations in the first period but failed to do so in the second, and one though not meeting his responsibilities in the first period did so in the second.

(e) Of 30 men who were minor offenders throughout the ten years, none met their economic responsibilities during the span, but 25 (83.3 per cent) though not meeting their financial obligations during the first five years assumed them in the second; 5 (16.7 per cent) did not meet their economic responsibilities either in the first or second five-year period.

(f) Of the 71 men who committed serious offenses throughout the ten years, only 15 (21.1 per cent) met their economic responsibilities throughout; 43 (60.6 per cent) did not accept their obligations; 11 (15.5 per cent), though meeting their responsibilities in the first five-year period, did not do so in the second; while 2, though neglecting to assume these responsibilities in the first five years, did so in the second.

INDUSTRIAL STATUS AND DELINQUENCY

Is there likewise manifest a high relationship between industrial stability and non-delinquency? Table 3 deals with this relationship. For the purposes in question it seems justifiable to combine into one category those men who were partially or completely successful industrially, thus permitting of a more liberal interpretation of industrial success.[2]

Again a comparison of the total incidence of partial or complete industrial successes (54.3 per cent) with the proportion of non-delinquents in the ten-year span who were partially or totally

[2] See definitions of *success* and *partial success*, under *Industrial History*, Appendix B, page 243.

TABLE 3. INDUSTRIAL STATUS IN TEN-YEAR SPAN CORRELATED WITH DELINQUENCY IN TEN-YEAR SPAN

INDUSTRIAL STATUS IN TEN-YEAR SPAN

DELINQUENCY IN TEN-YEAR SPAN	Partial or total success throughout		Failure throughout		Partial or total success in I, failure in II		Failure in I, partial or total success in II		Total	
	Number	Per cent	Number	Per cent	Number	Per cent	Number	Per cent	Number	Per cent
Non-delinquent throughout	73	97.4	2	2.6	0	–	0	–	75	100
Minor in Period I, non-delinquent in Period II	18	85.7	0	–	0	–	3	14.3	21	100
Serious in Period I, non-delinquent in Period II	6	42.7	2	14.6	0	–	6	42.7	14	100
Serious in Period I, minor in Period II	8	27.6	12	41.4	3	10.3	6	20.7	29	100
Minor throughout	38	50.7	24	32.0	3	4.0	10	13.3	75	100
Serious throughout	15	18.7	60	75.0	4	5.0	1	1.3	80	100
Non-delinquent in Period I, delinquent in Period II	9	90.0	0	–	1	10.0	0	–	10	100
Minor in Period I, serious in Period II	4	36.4	4	36.4	3	27.2	0	–	11	100
Total	171	54.3	104	33.0	14	4.4	26	8.3	315	100

$$C = .72$$

successful industrially (97.4 per cent), indicates a considerable relationship between the factor of industrial status and delinquency. This is reflected in the high coefficient of mean square contingency (.72). Detailed analysis shows the high association between the two factors in question still more clearly:

(a) Of 75 men who were non-delinquent throughout the ten years, 73 (97.4 per cent) were partial or total successes industrially (49 men being completely successful). Only 2 men were industrial failures throughout.

(b) Of 21 men who were minor offenders in the first five-year period and non-delinquent in the second, 18 (85.7 per cent) succeeded industrially; while 3, though failures in the first period, succeeded in the second.

(c) Of 14 men who were serious offenders in the first five-year period and non-delinquent in the second, 6 (42.7 per cent) succeeded industrially during the ten years; while a like number were unsuccessful in the first five years but succeeded in the second; and two men were industrial failures throughout the ten years.

(d) Of 29 men who were serious offenders in the first five-year period and minor offenders in the second, 8 (27.6 per cent) were industrially successful during the ten-year span, while 12 (41.4 per cent) failed industrially throughout the ten years; 6 (20.7 per cent), though failing in the first five years, succeeded in the second; and 3, though successful in the first period, failed in the second.

(e) Of 75 men who were minor offenders throughout the ten years, 38 (50.7 per cent) were industrially successful (partially or totally), a more detailed examination revealing that 26 of this group were only partially successful in both periods; while 24 (32 per cent) of those who were minor offenders during the ten years, were industrial failures. Ten men, though industrial failures in the first five years were partially or totally successful industrially in the second, and 3 men, though partially or totally successful in the first period, were failures in the second.

(f) Of the 80 men who were serious offenders during the ten

years, only 15 (18.7 per cent) were successful industrially thoughout and then only partially so. Of these 80 serious offenders, 60 (75 per cent) failed industrially throughout the ten years; 4, though partially or totally successful during the first five years, were industrial failures in the second, and one who failed industrially in the first five-year period succeeded in the second.

USE OF LEISURE AND DELINQUENCY

We consider next the degree of relationship between use of leisure and delinquent behavior. In Table 4 appears the correlation between these two factors.

A comparison of the proportion of the entire group who utilized their leisure time harmlessly during the ten-year span (28.3 per cent), with the proportion of non-delinquents who so employed their spare time (94.5 per cent), indicates that there is a marked relationship between the factor of leisure and the factor of delinquency, as does also the high coefficient of mean square contingency (.79). Detailed analysis reveals this association more clearly:

(a) Of 73 men who were non-delinquent during the ten-year span, 69 (94.5 per cent) utilized their spare time harmlessly.

(b) Of 20 men who were minor offenders in the first five-year period and non-delinquent in the second, 8 (40 per cent) employed their spare time harmlessly in both periods, while 11 men (55 per cent), though utilizing their leisure harmfully during the first five years, did not do so during the second. One man in this group spent his leisure time harmfully throughout the ten-year span.

(c) Of 30 men who were serious offenders in the first five years and minor in the second, all employed their leisure in harmful pursuits throughout the ten-year span.

(d) Of 77 men who were minor offenders during the ten years, 6 (7.8 per cent) did not spend their spare time harmfully; 3, though not indulging in harmful use of leisure during the first five years, did so during the second; while one, though using his spare time

TABLE 4. USE OF LEISURE IN TEN-YEAR SPAN CORRELATED WITH DELINQUENCY IN TEN-YEAR SPAN

DELINQUENCY IN TEN-YEAR SPAN	USE OF LEISURE IN TEN-YEAR SPAN									Total	
	Harmless throughout		Harmful throughout		Harmless in I, harmful in II		Harmful in I, harmless in II			Total	
	Number	Per cent	Number	Per cent	Number	Per cent	Number	Per cent		Number	Per cent
Non-delinquent throughout	69	94.5	2	2.8	2	2.7	0	–		73	100
Minor in Period I, non-delinquent in Period II	8	40.0	1	5.0	0	–	11	55.0		20	100
Serious in Period I, non-delinquent in Period II	3	30.0	0	–	0	–	7	70.0		10	100
Serious in Period I, minor in Period II	0	–	30	100.0	0	–	0	–		30	100
Minor throughout	6	7.8	67	87.0	3	3.9	1	1.3		77	100
Serious throughout	1	1.1	85	96.6	2	2.3	0	–		88	100
Non-delinquent in Period I, delinquent in Period II	3	30.0	0	–	7	70.0	0	–		10	100
Minor in Period I, serious in Period II	0	–	9	90.0	1	10.0	0	–		10	100
Total	90	28.3	194	61.0	15	4.7	19	6.0		318	100

$C = .79$

harmfully in the first period, did not do so in the second. But the great majority of the men in this group, 67 (87 per cent), utilized their leisure time harmfully during the ten years following the expiration of their Reformatory sentences.

(e) Of 88 men who were serious offenders during the ten years, only one did not spend his spare time harmfully; 2 men, though not indulging in damaging use of leisure in the first five years, did so in the second; while 85 of the men (96.6 per cent) employed their leisure hours harmfully during the ten-year span.

Conclusion

The consistent and substantial correlations between delinquent conduct during the ten-year period following expiration of the Reformatory sentence, and certain major aspects of the life activities of our men do not in themselves justify the conclusion that there is a *causal* relationship involved. Improvement in the assumption of economic responsibilities, for example, has not necessarily *preceded* and aided reformation in criminal conduct. There may, of course, be some interaction of the phenomena in question. However, at this point, the findings do not justify any conclusion other than that good family relationships, the assumption of economic responsibilities, successful industrial adjustment, and wise use of leisure, in large measure *accompany* non-delinquency.

It may well be that the improvement noted in previous chapters in respect to criminal conduct and in the other major aspects of the life activities of our group is in turn attributable to one or more influences not yet ascertained. To a consideration of this possibility, a later chapter is devoted.

Chapter VIII

CHARACTERISTICS OF REFORMED AND UNREFORMED

BEFORE proceeding to any consideration of the reasons for the general improvement which has occurred among the ex-inmates of the Massachusetts Reformatory, let us compare the characteristics of those who reformed and those who did not. The men classified as *reformed* are those who were non-delinquent throughout Period II, including those who had been delinquent in Period I. There were 118 men who, on this basis, could definitely be counted as reformed.[1] In contrast to these, there were 250 men who continued to recidivate for all or part of the second follow-up period.[2]

Our interest at the moment is merely in a descriptive comparison of those who reformed and those who did not, without any consideration of the significance of these differences in explaining reformation. The chapters following this one will be concerned with the latter problem.

In noting the differences between the reformed and unreformed it should be borne in mind that in the previous chapter it has already been shown that a high relationship exists between reformation in criminal conduct and improvement in the other aspects of life's activities.

Findings

PRE-REFORMATORY PERIOD: RESEMBLANCES AND DIFFERENCES

How did the reformed and unreformed *resemble* each other prior to their commitment to the Reformatory? The resemblances are indicated in Table 5.

Examination of this table shows that the reformed and unre-

---

[1] Among these are not included 19 men who were delinquent for part of Period II and non-delinquent toward the end of it. These 19 were omitted to insure the purity of the comparison for we do not know whether they will really continue to be non-delinquents.

[2] For details, see Chapter VI and also Appendix C, tables 2–51a through 2–59.

TABLE 5. RESEMBLANCES BETWEEN REFORMED AND UNREFORMED,
PRE-REFORMATORY PERIOD

FACTOR OF RESEMBLANCE	PER CENT AMONG REFORMED	PER CENT AMONG UNREFORMED
Both parents without formal education	84.7	81.7
One or both parents foreign, son native	53.1	50.7
Family in marginal economic circumstances	59.2	56.5
Offender moved about excessively	46.6	42.2
Offender did not attend church regularly or at all	88.1	92.7
Offender used leisure time harmfully	92.2	99.1
Offender began to work when under 15 years old	38.4	45.7
Offender arrested as often as once in nine months	43.3	45.0

formed resembled each other in the limited formal education of their parents; the extent to which the offenders were native-born sons of one or two foreign-born parents; the economic circumstances of their parents; their excessive moving about within one city or from one city to another during the years prior to their commitment to the Reformatory; their neglect of church duties. The reformed and unreformed also closely resembled each other in their use of leisure time; their early entrance into industrial life; and in the frequency of arrest of those among them who actually came into contact with the law. Some or all of these factors may have been of significance in the origin of their delinquencies, but clearly they must be regarded as complacent factors (i.e., without influence) in any explanation of why some of the men ultimately reformed while others continued in crime.

Now what of the pre-Reformatory *differences* in the characteristics of the reformed and unreformed? These are listed in Table 6.

The reformed and unreformed differed somewhat from each other in that fewer of the unreformed were foreign born; a greater proportion of them were under 14 years of age when they first showed delinquent tendencies; a greater proportion of the unreformed left home when they were under 14 years of age (either because of the break-up of the home following death of one of

TABLE 6. DIFFERENCES BETWEEN REFORMED AND UNREFORMED,
PRE-REFORMATORY PERIOD

FACTOR OF DIFFERENCE	PER CENT AMONG REFORMED	PER CENT AMONG UNREFORMED
Offender foreign-born	26.7	14.3
Parents and/or one or more siblings delinquent	56.5	78.9
Offender under 14 at first delinquency	29.3	43.2
Offender first left home when under 14 years old	33.3	45.9
Offender was unskilled worker	46.1	59.9
Offender's work habits poor	37.2	57.5
Offender failed to meet his economic responsibilities	69.6	87.6
Offender failed in his family relationships	53.6	68.2
Offender committed serious (as opposed to minor) crimes	73.8	86.7
Offender was arrested prior to offense for which committed to Reformatory	78.7	94.4
Offender had penal experiences prior to Reformatory commitment	33.3	67.4

the parents or because they ran away from home or had been committed to correctional institutions or placed in foster homes). Those who reformed and those who did not also differed somewhat from each other in their family relationships. Of those who did not reform, a greater proportion had, during the pre-Reformatory period, committed serious (as distinguished from minor) offenses; and a greater proportion of them had been arrested on one or more occasions prior to the offense for which they were sentenced to the Reformatory.

It is clear that the pre-Reformatory differences between the reformed and unreformed are not very marked, except for the fact that those who reformed came, in much less measure, from families in which parents or (and) siblings had also been delinquent; that they had to a far lesser extent been incarcerated; that their work habits were far better than of those who continued to recidivate; and that they to a far greater extent met their economic responsibilities prior to their commitment to the Reformatory.

REFORMATORY AND PAROLE PERIOD: RESEMBLANCES AND DIFFERENCES

How did the reformed and unreformed *resemble* each other at the time of their commitment to the Reformatory, during their incarceration, and while on parole? These resemblances are listed in Table 7.

TABLE 7. RESEMBLANCES BETWEEN REFORMED AND UNREFORMED, REFORMATORY AND PAROLE PERIODS

FACTOR OF RESEMBLANCE	PER CENT AMONG REFORMED	PER CENT AMONG UNREFORMED
Offender was 21 or under at time of Reformatory commitment	72.5	68.1
Offender was committed to Reformatory for commission of a major offense (mostly crimes against property)	90.5	93.3
Offender committed offense for which sent to Reformatory, in company with others	61.4	59.9
Offender's physical condition on entrance to the Reformatory was good	95.6	88.5
Inmate had two or more occupational experiences in the Reformatory	82.8	81.5
Inmate was held in the Reformatory for a year or longer	77.6	80.7
Parolee was on parole for a year or longer	88.5	88.8
Parolee had supervision during parole by a parole officer	84.7	89.4
Parolee seen by parole officer on the average of once in less than six months	88.6	89.6

From the table it is evident that an equal proportion of reformed and unreformed were 21 or under at the time of their commitment to the Reformatory; that by far the greatest proportion of both groups of men were sentenced for a major offense (mostly a property crime); that an equal proportion of the reformed and unreformed committed this particular offense with accomplices. Those who reformed also resembled those who continued to be criminal, in their state of health at the time of their commitment, in the number of occupational experiences which they had in the Reformatory, in the length of time during which they were held in the institution. They also resembled each other in the length of time during which they were on parole, and in the extent and kind of parole supervision they experienced.

Turning now to a consideration of the *differences* between those who reformed and those who did not, Table 8 reveals the nature of these differences.

TABLE 8. DIFFERENCES BETWEEN REFORMED AND UNREFORMED, REFORMATORY AND PAROLE PERIODS

FACTOR OF DIFFERENCE	PER CENT AMONG REFORMED	PER CENT AMONG UNREFORMED
Psychometric examination in Reformatory revealed inmate to be feebleminded or of borderline intelligence	33.6	42.2
Psychiatric examination in Reformatory revealed inmate to have mental abnormality (disease, distortion, or marked liabilities of personality)	7.6	51.2
Inmate committed offenses in Reformatory	73.3	87.3
Inmate committed serious offenses in Reformatory	61.2	75.3
Inmate committed offenses frequently in Reformatory	42.2	57.5
Inmate was a fair or poor worker in Reformatory	21.6	32.1
Parolee violated conditions of parole	33.7	54.0

An examination of this table shows that the greatest difference between the reformed and unreformed lies in their mental condition—only 7.6 per cent of those who ultimately reformed having, upon psychiatric examination at the Reformatory, revealed any mental abnormality (disease, distortion, or marked liabilities of personality, this latter referring mainly to excessive emotional instability), as compared with 51.2 per cent among those who continued to be delinquent or criminal. The other differences are not nearly so marked. Nevertheless, more of those who did not reform than of those who did were feebleminded or of borderline intelligence; more of them committed serious offenses while in the Reformatory; and the former violated institutional rules with greater frequency than those who ultimately reformed. Likewise proportionally more of those who later continued to be delinquent were only fair or poor workers in the Reformatory. And more of them were total failures in respect to criminal conduct during parole.

FIRST FIVE-YEAR FOLLOW-UP PERIOD: RESEMBLANCES AND DIFFERENCES

Any points of *resemblance* between those who reformed and those who did not practically cease after the expiration of the Reformatory sentence. *With the removal of all control—whether in the institution or in the community under parole supervision—the traits and conditions of the reformed and unreformed become sharply differentiated.* Except for the fact that both groups of men were of the same age distribution at the beginning of the first follow-up period, that three-fourths of both groups lived in cities throughout Period I, and that a like proportion did not during the first five-year period utilize the occupational training which they had acquired in the Reformatory, they cease to resemble each other.

The *differences* between those who reformed and those who continued to be delinquent now become, with slight exceptions, much more marked than they have been up to this point. This is evident from Table 9.

An examination of this table shows that those who did not reform made their homes to a far greater extent than did those who reformed, in neighborhoods where the influences were unwholesome; that the former likewise lived to a far greater extent in homes in which the physical conditions were poor; that far more of the unreformed than of the others moved about excessively either within one city or from one city to another; that the former were far less stable in their household relationships than the latter; and that proportionally fewer of the unreformed lived throughout the first period outside of institutions. Those who continued to be

TABLE 9. DIFFERENCES BETWEEN REFORMED AND UNREFORMED,
FIRST FIVE-YEAR FOLLOW-UP PERIOD

FACTOR OF DIFFERENCE	PER CENT AMONG REFORMED	PER CENT AMONG UNREFORMED
Neighborhood influences poor	15.3	57.5
Physical aspect of home poor	11.6	50.3
Excessive mobility	25.0	69.2
Excessively unstable household	11.5	53.6
Lived in community throughout five-year period	79.3	39.9
Still single at end of period	25.9	52.5
Conjugal relations poor	4.9	48.2
Failure in family relationships	13.9	67.3
In comfortable economic circumstances	24.1	0
Dependent on others for support	6.1	15.9
Dealt with by social agencies	16.1	27.1
Failed to meet economic responsibilities	10.3	46.7
Unskilled worker	26.1	47.0
Poor work habits	9.9	51.7
Engaged in some illicit occupation	3.5	36.0
Irregular worker	13.6	51.5
Held job on the average of less than three months	14.1	53.3
Average earnings less than $25 weekly	41.0	60.0
Industrial failure	12.6	62.9
Did not attend church	36.7	50.6
Patronized harmful places of recreation	19.0	94.1
Had harmful companions	21.4	94.2
Used leisure time to further self educationally	9.0	1.5
Did not belong to any constructive (or harmless) organization for use of leisure time	75.2	93.8
Used leisure time harmfully	21.0	93.9

delinquent and those who reformed also differed markedly from one another in their conjugal and family relationships, far more of them still being single at the end of the first five-year period than of those who reformed; far more of those among the unreformed who were married than among the reformed had poor conjugal relationships; and far more of the former failed in their family responsibilities.

Not one of the unreformed was during Period I in comfortable economic circumstances, while a fourth of those who reformed in that or the next five-year period were in this favorable economic class; and more of the unreformed than of the reformed had to depend on others for support during the first five-year period. Likewise, more of the unreformed than of those who abandoned their criminal ways had to be assisted in one way or another by social service agencies; more of the former failed to meet their economic responsibilities. More of them were unskilled and irregular workers, had poor work habits, and engaged in some illicit occupation during Period I. More of them held their jobs on the average of less than three months than did those who reformed; they earned less than those who reformed and they were to a far greater extent industrial failures than those who became non-delinquent either in Period I or Period II.

During the first five-year period a greater proportion of those who continued to be delinquent neglected their church duties than did those who were already, or in the second five-year period became, non-delinquent. A far greater proportion of the unreformed patronized unwholesome places of recreation, had undesirable companions, did not belong to any organizations for the constructive or harmless use of leisure time, and altogether utilized their leisure far more harmfully than did those who were already or who later reformed.

SECOND FIVE-YEAR FOLLOW-UP PERIOD: RESEMBLANCES AND DIFFERENCES

As in the first follow-up period so during the second five years, there are practically no resemblances between those who reformed and those who continued to recidivate with the exception of the three factors of resemblance already noted: age distribution, residence in cities, and failure to utilize the occupations learned in the Reformatory.

As part of the general differentiation that comes with the passage of time, the differences between those who were non-delinquent in the second period and those who continued to be delinquent, become in many respects even more sharpened than they were in the first. This is evident from a study of Table 10.

TABLE 10. DIFFERENCES BETWEEN REFORMED AND UNREFORMED, SECOND FIVE-YEAR FOLLOW-UP PERIOD

FACTOR OF DIFFERENCE	PER CENT AMONG REFORMED	PER CENT AMONG UNREFORMED
Neighborhood influences poor	4.5	54.6
Physical aspects of home poor	5.5	47.1
Excessive mobility	16.7	62.1
Excessively unstable household	6.9	52.3
Lived in community throughout five-year period	98.2	41.1
Still single at end of period	16.5	48.0
Conjugal relations poor	4.3	44.7
Failure in family relationships	7.0	73.1
In comfortable economic circumstances	23.5	2.6
Dependent on others for support	7.0	26.3
Dealt with by social agencies	26.8	47.6
Fails to meet economic responsibilities	4.7	52.3
Unskilled worker	17.7	49.4
Poor work habits	.9	42.5
Engaged in some illicit occupation	0	28.0
Irregular worker	6.5	46.2
Held job on average of less than three months	8.6	46.3
Average earnings less than $25 weekly	38.2	61.8
Industrial failure	3.6	57.8
Did not attend church	35.0	56.6
Patronized harmful places of recreation	4.6	92.0
Had harmful companions	4.5	93.5
Used leisure time to further self educationally	9.0	1.5
Did not belong to any constructive (or harmless) organization for use of leisure time	76.0	91.0
Used leisure time harmfully	4.5	96.2

A comparison of this table with Table 9, in which the differences between the reformed and unreformed in Period I were presented, reveals the sharper differentiation between the two groups in almost all the factors involved. There is no need to detail these differences because they occur in the same factors as for the first follow-up period, except that in many of them the differences are even greater than they were in Period I.

Conclusion

The broadening differentiation with the passing of the years between those who reformed and those who continued to recidivate, raises the question of the reasons for this increasing divergence of the two groups of men from each other. Why did some reform and others not? Do the differences between the two groups of men account for their behavior, or are they the natural accompaniments of it? It has already been noted in the previous chapter that there is a high degree of relationship between reformation and change (improvement) in the other major aspects of the careers of our men. *Is this relationship of itself causal or is it in turn caused by some other influence?*

To this question we turn our attention in the next chapter.

Chapter IX

INFLUENCES MAKING FOR REFORMATION

IN Chapter VII was revealed the existence of a high association between non-delinquency and the favorable aspects of other major factors in the careers of our men—successful family relationships, assumption of their economic responsibilities, good industrial adjustment, and harmless use of leisure. As already suggested, this does not necessarily imply the existence of a causal relationship between non-delinquency and these other factors. But the high correlation at least raises the question whether the general improvement in family, economic, and like aspects of the careers of our men explains the reduction which has actually occurred in criminality (or *vice versa*); or whether still other factors largely account for the reduction in recidivism and in turn for the improvement which has occurred in the other aspects of the life activities of our men.

In attempting to answer this basic query we are justified in treating "success" in criminal conduct as a fairly accurate index of "success" in the other respects noted above; for non-delinquency has already been found to be very highly related to the favorable aspects of other major activities in the life careers of our men.[1]

Method of Analysis

To determine which factors can properly be credited with reformation in criminal behavior (and improvement in other conduct as well) we must compare the incidence of non-delinquency among our ex-prisoners during Period I and Period II in respect to each of the factors involved in this research and contrast this, in every instance, with the *total* incidence of non-delinquency in the entire group of cases to see which factors have contributed a signifi-

[1] See Chapter VII.

cantly greater proportional increase of non-delinquents than occurred in the group as a whole. Table 11 illustrates the method of
analyzing the factors.

TABLE 11. NON-DELINQUENCY IN PERIODS I AND II BY
INTELLIGENCE GROUPINGS

INTELLIGENCE GROUPING	NON-DELINQUENTS IN PERIOD I		NON-DELINQUENTS IN PERIOD II		PROPORTIONAL INCREASE IN NON- DELINQUENCY
	Number	Per cent*	Number	Per cent*	
Normal	36	31.6	43	37.7	1.2
Dull	24	26.4	28	30.8	1.2
Borderline	13	18.6	22	31.4	1.7
Feebleminded	10	16.1	14	22.6	1.4
Total	83	24.6	107	31.8	1.3

* The percentages are based on the total number of cases within each subcategory.

Examination of the table shows that as between Period I and
Period II the greatest proportional increase in non-delinquency has
occurred within the subgroup who are of *borderline* intelligence.
Of this category 18.6 per cent had been non-delinquent in Period I,
while 31.4 per cent were non-delinquent in Period II. This represents a proportional increase in non-delinquency of 1.7. It will be
seen that this increase in non-delinquency in Period II among those
of borderline intelligence is greater than the increase for the entire
group of cases represented in the factor of *Intelligence,* for which
the proportional change in non-delinquency in Period II as compared with Period I is only 1.3.

Each one of the following factors of this research has been subjected to a similar analysis:

Family Background
 1. Nativity of parents and sons
 2. Education of parents
 3. Economic status of parents
 4. Family delinquency

Personal History Prior to Reformatory Commitment
5. Nativity of offender
6. Intelligence
7. Mental condition (disease or distortion)
8. Age at leaving home
9. Mobility
10. Age offender began work
11. Work habits
12. Skill
13. Economic responsibility
14. Family relationships
15. Use of leisure
16. Church attendance
17. Age at offender's first known delinquency
18. Prior arrests
19. Penal experiences
20. Delinquency

Reformatory History
21. Age at time of offender's commitment to Reformatory
22. Offense for which committed to Reformatory
23. Commission of offense alone or with others (associates in crime)
24. Physical condition on entrance to Reformatory
25. Kind of worker in Reformatory
26. Number of occupational experiences in Reformatory
27. Conduct in Reformatory
28. Frequency of commission of offenses in Reformatory

Parole History
29. Supervision during parole, length of
30. Delinquency during parole

Periods I and II: Environmental Factors
31. Household stability
32. Mobility
33. Neighborhood—type
34. Neighborhood—influences
35. Home—physical condition of

Periods I and II: Family Relationships
36. Marital status at end of period
37. Relation to nearest relatives
38. Family relationships

Periods I and II: Economic Responsibility
39. Economic condition
40. Dependents
41. Disposition of earnings
42. Social services rendered
43. Economic responsibility

Periods I and II: Industrial History
44. Steadiness of employment
45. Work habits
46. Skill
47. Used occupation taught at Massachusetts Reformatory
48. Longest period of time held job
49 Average period of time held job
50. Highest wage weekly
51. Average wage weekly
52. Usual reason for leaving work
53. Illegitimate occupation
54. Industrial history

Periods I and II: Leisure and Habits
55. Companionship
56. Haunts
57. Educational activities
58. Society member
59. Church attendance
60. Leisure and habits

Periods I and II: Mental Condition
61. Mental condition (disease or distortion)
62. Emotional stability

Periods I and II: Age
63. Age at beginning of period

The reader is referred to Appendix F in which are presented the tables for each of these factors, as illustrated by Table 11 above.

Obviously, those subcategories of the factors in which the proportional increase in non-delinquency in Period II as compared with Period I is no greater than for the entire number of cases represented by the particular factor, may be regarded as *complacent,* that is, as not having had any influence on the increase in the proportion of non-delinquency with the passage of time. Obviously, also, the explanation for increased reformation is not to be found in those subcategories of the factors in which the proportional increase in non-delinquency in Period II is *less* than for the entire group of cases represented by that factor.

It is rather to those factors within one or more subcategories of which the increase in non-delinquency in Period II is *significantly in excess* of non-delinquency in Period I (as tested in terms of the standard deviation),[2] to which we must turn for reasonable explanation of the reasons for reformation.

Findings

SIGNIFICANT FACTORS

The factors we are examining in order to find explanations for the improvement which has occurred in delinquent behavior in Period II as compared with Period I include those which reflect the family and personal history of the men prior to their commitment to the Reformatory, during their incarceration in the Reformatory, and during parole from the Reformatory. These factors, as well as the ones concerned with the conditions and circumstances of the men during the follow-up periods, must be included in any consideration of the probable reasons for increasing reformation with the passage of time, in order that account may be taken of the possibility that native endowment and previous circumstances have as significant a bearing upon ultimate reformation as do the factors more nearly related to it in point of time.

---

[2] See Appendix F, pp. 377 *et seq.,* for a description of the formula utilized. This formula was advised by Dr. Carl Doering, statistician at the Harvard School of Public Health.

A close examination of all the factors studied (63, as above listed and as detailed in Appendix F) with a view to determining which ones tend to explain increased reform, reveals that only within the factor of *Aging* (or maturation) was the increase in the proportion of non-delinquents sufficiently great to be statistically significant when tested by the standard deviation. Upon cursory inspection other factors, such as *Intelligence* (Table 11 above), *Mental condition at time of commitment to Reformatory* (Appendix F, 7), *Pre-Reformatory use of leisure* (Appendix F, 15), *Pre-Reformatory penal experience* (Appendix F, 19), and several others, appeared to contain categories that were related significantly to increasing non-delinquency. But consideration of such factors in the light of the standard deviation served to eliminate all but the factor of *Aging*.

AGING AND REFORMATION

A closer examination of this particular factor is therefore necessary.

TABLE 12. NON-DELINQUENCY IN PERIODS I AND II BY AGE GROUPINGS

AGE AT BEGINNING OF PERIOD*	NON-DELINQUENTS IN PERIOD I		NON-DELINQUENTS IN PERIOD II		PROPORTIONAL INCREASE IN NON-DELINQUENCY
	Number	*Per cent*	*Number*	*Per cent*	
Under 21	11	23.4	0	0	0
21 to 25	40	23.7	12	25.5	1.1
26 to 30	29	30.2	59	34.9	1.2
31 to 35	5	14.7	34	34.3	2.3
36 to 40	3	21.4	8	23.5	1.1
41 and over	0	0	3	21.4	0
Total	*88*	*24.4*	*116*	*32.3*	*1.3*

* *Age at beginning of the period* is used instead of *Age at the end of the period* because a man to be considered non-delinquent in Period I or Period II actually had to be a non-offender throughout the whole of the five-year period, meaning that he was already a non-offender by the beginning of the period.

Inspection of Table 12 shows that *there was 2.3 times the proportion of non-delinquents in the 31–35 year age span by the beginning of Period II as there had been in this age span at the beginning of*

Period I, while the proportional increase in non-delinquency with the passage of time for all the men was only 1.3. A testing of the significance of the ratio of 2.3 by the standard deviation indicates that this ratio is not a chance phenomenon associated with the unreliability of the sample but is truly significant.

Table 12 does not indicate, as might at first glance appear, that 31–35 years is the most significant or likely age of reformation. It will be seen that the *absolute* percentage of non-delinquency in the 31–35 year age group in Period I is only 14.7 per cent and that the highest incidence of non-delinquency in that period (30.2 per cent) occurs not in the 31–35 year span but rather in the 26–30 year span. The reason for the high incidence of non-delinquency among those who were 31–35 at the beginning of Period II is not that this particular age span (which would be 36–40 by the end of Period II) is the most favorable to reformation, but that those who were between 26 and 30 years of age at the beginning of Period I and were already *then* non-delinquents have in Period II (by which time they were five years older) been included with those who did not reform until the *second* period. The 2.3 ratio of improvement in the age span of 31–35 means, therefore, that the passage of time brings about an *accumulation* of those inclined to reform at various age spans, this accumulation reaching its peak at 31–35 years. Beyond this period there appears to be a marked decrease in the proportion of non-delinquents and therefore in further reformation. In other words, if reformation has not occurred by the thirty-sixth year, it is less likely to occur thereafter.

The substantial increase in non-delinquency in the 31–35 year span from 14.7 per cent at the beginning of Period I to 34.3 per cent by the beginning of Period II is, therefore, due to the fact that within that age span have been assembled both those of earlier age groups who were already reformed by the beginning of Period I and were between 31 and 35 years of age at the beginning of Period II, and those who did not reform until reaching the second period. However, the cumulative effect not only continues to the age of 35, but also *ceases* after that age.

It is therefore in the factor of *Aging* that we must seek the principal explanation for reform. This does not mean that aging completely accounts for reformation. Other influences, which have not been statistically treated in this research may also be involved in some individual instances. For example, intensive case analysis appears to show that certain offenders reformed (or improved) when living in a simple environment, perhaps in the country far removed from the complexities and temptations of city life. This is especially true of certain types of feebleminded offenders. In a few instances reformation appears to have been due largely to being under the very close supervision of relatives, or a wife, or an employer. In several cases, fear of recommitment appears to have been the most potent and direct reformative agent. Were the protections and restraints which have been placed around these particular ex-prisoners removed, it is very likely that they would revert to criminality.

However, in view of the fact that the analysis of 63 factors reflects almost every aspect of the lives of our men, it seems reasonable to assume that because *Aging* is the only factor which emerges as significant in the reformative process when our cases are analyzed *en masse,* the *principal* (though not necessarily the only) explanation of the reform which has occurred in our group is to be found in that factor.

The actual age at which reformation occurred now becomes of particular interest. Of the 118 men who could be classified as nondelinquent in Period II, 16.1 per cent had reformed when they were younger than 21; 33.8 per cent when they were but 21 to 25; 31.3 per cent when they were between 26 and 30; 14.4 per cent between 31 and 35; and 4.1 per cent when they were 36 and over. Evidently, the peak age of reformation for the kind of delinquents who are sent to the Massachusetts Reformatory is the ten-year span between

21 and 30 years. *Why reformation then declines and dwindles to almost nil after 36 will be considered in the next two chapters.*

Conclusion

The factor of *Aging* (maturation) emerges, then, as one of great significance in the reformative process. No other factor, at least among those included in this research, appears to have any significant influence upon reformation. The sheer passage of time, with the maturation that accompanies it, seems to be the key to an understanding of the reasons for reformation.

Furthermore, in the light of the evidence, we must conclude that the general improvement which has occurred in the major aspects of the lives of our men and which was found to be highly related to freedom from criminal conduct, is also in large measure due to aging or maturation. Whether the component elements of this process are largely biological or psychological or social is a question which we cannot answer within the confines of the present research.

However, it is obviously necessary to subject the factor of *Aging* to closer scrutiny in order that we may have a clearer idea of *why it plays so important a part in the reformative process.* To this we turn our attention in the next chapter.

Chapter X

AGING AND ITS ACCOMPANIMENTS

IN the previous chapter it became evident that the factor of *Aging* (maturation) is the most significant one of the 63 factors included in this research, in explaining the decrease in criminality that has occurred among our ex-prisoners since the expiration of their sentences from the Reformatory. It is of course possible that there are other factors which play some part in the reformative process, but in view of the fact that practically every phase of a life career is somehow considered or reflected among the 63 factors studied, it seems safe to conclude that the factor of *Aging* remains the most important one in bringing about, or at least in facilitating, reformation.

It therefore becomes necessary that we more fully understand this aging process. What happens with advancing years that helps to explain the influence of *Aging* upon reformation? To arrive at any conclusions regarding this influence, we have subjected to analysis the factor of age (at the beginning of the second five-year period) as it relates to all the pertinent factors of the second five years in order to see how the various age groups differ from one another.[1] These factors have been divided into the following major groupings:

(a) Delinquency
(b) Environmental conditions
(c) Family relationships
(d) Assumption of economic responsibilities
(e) Industrial status
(f) Use of leisure
(g) Mental condition

[1] At the beginning of Period II, 62 men were between 21 and 25 years old; 213 were 26–30; 116 were 31–35; 63 were 36 and over.

Detailed analysis follows of the relationship of aging to the various factors that comprise each one of these major aspects of the life careers of our men.

Findings

AGING AND DELINQUENCY

What changes occur in delinquent behavior with advancing years? It has already been established in the previous chapter that such reformation as has occurred is largely explained by the factor of aging or maturation. It will be recalled that by the beginning of Period I, 21.5 per cent of the entire group of men were non-delinquent while by the beginning of the second five-year period 32.1 per cent were non-delinquent. However, the essence of the improvement can best be seen by focusing attention on behavior in the various age spans. Thus, 27.7 per cent of those who were between 21 and 25 years of age at the beginning of the second five-year period were non-delinquent. This proportion was exceeded by those who were between 26 and 35 years, in which group 34 per cent were then non-delinquent, decreasing to 24.5 per cent of non-delinquents among those who were 36 or older by the beginning of the second five-year period. The proportion of serious offenders was 44.6 per cent among those who were 21 to 25 years old at the beginning of Period II and only 27.3 per cent among those who were 31 to 35; but was again high (40.8 per cent) among those who were 36 and over at the beginning of the second five-year period.

Turning now to arrests, 58.3 per cent of those who were between 21 and 25 years old at the beginning of the second follow-up period were apprehended during the period as compared to 51 per cent of those who were between 31 and 35. In the succeeding age span of 36 and over there was a higher incidence of men arrested than in the younger groups—62.5 per cent. Considering next the proportions of men who have had penal experiences during the second five-year period a similar changing incidence with age is noted: from 45.6 per cent of those who were 21 to 25 years old at the beginning of the second five-year period to 29.5 per cent of those who were 31 to 35 years of age; but of those who were 36 and over at the beginning of the second period the much higher proportion of 51 per cent served time in penal institutions.

Even at this point it becomes evident that the greatest improvement occurs in the younger age groups (usually in the 26–35 year span); and that a decline sets in after approximately the thirty-sixth year. In studying the character of the predominant offenses of the group in the various age spans, we begin to see more clearly the significant changes that occur with the passage of time. Of those who were between 21 and 25 at the beginning of the second five-year period, 31.3 per cent typically committed offenses against property. This proportion was reduced in the older age spans to only 10.8 per cent among those who were 36 and over. The gradual change with advancing years in the characteristic commission of offenses against property was in part absorbed by an increase in the proportion of men who were predominantly drunkards; there were 25 per cent of drunkards among those who were 21 to 25 years of age at the beginning of the second five-year period, rising to 62.2 per cent among those who were 36 and over by the beginning of the second five-year period.

In considering the question of the commission of criminal acts alone or with companions, it is significant that up to the thirty-sixth year a little over half the men committed their offenses alone, the remainder carrying out their depredations in companionship with several others. Among those older than 36, however, 71.4 per cent of the men were lone offenders. This is partly explained by the fact that where anti-social behavior persists, the nature of the offenses committed changes with the passage of time from the more aggressive kind of criminality reflected in offenses against property to the less aggressive. This phenomenon, in turn, is probably related to the biologic and psychologic changes that come at certain ages. In cases where the aggressive type of criminality persists, it does so more because it is an expression of some continuing deep-seated urge or need of the organism than because of incitement by companions. The "gang spirit," whatever its psychologic constituents may be, is found to be practically inoperative in the later years (see p. 119); hence, if criminal conduct persists despite advancing years, "ganging" cannot be held responsible for it.

In Table 13 are briefly summarized the factors which have been discussed in this section on aging and delinquency.

TABLE 13. NATURE OF DELINQUENCY IN PERIOD II BY AGE
GROUPINGS (PERCENTAGES)

AGE AT BEGINNING OF PERIOD II	Non-de-linquents	Serious de-linquents	Arrests	Penal experiences	Predominantly offenders against property	Pre-dominantly drunkards	Lone offenders
				NATURE OF DELINQUENCY			
21 to 25	27.7	44.6	58.3	45.6	31.3	25.0	54.5
26 to 30	34.7	32.4	54.2	33.9	22.9	27.5	54.8
31 to 35	34.3	27.3	51.0	29.5	16.9	44.6	55.3
36 and over	24.5	40.8	62.5	51.0	10.8	62.2	71.4

It must already be evident from this analysis that improvement in conduct occurs with advancing years until approximately the thirty-sixth year. Beyond that the incidence of improvement drops markedly.

AGING AND ENVIRONMENTAL CIRCUMSTANCES

What changes take place in environmental circumstances with advancing years? First may be mentioned a decrease in excessive moving about (from one part of the city to another or from city to city), as seen by the fact that while 58 per cent of our men who were 21 to 25 years of age at the beginning of Period II moved about excessively, the proportion was lower (41.5 per cent) among those who were between 31 and 35 years old, but increased to 49 per cent among those who were 36 and over at the beginning of the second five-year period. Another evidence of change as related to aging lies in the fact that while only 6.7 per cent of those in the 21–25 year span were living in good neighborhoods during Period II, 17 per cent among those who were between 26 and 35 years old had the benefit of good surroundings. Again a drop in incidence of a favorable condition is noted, however, in the older group, for only 9.3 per cent of those who were 36 or over lived in good neighborhoods during the second five-year period. A like change related to aging occurs in the proportion of men living in homes of which the physical conditions might be considered adequate. Thus, about one-third of those who were between 21 and 30 resided in good homes during the second period; this proportion was raised to 41 per cent among those in the 31 to 35 year span; but lowered to 27.3 per cent among those who were 36 or over at the beginning of the second five-year period. There is a like increase related to advancing years up to 36 in the proportion of men who lived in homes in which the moral influences could be considered satisfactory. The incidence increased from about one-third of the men who were between 21 and 30 years of age, to 46.2 per cent of those who were between 31 and 35 years old; but of those who were 36 or over, slightly less than a third were living in homes with adequate moral standards.

Considering now these surrounding circumstances of our men in summary (that is, as a composite picture of neighborhood influences, the physical characteristics of the homes, and the moral standards of the homes), the typical pattern of increasingly favorable conditions related to advancing years up to the thirty-sixth year, emerges sharply. Those who were 21 to 25 years of age at the beginning of the second five-year period enjoyed a 20 per cent incidence of favorable environing conditions, those who were 31 to 35 years, a 28.1 per cent incidence, the proportion decreasing to 23.3 per cent among those who were 36 or older.

Thus, in analyzing the environmental conditions surrounding our men, the same trends are evident with the passage of time that were revealed in a consideration of their delinquent conduct—a rising incidence of improvement until approximately the age of

36, followed by a decline. This would seem to indicate, or at least to raise the reasonable hypothesis, that *the maturation process reaches its peak before the thirty-sixth year,* and that those persons who have not gained stability by that time are not very likely to do so in any fundamental sense thereafter.

In Table 14 are briefly summarized the findings presented in this section.

TABLE 14. ENVIRONMENTAL CIRCUMSTANCES IN PERIOD II
BY AGE GROUPINGS (PERCENTAGES)

AGE AT BEGINNING OF PERIOD II	ENVIRONMENTAL CIRCUMSTANCES				
	Moved about excessively	Good neighborhood influences	Good physical homes	Good moral standards	Good environmental conditions
21 to 25	58.0	6.7	34.1	38.6	20.0
26 to 30	45.8	16.9	31.5	39.7	25.3
31 to 35	41.5	17.0	40.9	46.2	28.1
36 and over	49.9	9.3	27.3	32.6	23.3

AGING AND FAMILY RELATIONSHIPS

Is the trend already noted in regard to criminal conduct and environmental circumstances likewise evident in respect to improvement in family relationships with advancing years until approximately 36? Consideration of the relationships of our men to their nearest relatives reveals that half (52 per cent) of those who were between 21 and 30 years of age were on terms of friendliness with their nearest relatives; this proportion was bettered with aging until it amounted to almost two-thirds (63.4 per cent) among the men who were between 31 and 35 years of age at the beginning of the second period; but among those who were 36 or older there again occurred the typical decline to 43.7 per cent. A like trend is manifest in the attitude of the relatives to the men: almost two-thirds (63.6 per cent) of those who were between 21 and 30 at the beginning of the second period were regarded with friendliness by their nearest relatives; this proportion was raised to 72.5 per cent among those who were 31 to 35 years old, but dropped to 50 per cent among those who were 36 or over.

What of the changes in the marital status of the men with advancing years? Among those who were 21 to 25 years of age at the beginning of the second period, 56 per cent were still single. A substantially lower incidence—only 34.3 per cent—existed among those who were 31 to 35 years of age; but of the group who were 36 and older by the beginning of the second period, the proportion of men who were still single was 43.3 per cent, indicating that if a man has not married by the time he is 35, he is less likely to do so thereafter than when he was younger. Among those who were 21 to 25 years old at the beginning of Period II, almost a third were married and living with their wives. This proportion was higher (46.3 per cent) among those who were 31 to 35 years old and lower (32.1 per cent) among those who were 36 and older.[2] As to the changing attitude of the men toward their children with advancing years (including illegitimate children to whose mothers the men were not married), among those who were between 21 and 30 years old at the beginning of the second period over half (56.5 per cent) were both fond of their children and took proper care of them; this proportion increased to 72.9 per cent among those who were between 31 and 35 years old and decreased to 63.6 per cent among those who were 36 and over.

Consider, now, the men's family relationships on the whole (i.e., their relationship to their wives and children if they were

[2] It should be noted, however, that of those who were married and living with their wives at the beginning of Period II, there was a steadily increasing assumption of marital responsibilities with advancing years from 55.6 per cent of those who were between 21 and 25 years of age at the beginning of Period II to 72.2 per cent among those who were 36 and older at the beginning of the period, so that apparently those men who remain with their wives increasingly assume their marital responsibilities even beyond the age of 35. The same may be said of the conjugal relationships of the men who were married and actually living with their wives at the beginning of the period, for there has been an increase from 51.9 per cent of those whose conjugal relationships might be considered good among the men who were 21 to 25 years of age at the beginning of Period II to 72.2 per cent of those who were 36 and over at the beginning of that period.

married men; to their children if they had been separated, divorced, or widowed before the beginning of the second five-year period; to their parents and siblings if they were unmarried men or had been separated prior to the beginning of the five-year period and had no children). In this connection it will be recalled that the standard of socially acceptable conduct in regard to family relationships which has been adopted for our purpose is the following: The man must not be harming his family in any way deemed injurious to the institution of the family; that is, if married, he must not neglect or desert his wife or children during the period under consideration and must not be separated or divorced from his wife during that period, must not have illicit relations with other women, nor be abusive to his wife or children, not be continually away in the evening, if this is not necessary to his business. If single, separated, widowed, or divorced before the beginning of the period and living away from home, he must be in touch with his parents or nearest relatives. If living at home, he must give evidence that he considers it more than merely a convenient place to sleep and eat in.

TABLE 15. FAMILY RELATIONSHIPS IN PERIOD II BY AGE
GROUPINGS (PERCENTAGES)

AGE AT BEGINNING OF PERIOD II	FAMILY RELATIONSHIPS				
	Friendly to nearest relatives	Relatives friendly to man	Married and living with wife at beginning of period	Fond of children and takes care of them	Successful in family relationships
21 to 25	52.0	63.6	32.2	56.5	40.0
26 to 30	49.1	58.8	36.6	52.8	48.8
31 to 35	63.4	72.5	46.3	72.9	57.3
36 and over	43.7	50.0	32.1	63.6	48.8

On the basis of this criterion, an increasing incidence of success in family relationships is noted with advancing years up to 36; for 40 per cent of our men who were between 21 and 25 years old at the beginning of the second period had good family relationships, the proportion increasing to 57.3 per cent of those who were between 31 and 35, but declining to 48.8 per cent among those who were 36 or over.

Obviously, the same trend is manifest in the family relationships of our men that was noted in their delinquent conduct and in their environmental circumstances—an improvement up to about the age of 36 and a decline thereafter.

The factors discussed in this section are summarized in Table 15.

AGING AND ECONOMIC RESPONSIBILITY

What changes occur with the passage of time in the assumption of economic responsibilities? First, with advancing years there is an increase in the proportion of men who carry insurance. Thus, among those who were 21 to 25 years of age at the beginning of the second five-year period 37.8 per cent were insured; the proportion increased to a little over half of those who were 26 to 35 years of age, but among those who were 36 or over, the incidence declined to 40.5 per cent. A like fluctuation in incidence is found with regard to savings. Among those who were between 21 and 25 at the beginning of Period II, 14 per cent had some savings; in the 26–35 year group a fourth of the men had savings, while among those 36 or over this proportion declined to 20.9 per cent. In regard to the general economic condition of the men, there has occurred an increase in the proportion of those in comfortable circumstances with the passage of time, from 6.1 per cent in the 21 to 25 year age span to 11 per cent of those who were between 26 and 35, followed by a decrease to 6.5 per cent of those who were 36 or older. The steady decline in the proportion of men in marginal circumstances with advancing years—from 77.6 per cent of those who were between 21 and 25 years old at the beginning of Period II to 60.9 per cent of those who were then 36 or over—is largely absorbed by an increase in the proportion of those who were totally dependent on relatives or social agencies for support—from a little less than one-fifth of the men who were between 21 and 35 years old at the beginning of Period II to almost one-third of those who were then 36 or older.

Summarizing, now, the subject of assumption of economic responsibilities (which refers to the men's support of their wives and children and/or other dependents), it is found that a little over half of those who were between 21 and 35 years of age at the beginning of the second period, were assuming their economic obligations, while only 40 per cent of those who were 36 or over were doing so.

Once again, then, the same general accumulation of improvement is evident until approximately the thirty-sixth year, after which there is a decline. In Table 16 are briefly summarized the findings of this section.

TABLE 16. ECONOMIC RESPONSIBILITY IN PERIOD II
BY AGE GROUPINGS (PERCENTAGES)

AGE AT BEGINNING OF PERIOD II	ECONOMIC RESPONSIBILITY				
	Carries insurance	Has savings	In comfortable circumstances	Dependent on others for support*	Meets his economic responsibility
21 to 25	37.8	14.0	6.1	16.3	53.1
26 to 30	53.5	25.5	10.8	17.2	56.2
31 to 35	52.0	27.4	11.7	19.2	52.6
36 and over	40.5	20.9	6.5	32.6	40.0

* Not because of industrial depression.

AGING AND INDUSTRIAL STATUS

What changes take place in industrial status with advancing years? Of those of our men who were between 21 and 25 years old at the beginning of Period II, 21.3 per cent worked steadily during that period. This proportion was raised to 36.7 per cent among those who were 31 to 35 years old and lowered to 20.8 per cent among those who were 36 or over. Likewise the incidence of men with good work habits rose from 34.8 per cent among those who were between 21 and 25 years old at the beginning of Period II to approximately 45 per cent in the group who were between 26 and 35; and this too was followed by the typical decline in incidence to only 29.8 per cent among those who were 36 or over.

In regard to occupational skill, about two-thirds of the men who were between 21 and 35 at the beginning of Period II could be classified either as semi-skilled or skilled workers, but of those who were 36 and over only 46.5 per cent could be so classified, so that beyond roughly the thirty-fifth year there once more occurs a drop in the incidence of a favorable condition—this time, occupational skill. Industrial stability, as manifest by engagement in one type of occupation rather than in several during the second period, also follows the pattern of age already stressed. Among the men who were between 21 and 25 years old, 45 per cent had engaged in only one kind of work during Period II. The incidence rose to 64 per cent among those who were between 31 and 35 years old; but again there was a decline to 56.2 per cent among those who were 36 or over and engaged in only one occupation throughout Period II.

Analysis of the character of the usual occupation followed by these men indicates that among those who were 36 and over there was an increasing incidence of idleness as contrasted with the previous age spans, and also a rising trend toward rough labor, farm work, and odd jobs of various kinds together with a decrease of employment in factories, in clerical occupations, and in trades.

In regard to the average length of employment, the typical age pattern is again evident. This is shown by the fact that among those who were 21 to 25, 34.3 per cent held their jobs on the average of a year or more, and in the 26–35 group 44 per cent were as steadily employed; while only 28.6 per cent of those who were 36 and over held their jobs on the average of a year or longer. The same general trend is evident in the earnings of the men. Among those who were 21–25 years old, an average weekly wage of less than $15 was earned by only 10 per cent of the men. The 26–30 year group contained 16.7 per cent who earned such an average wage, while among those who were 36 or older, 14.5 per cent earned less than $15 a week on the average.

Summarizing the changing industrial status with advancing years we find that successful industrial adjustment increased from 18.7 per cent among those who were 21 to 25 years old at the beginning of Period II, to 30 per cent among the group who were then 31 to 35 years old; but declined in incidence to 17.4 per cent among the men who were 36 or older.

In their industrial status, therefore, as in their assumption of economic responsibilities, in their family relationships, in their environmental circumstances, and in their delinquent conduct a trend toward improvement, i.e., a rising incidence in favorable conditions, is manifest until approximately the thirty-sixth year, beyond which occurs a reversal.

In Table 17 are summarized the findings of this section.

TABLE 17. INDUSTRIAL STATUS IN PERIOD II BY AGE
GROUPINGS (PERCENTAGES)

			INDUSTRIAL STATUS				
AGE AT BEGINNING OF PERIOD II	Steadily employed	Good work habits	Semi-skilled or skilled worker	Engaged in one type of work only	Holds jobs on average of a year or longer	Average earnings less than $15 a week	Industrial status successful
21 to 25	21.3	34.8	65.2	45.0	34.3	10.0	18.7
26 to 30	28.4	46.5	61.8	58.2	44.9	16.7	26.7
31 to 35	36.7	42.9	69.4	64.0	43.6	14.5	30.0
36 and over	20.8	29.8	46.5	56.2	28.6	43.5	17.4

AGING AND USE OF LEISURE

Are there any changes evident in the character of the use of leisure with the passage of time? First of all it is clear that with maturation there occurred a decline in the proportion of men having harmful companions—from 66.7 per cent among those who were between 21 and 25 at the beginning of Period II, to 58.6 per cent among those who were between 31 and 35; but again a reversal is apparent beyond that age span, for the incidence of harmful companionships increased to 71.1 per cent among the men who were 36 or over. If we may generalize from our sample of cases, it would appear that the most active period for criminalistic "ganging" seems to lie between the ages of 26 and 30, for during that age span 43.8 per cent of our group were members of gangs as contrasted with only 10 per cent in the 21 to 25 year span and 9 per cent and 8 per cent in the 31 to 35 year period and the 36 year and over span. In respect to this particular factor, therefore, the general maturation pattern is somewhat atypical.

In regard to patronizing places of recreation, there has occurred a decrease in resort to questionable places of recreation from 67.4 per cent among those who were between 21 and 25 years old to 55.8 per cent among those who were between 31 and 35; but, as in so many other respects, aging increased the incidence of this un- desirable expression of behavior; for among those who were 36 and over at the beginning of the second period, 65.1 per cent patronized undesirable haunts. The proportion of men utilizing some of their leisure time by hanging about on street corners also decreased as between the two lower age spans from 57.1 per cent among those who were between 21 and 25, to 40.3 per cent among those who were between 31 and 35; and the now familiar rise in incidence beyond the latter age span is once more apparent, for of those who were 36 and over at the beginning of Period II, 62.5 per cent indulged in street life.

Summarizing, now, the subject of use of leisure (which includes a consideration of our ex-prisoners' companions, recreations, and habits) we find that there was a decrease in the incidence of harm- ful use of leisure from 70.8 per cent of those who were between 21 and 25, to 61.7 per cent of those who were between 31 and 35, but an increase to 72 per cent among those who were 36 and over at the beginning of Period II.

Once again, therefore, the pattern is that of improvement up to the thirty-sixth year followed by decline beyond that age. In Table 18 is a summary of the findings discussed in this section.

TABLE 18. USE OF LEISURE IN PERIOD II BY AGE
GROUPINGS (PERCENTAGES)

AGE AT BEGINNING OF PERIOD II	USE OF LEISURE				
	Harmful companionships	Member of gang	Patronizes harmful places of recreation	Indulges in street life	Uses leisure time harmfully
21 to 25	66.7	10.0	67.4	57.1	70.8
26 to 30	61.4	43.8	61.3	45.9	64.0
31 to 35	58.6	9.1	55.8	40.3	61.7
36 and over	71.1	8.1	65.1	62.5	72.0

AGING AND MENTAL CONDITION

Only one more aspect of the life careers of our men remains to be considered in relation to advancing years and that is the factor which reflects the mental make-up or personality of our group. First, as to emotional instability, some two-thirds of the men who were between 21 and 25 at the beginning of Period II showed evidences of marked emotional instability during this period. This proportion remained about the same in the 26–30 and 31–35 age spans but rose to the excessively high incidence of 87.5 per cent among those who were 36 and over at the beginning of Period II. Turning now to the associated factor of mental disease or distortion, it is likewise found that the proportion of men with some mental condition noted by psychiatrists at one stage or another (such as a psychosis, constitutional psychopathy or psychopathic personality or "traits," alcoholism, drug addiction, neurasthenia, and the like) has increased from 60 per cent among those who were 21 to 35 years old at the beginning of Period II, to 80 per cent among those who were 36 and older.

In this factor, then, as in those previously discussed, a decline in favorableness occurred after the thirty-fifth year, although the incidence in the lower age spans remained about the same through-out. These findings are briefly summarized in Table 19.

TABLE 19. MENTAL CONDITION IN PERIOD II BY AGE
GROUPINGS (PERCENTAGES)

AGE AT BEGINNING OF PERIOD II	MENTAL CONDITION	
	Emotionally unstable	Mental aberration or imbalance
21 to 25	68.9	62.7
26 to 30	65.5	64.9
31 to 35	68.4	61.7
36 and over	87.5	80.0

Conclusion

Before stating any conclusions, it would be well briefly to review the findings in regard to the changes which occurred with time in the various phases of the life careers of our criminals. In the following respects there was a progressive improvement from the twenty-first to the thirty-sixth year followed by a decline in the incidence of favorable factors or conditions: seriousness of de-linquency, arrests, penal experiences, mobility, environmental con-ditions, marital status, family relationships, regularity of em-ployment, uniform type of employment, industrial adjustment, companionships, places of recreation, street life, use of leisure.

In the following factors the incidence of improvement also rose to the thirty-sixth year and was then followed by a decline but those who are 21–25 and 26–30 years old resemble each other very closely: character of physical home, moral standards, attitude toward relatives, attitude of relatives to the men, attitude of the men toward their children.

In the following factors the proportion of improvement also rose in the spans from 21 to 35 years and then declined, but there is a close resemblance between those who are 26–30 years old and those who are 31–35: proportion of non-delinquency, good neighborhood influences, carrying of insurance, having savings, having good work habits, holding jobs on the average of a year or longer, earning more than $15 a week on the average.

We have noted a progressive decrease with the passage of time in the proportion of men who characteristically commit offenses against property, and a progressive increase in the proportion of drunkards. We have also noted that the peak of the ganging period occurs in the 26–30 year age span and that there is a sharp decline thereafter.

There is a small group of factors in which no change with advancing years was evident until approximately the age of 36, when there occurred a marked increase in incidence of unfavorable conditions: committing offenses alone, being dependent on others for support, failing to meet economic responsibilities, being an unskilled worker, earning on the average of less than $15 a week, showing marked emotional instability, having a serious mental aberration or imbalance.

The major conclusion that emerges from this chapter is the fact of a rising trend toward improvement in all aspects of the activities of our men accompanying the passage of time (aging or maturation). This proceeds to approximately the age of 36, beyond which there is retrogression to less favorable conditions. The decline in incidence of the favorable conditions beyond that age suggests that among our particular group of criminals at any rate, the process of improvement in large measure ceases by the time the age of 36 is reached.[3]

On the basis of the evidence it is reasonable to conclude that the improvement in practically all aspects of the careers of our offenders, which continues to about the thirty-sixth year, is naturally to be expected as an accompaniment of growth or maturation, to which may in turn largely be attributed such reformation as has occurred. Some offenders "age" more rapidly than others and are

---

[3] From these findings we do not of course generalize to other groups of criminals or to non-criminals.

therefore likely to "settle down" earlier; many do not reach "years of discretion" until the middle thirties. But those who have not reformed by the thirty-sixth year are less likely to do so thereafter, since improvement in almost every aspect drops markedly beyond the 30–35 year age span. It remains to be seen, of course, as we continue to follow these men through the years, whether there will later appear another typical period of reformation, and if so, whether the reasons can be found in the aging process or in something else.

But if aging is so important a factor in bringing about reformation, why is it that so many offenders do not reform despite the passage of time? Are there, in other words, conditions or forces operative in some cases that prevent or perhaps unduly retard their improvement?

To this question we turn our attention in the next chapter.

Chapter XI

FACTORS IMPEDING REFORMATION

I N the two previous chapters it has been ascertained that aging (maturation) is the chief influence upon both reformation and the improvement which has occurred in all the major aspects of the life activities of our men. We have discovered also that this general improvement proceeds until approximately the thirty-sixth year and then declines. Presumably this is the normal curve of growth or maturation in the criminalistic group represented by our sample of cases. Only continuing follow-up studies of offenders will indicate, however, whether or not this tentative conclusion is justified.

We must now turn our attention to a determination of those factors which in certain cases somehow prevent reformation (or perhaps delay it) despite the passage of time.

Findings

MENTAL CONDITION AS MAJOR IMPEDIMENT TO REFORMATION

Although a marked improvement has occurred with the passage of the years in the traits and major life activities of the offenders we are studying, this cannot be said in respect to their mental condition (mental disease or aberration). This fact becomes evident from Table 20.

This lack of improvement in respect to mental condition is evidently a serious impediment to the reformative process—a conclusion substantiated not only by the detailed statistical analysis to follow but also by an intensive case analysis of the men who did not reform. As this analysis was made independently of, and long before, the statistical study of the cases in the mass was begun, it is of particular significance. It showed that in nine-tenths of the cases the failure of the men to improve appeared, on consideration of the factors and mechanisms in each case, to be clearly due to some mental or marked personality abnormality—psychosis, psychopathy, alcoholism, sex perversion, drug addiction, great emotional instability, and the like.[1]

TABLE 20. PERCENTAGE COMPARISON OF MAJOR ASPECTS OF LIFE
ACTIVITY IN PERIOD II AND IN PRE-REFORMATORY PERIOD*

	PRE-REFORMATORY PERIOD	PERIOD II	PERCENTAGE OF IMPROVEMENT
Non-delinquent	.9	32.1	31.2
Succeeds in family relationships	32.4	50.0	17.6
Meets economic responsibility	17.6	60.8	43.2
Good worker	19.8	41.2	21.4
Harmless use of leisure	3.6	34.2	30.6
No mental disease or disturbance	27.7	34.3	6.6

* For full details see Appendix D, *Period-Comparison Tables.*

Evidence gained from a comparison of the pre-Reformatory, Reformatory, and parole characteristics of those who ultimately reformed and those who continued to recidivate[2] reveals that by far the greatest difference between the two groups is to be found in their mental condition (diagnosis of which was made at the time of their commitment to the Reformatory). This is seen from Table 21 in which are presented the factors in which those who subsequently reformed and those who continued to recidivate differed to *more than a slight degree* prior to the expiration of their Reformatory sentences.

It now becomes of the utmost importance to analyze more closely the significance of the factor of mental deviation in a psychiatric sense.

[1] In the remaining 10.7 per cent of the cases the apparent reasons for the failure of the men were unfortunate marriage in 6.3 per cent, low ethical standards in 1.7 per cent, the habit of delinquency in 1.1 per cent; in one case desire for money, in one case "the hazard of success" (too high wages), and in one case the industrial depression.

[2] For a more detailed comparison of the characteristics of those who reformed and those who continued to recidivate, see Chapter VIII.

TABLE 21. COMPARISON OF INCIDENCE OF PRE-REFORMATORY, RE-
FORMATORY, AND PAROLE FACTORS IN REFORMED AND
UNREFORMED UP TO EXPIRATION OF
REFORMATORY SENTENCE

	PER CENT AMONG REFORMED	PER CENT AMONG UN-REFORMED	PROPORTIONALLY GREATER INCIDENCE AMONG UN-REFORMED
Delinquency in family	56.5	78.9	1.4
Under 14 at first delinquency	29.3	43.2	1.5
Pre-Reformatory arrests	78.7	94.4	1.2
Pre-Reformatory penal experiences	33.3	67.4	2.0
Serious offender in pre-Reformatory period	73.8	86.7	1.2
Poor work habits in pre-Reformatory period	37.2	57.5	1.5
Failed in family relationships in pre-Reformatory period	53.6	68.2	1.3
Failed in economic responsibilities in pre-Reformatory period	69.6	87.6	1.3
Committed offenses in Reformatory	73.3	87.3	1.2
Committed offenses frequently in Reformatory	42.2	57.5	1.4
Fair or poor worker in Reformatory	21.6	32.1	1.5
Violated conditions of parole	33.7	54.0	1.6
Mental disease or disturbance at time of commitment to Reformatory	7.6	51.2	6.7

COMPARISON OF MENTAL DEVIATES AND NORMALS

In comparing the characteristics of the men with and those without mental deviations of one sort or another,[3] we are confining ourselves to a consideration of their characteristics in the *second* five-year period, for the reason that so far as the present investigation is concerned, it is within this period that the maximum *accumulation* of non-delinquency has occurred. Such examination reveals that *the men having mental deviations of one kind or an-*

[3] Without consideration of intelligence.

*other differ markedly, in other respects as well, from those who
may be considered of normal personality.* This finding becomes
all the more striking in the light of the fact that the two groups—
mentally normal and mentally abnormal—were of essentially the
same age distribution at the beginning of Period II, so that the
differences in their characteristics, about to be presented, certainly
do not hinge upon any difference in their ages (Table 22).

TABLE 22. PERCENTAGE DISTRIBUTION BY AGE OF MENTAL DEVIATES
AND NORMALS AT BEGINNING OF PERIOD II

	AGE 21 TO 25	AGE 26 TO 30	AGE 31 AND OVER
Mental deviates	13.6	46.4	40.0
Normals	15.4	48.0	36.6

TABLE 23. PERCENTAGE COMPARISON OF CRIMINAL CONDUCT OF
MENTAL DEVIATES AND NORMALS IN PERIOD II

	NORMALS	MENTAL DEVIATES	DIFFERENCE
Unreformed	21.1	92.0	70.9
Serious offender	9.0	49.1	40.1
Arrested	18.9	63.4	44.5
Penal experiences	10.7	55.4	44.7
Offense committed alone	46.2	61.6	15.4
Used aliases	23.8	41.9	18.1

It will be apparent from Table 23 that there is a marked difference
between the characteristics of those with mental disease, aberration, or marked emotional instability, and those without such
mental or personality deviations. An examination of this table
clearly indicates that a far higher percentage of mental deviates
than of "normals" continue to be criminalistic; that a much higher
proportion of the former continue to be serious offenders, that
many more of them are arrested and many more have penal experiences, that more of them commit their offenses alone rather
than in company with others, and that more of them use aliases.

In regard to the attributes of criminal conduct, therefore, it can safely be said that the failure to reform despite the aging process, is in great measure chargeable to the influence of abnormal mental condition; for the men presenting marked mental and personality deviations continue their delinquencies (and serious crimes) to a far greater extent than those who do not have such mental and emotional handicaps.

An equally typical difference is manifest in the use of leisure time by the two groups of men during Period II.

TABLE 24. PERCENTAGE COMPARISON OF USE OF LEISURE BY MENTAL
DEVIATES AND NORMALS IN PERIOD II

	NORMALS	MENTAL DEVIATES	DIFFERENCE
Did not attend church	29.6	60.5	30.9
Participated in educational activities	11.6	2.7	8.9
Harmful companions	19.4	87.7	68.3
Belonged to "gang"	4.1	11.0	6.9
Frequented harmful places of recreation	16.3	87.2	70.9
Idled about streets	10.0	77.1	67.1
Had bad habits	24.5	94.0	69.5
Used leisure harmfully	20.9	90.9	70.0

From Table 24 it is evident that a far higher percentage of those with abnormal mental conditions or deviations than of those without them, did not attend church during the second five-year period; that fewer of the former than the latter participated in any educational activities; that far more mental deviates than mentally normal had harmful companionships, more of the former belonged to gangs, far more patronized harmful places of recreation, far more idled about the streets and far more had bad habits.

Summarizing the indices of use of leisure within the two groups of men, we find that 90.9 per cent of those with mental abnormalities utilized their spare time harmfully during the second five-year period compared to but 20.9 per cent of those without pathological mental conditions or personality deviations. From all this evidence it is clear that there is a marked difference in the characteristics and behavior of the men diagnosed as having mental abnormalities and those not having them, the former group utilizing their spare time far more harmfully than the latter.

TABLE 25. PERCENTAGE COMPARISON OF ENVIRONMENTAL CIRCUM-
STANCES OF MENTAL DEVIATES AND NORMALS IN PERIOD II

	NORMALS	MENTAL DEVIATES	DIFFERENCE
Moved about excessively	12.1	65.5	53.4
Poor physical home	3.9	45.3	41.4
Poor moral standards	10.5	52.5	42.0
Poor neighborhood influences	5.9	53.9	48.0
Poor environmental conditions	4.9	47.8	42.9

Likewise in regard to environmental circumstances during Period II, a comparison of those with mental deviations and those without them shows that the former contrast most unfavorably with the latter. It will be seen from Table 25 that a far greater percentage of the mental deviates than of the normals moved about excessively during the second period, lived in homes in which the physical conditions were unsatisfactory and the moral standards low, and resided in neighborhoods in which the surrounding influences were harmful.

Summarizing the environmental circumstances of the two groups of men during the second five-year period, we find that in almost one-half the cases of those with mental or emotional disturbances, the environing conditions were poor, compared with 4.9 per cent among those who had no mental aberrations.

Similarly, in regard to their family relationships, the men having mental deviations fulfilled to a far less extent the obligations of family life than did those who did not suffer from mental abnormalities or marked emotional disturbances. This is evident from Table 26 which shows that a far lower percentage of the men having mental aberrations, than of those without them, kept in touch with their nearest relatives; and that in a far greater per-

centage of the former than of the latter were the relatives themselves indifferent or hostile to the offenders. It is a striking fact,
also, that a far higher proportion of those with mental conditions
than of the normal were still single by the end of Period II; and
that among the former who were married, a far higher percentage
neglected their marital responsibilities, were grossly incompatible
in their conjugal relations, and were neglectful of their children.

TABLE 26. PERCENTAGE COMPARISON OF FAMILY RELATIONSHIPS OF
MENTAL DEVIATES AND NORMALS IN PERIOD II

	NORMALS	MENTAL DEVIATES	DIFFERENCE
Rarely in touch with relatives or only when in need	15.8	62.3	46.5
Relatives indifferent or hostile to offender	12.9	47.8	34.8
Still single at end of Period II	18.0	44.1	26.1
Conjugal relations poor	6.7	45.8	39.1
Attitude to children poor	5.4	43.1	37.7
Neglected marital responsibilities	6.7	73.5	66.8
Failed in family relationships	14.3	71.6	57.3

Summarizing the family relationships of these two groups of
men, we find that of those who had mental abnormalities or deviations, 71.6 per cent were failures in their family relationships
during Period II, as compared with but 14.3 per cent of those who
did not have such psychotic or psycopathic deviations.

Similarly, in regard to the assumption of their economic responsibilities, those with mental abnormalities behaved far less
favorably than those not having them. This is evident from
Table 27.

The table indicates that a far lower percentage of the men with
mental deviations than of the others carried insurance or had any
savings; that considerably more of the former than of the latter
were dependent on others for support during the second period
(and this not by reason of the industrial depression); that far more

of the mentally deviant than of the normal had been dealt with by social agencies—a finding which would indicate that they so grossly mismanaged their affairs that, through one source or another, social agencies found it necessary to step into the situation and assist the men and their families in various ways.

TABLE 27. PERCENTAGE COMPARISON OF ASSUMPTION OF ECONOMIC
RESPONSIBILITIES BY MENTAL DEVIATES AND
NORMALS IN PERIOD II

	NORMALS	MENTAL DEVIATES	DIFFERENCE
Carried insurance	85.1	26.8	58.3
Had savings	51.5	8.8	42.7
Dependent on others for support	4.6	24.0	19.4
Dealt with by social agencies	27.9	50.3	22.4
Failed to meet economic responsibilities*	6.2	55.7	48.5

* Not because of industrial depression.

Summarizing the indices of assumption of economic responsibilities by these two groups of men, we find that 55.7 per cent of those with mental abnormalities failed to meet their economic responsibilities (and for reasons not related to the industrial depression) as compared with but 6.2 per cent of those who did not have any mental or personality difficulties.

In regard to the industrial status of the two groups of men during the second five-year period it is further clear that those with diagnosed mental deviations behaved far less favorably than did those not having them.

Table 28 shows that a far higher percentage of the men with mental abnormalities than those without them were irregular workers, had poor work habits, lost their positions through their own fault, were unskilled workers, were employed in more than one kind of occupation during the second period, worked partially or wholly in illegitimate employment, earned on the average of less than $15 weekly, and held their jobs on an average of less than three months.

Summarizing their industrial status during the second five-year period we find that 59.7 per cent of those with mental conditions or aberrations had to be classified as industrial failures as compared with but 4.7 per cent of the men who did not have such mental or emotional disturbances.

TABLE 28. PERCENTAGE COMPARISON OF INDUSTRIAL STATUS OF
MENTAL DEVIATES AND NORMALS IN PERIOD II

	NORMALS	MENTAL DEVIATES	DIFFERENCE
Irregular worker	5.5	59.4	53.9
Poor work habits	3.7	41.8	38.1
Lost jobs through own fault	7.7	72.9	65.2
Unskilled worker	17.8	49.7	31.9
Employed in more than one kind of occupation	31.4	51.8	20.4
Earned on average less than $15 weekly	3.2	29.0	25.8
Held jobs on average less than three months	8.1	65.4	57.3
Industrial failure	4.7	59.7	55.0

TABLE 29. SUMMARY OF PERCENTAGE COMPARISON IN MAJOR FACTORS
BETWEEN MENTAL DEVIATES AND NORMALS IN PERIOD II

	NORMALS	MENTAL DEVIATES	DIFFERENCE
Unreformed in criminal conduct	21.1	92.0	70.9
Harmful use of leisure	20.9	90.9	70.0
Poor environmental conditions	4.9	47.8	42.9
Failure in family relationships	14.3	71.6	57.3
Failure in meeting economic responsibilities*	6.2	55.7	48.5
Industrial failure	4.7	59.7	55.0

* Not because of industrial depression.

Turning now to a general summary of the major differences in Period II between the men suffering from mental abnormalities or having marked liabilities of personality and those who were free of any such psychiatric conditions or traits, it becomes certain that *there is a marked difference in the performance of the two groups in favor of those without mental or emotional difficulties.* As shown in Table 29, the greatest difference lies in the failure of the abnormal to reform despite the passage of time with its accompanying process of maturation that, as we have seen in the two previous chapters, largely accounts for the reform which did occur.

Conclusion

The foregoing discussion has, it seems to us, quite clearly shown that although the process of maturation (which proceeds up to roughly the thirty-sixth year) is the most pervasive operating influence on reformation, it is subject to blocking or retardation by mental or personality deviations. Whether this hampering of the natural process of maturation will continue into the years not yet covered by the present investigation and become even more marked, remains for further follow-up studies to disclose.

In the meantime, however, the findings already suggest that mental hygiene and psychiatric services should be of value not only in the pre-Reformatory and Reformatory stages of criminal careers, but in the subsequent periods. Obviously, in many cases, the natural tendency to improvement of behavior that comes with advancing age needs to be released or facilitated by the skill of the psychiatrist, so that the benign influence of aging on reformation may proceed with as little obstruction as possible.

Chapter XII

PREDICTING CRIMINAL CONDUCT FOLLOWING
EXPIRATION OF SENTENCE

THE final problem to which we need to devote ourselves in the present investigation deals with the prognostication of behavior at a sufficiently early stage in criminal careers to make possible more effective treatment of offenders. Because a second five-year period has elapsed since the expiration of the sentences of our men to the Reformatory, it now becomes possible to predict, on the basis of significant factors in their lives, the probable behavior over *a ten-year span* following expiration of sentence from the Reformatory of other offenders with similar characteristics.

For some time the authors have been concerned with the problem of redefining and implementing the traditional indeterminate sentence in a way to make its use more realistic and effective. The beginnings of such a use now become more evident as we see that it is feasible to predict with sufficient accuracy the behavior of offenders over a ten-year span.

Prediction Table

METHOD OF CONSTRUCTING PREDICTION TABLE

It will be recalled from previous chapters that as regards recidivism the behavior classifications for the ten-year period following the expiration of sentence from the Reformatory are as follows:

(a) Non-delinquent throughout
(b) Minor delinquent throughout
(c) Serious delinquent throughout
(d) Non-delinquent in Period I, delinquent in Period II
(e) Minor delinquent in Period I, non-delinquent in Period II
(f) Minor delinquent in Period I, serious delinquent in Period II
(g) Serious delinquent in Period I, minor delinquent in Period II
(h) Serious delinquent in Period I, non-delinquent in Period II

By relating the pre-Reformatory factors to delinquent behavior during the ten-year period it was found that twenty-six factors in the careers of our men showed a considerable relationship to criminal behavior over the ten-year span[1] as determined by inspection of correlation tables and by the coefficients of mean square contingency.[2] Five factors among those which bore the highest relationship to recidivism or reform were chosen as the basis of a prediction table. Actually eight factors bore a relationship of .20 or more to delinquent behavior in the ten-year span—an association sufficiently high to give exceptional predictive value. However, three of these were eliminated in order to avoid the use of too many factors that are more or less constituents of the factor of delinquency—namely, *Pre-Reformatory use of leisure, Pre-Reformatory criminality, Pre-Reformatory penal experience.*

The five pre-Reformatory factors which were utilized in the construction of the prognostic instrument were, then:

PRE-REFORMATORY FACTORS	CONTINGENCY COEFFICIENT
(a) Age at first delinquency	.23
(b) Mental condition (disease or distortion)	.43
(c) Arrests	.25
(d) Economic responsibility	.28
(e) Work habits	.35

A comparison with the pre-Reformatory factors that were found to be highly predictive of behavior in Period I (as reported in *500 Criminal Careers,* pages 281 and 282) shows that the factor

[1] These factors are as follows: Nativity of parents and sons; Education of parents; Economic status of parents; Criminality or delinquency in family; Nativity of offender; Mobility; Church attendance; Family relationships; Age at leaving home; Age at beginning work; Work habits; Industrial skill; Economic responsibility; Use of leisure; Age at first known delinquency; Arrests preceding arrest for which sent to Reformatory; Frequency of arrests; Pre-Reformatory criminality; Pre-Reformatory penal experiences; Age at time of sentence to Reformatory; Seriousness of offense for which men were committed to Reformatory; Type of offense for which men were committed to Reformatory; Commission of offense alone or with others; Physical condition at entrance to Reformatory; Intelligence grade; Mental disease or distortion.

[2] For the significance of the mean square contingency coefficient see note 1, p. 77.

Work habits was then also highly predictive (C = .42); as was also the factor of *Arrests* (C = .29), the factor of *Economic responsibility* (C = .27), and the factor *Mental disease or distortion* (C = .26). The factor *Penal experiences* was then also highly predictive (C = .29), but this particular factor has now been eliminated from the prediction table for the reason already stated. The same is true of the factor *Pre-Reformatory criminality* (in *500 Criminal Careers* designated as *Frequency and seriousness of pre-Reformatory criminality*) which then showed a relationship of .36 and is now also highly related to outcome but is not used in the construction of the prediction table because it is a component of the factor, *Pre-Reformatory delinquency.*

It will be seen, therefore, that of the eight factors which were sufficiently related to behavior throughout the ten-year span to be used in constructing the present prediction table, five had also been utilized in the construction of the table predicting criminal conduct during the first five years. The only differences to be noted are that the factor *Work habits* is not now quite so highly predictive as it was before (C = .35: .42); while the factor *Mental condition* is more predictive of delinquent conduct over the ten-year period than it was in the first five years (C = .43: .26).

The factor of *Age at first delinquency,* utilized in the present prediction table and not in the first one, is still as highly predictive of future behavior as it was before (C = .23: .22).[3]

PREDICTIVE FACTORS

In *500 Criminal Careers,* Chapter XVIII; in *Five Hundred Delinquent Women,*[4] Chapter XVII; and in *One Thousand Juvenile Delinquents,*[5] Chapter XI, the method developed in constructing prediction tables has been described in detail. There is, therefore, no need to repeat a description of this procedure, which has not been modified for the present purpose.

---

[3] See *500 Criminal Careers,* p. 248.　　　　[4] New York, Alfred A. Knopf, 1934.
[5] Harvard University Press, 1934.

The factors which were selected for the construction of the particular prediction table with which this chapter is concerned have already been listed. Their subcategories will now be presented together with their non-delinquency rates ("success") over the ten-year follow-up period:

FACTORS AND SUBCATEGORIES	PERCENTAGE INCIDENCE OF NON-DELINQUENCY
1. Work Habits	
Good	49.1
Fair	19.2
Poor	11.4
2. Economic Responsibility	
Fair	46.2
Poor	15.7
3. Age at First Known Delinquency	
14 and over	28.0
Under 14	12.1
4. Prior Arrests	
No	48.6
Yes	17.3
5. Mental Disease or Distortion	
None	34.3
Psychotic	3.2
Psychopathic	0

From the above it will be seen that, for example, of those who had *good* work habits in the pre-Reformatory period, 49.1 per cent were non-delinquent during the ten-year period; of those whose work habits were *fair,* but 19.2 per cent were non-delinquent in the ten-year period; while among the men whose work habits were *poor* prior to their commitment to the Reformatory, only 11.4 per cent were non-delinquent during the ten-year period. Each one of the other four factors may be similarly analyzed.

The next step in the construction of the prognostic table is to determine the upper and lower limits of the non-delinquency score. This is derived by summating the highest non-delinquency rates existing in each of the five factors (206.2) and the lowest (56.5). Next are established score classes within the upper and lower limits just determined, at intervals of 25. Finally, each man is classified according to his particular score. Within such 25-point intervals, Table 30 has been derived.

A careful examination of the table indicates that it is possible to make some contractions of it which would increase its usefulness. First of all, we may omit the group of those who were *Nondelinquent in Period I and Delinquent in Period II,* because there are only 5 such cases. We may also omit for the present purpose the group who were *Minor delinquents in Period I and Serious delinquents in Period II,* since there are only 7 of these. A further examination of the table also indicates that score classes of 50 would more sharply point up the differences between the cases in each score class than the finer classification. On the basis of these considerations two tables (Tables 31 and 32) were finally arranged, the first of which is more detailed than the second and either one of which should be useful in determining in advance the probable subsequent careers of Reformatory graduates over a ten-year span following completion of sentence.

From Table 31 it will be seen that a man scoring more than 175 in respect to the five predictive factors in question has 8 out of 10 chances (80 per cent out of 100 per cent) of becoming and remaining a non-delinquent after the expiration of his sentence to the Reformatory; and there are but 2 out of 10 chances of his continuing to be a minor delinquent throughout the ten-year period. There is probably no chance of so favorably situated an ex-inmate of the Reformatory being a serious offender in the first or second half of a ten-year span following the expiration of his sentence. It appears also from this table that a man with a score between 150

TABLE 30. NON-DELINQUENCY SCORE RELATED TO OUTCOMES IN THE TEN-YEAR SPAN (UNCONTRACTED)

NON-DELINQUENCY SCORE	DELINQUENCY IN PERIODS I AND II								Total
	Non-delinquent throughout	Minor throughout	Serious throughout	Non-delinquent in I, delinquent in II	Minor in I, non-delinquent in II	Minor in I, serious in II	Serious in I, minor in II	Serious in I, non-delinquent in II	
	Num-ber / Per cent	Num-ber / Per cent	Num-ber / Per cent	Num-ber / Per cent	Num-ber / Per cent	Num-ber / Per cent	Num-ber / Per cent	Num-ber / Per cent	Num-ber
56.5–75		11 25.6	17 39.5	2 4.7	1 2.3	4 9.3	6 13.9	2 4.7	43
75–100	6 8.8	20 29.4	26 38.2	1 1.5	3 4.4	1 1.5	6 8.8	5 7.4	68
100–125	15 30.6	9 18.4	12 24.5	0 –	6 12.2	2 4.1	3 6.1	2 4.1	49
125–150	6 40.0	2 13.3	4 26.7	0 –	0 –	0 –	2 13.3	1 6.7	15
150–175	7 46.7	1 6.7	2 13.3	2 13.3	1 6.7	0 –	1 6.7	1 6.6	15
175–206.2	8 80.0	2 20.0	0 –	0 –	0 –	0 –	0 –	0 –	10
Total	42 21.0	45 22.5	61 30.5	5 2.5	11 5.5	7 3.5	18 9.0	11 5.5	200*

* In this and the succeeding tables only those cases could be utilized about which all the factors involved were known.

TABLE 31. NON-DELINQUENCY SCORE RELATED TO OUTCOMES IN THE TEN-YEAR SPAN (FIRST CONTRACTION)

DELINQUENCY IN PERIODS I AND II

NON-DELINQUENCY SCORE	Non-delinquent throughout		Delinquent in I (serious or minor), non-delinquent in II		Minor throughout		Serious throughout		Serious in I, minor in II		Total	
	Num-ber	Per cent	Num-ber	Per cent	Num-ber	Per cent	Num-ber	Per cent	Num-ber	Per cent	Num-ber	Per cent
Less than 150	27	16.6	20	11.0	42	25.8	59	36.2	17	10.4	165	100
150–175	7	53.8	2	15.4	1	7.7	2	15.4	1	7.7	13	100
175–206.2	8	80.0	0	–	2	20.0	0	–	0	–	10	100
Total	42	22.3	22	11.7	45	23.9	61	32.4	18	9.7	188	100

C = .39

TABLE 32. NON-DELINQUENCY SCORE RELATED TO OUTCOMES IN
THE TEN-YEAR SPAN (SECOND CONTRACTION)

NON-DELINQUENCY SCORE	DELINQUENCY IN PERIODS I AND II							
	Non-delinquent throughout		Delinquent in I, non-delinquent in II		Delinquent throughout (minor or serious)		Total	
	Num-ber	Per cent	Num-ber	Per cent	Num-ber	Per cent	Num-ber	Per cent
Less than 150	27	16.6	20	11.0	118	72.4	165	100
150–175	7	53.8	2	15.4	4	30.8	13	100
175–206.2	8	80.0	0	–	2	20.0	10	100
Total	42	22.3	22	17.1	124	60.6	188	100

$$C = .37$$

and 175 has a little over 5 out of 10 chances of being non-delinquent throughout the 10-year period, 1½ out of 10 chances of eventually becoming non-delinquent, 1½ chances in 10 of being a serious delinquent throughout, and less than one chance in 10 of becoming a minor delinquent during any part of the ten-year period. It appears also from this table that a man whose non-delinquency score is less than 150 has but 1½ chances in 10 of becoming a non-delinquent after the expiration of sentence from the Reformatory; 3½ chances in 10 of being a serious offender throughout; 2½ chances in 10 of being a minor delinquent during the ten years; and only one chance in 10 of being a serious delinquent in the first period and a minor delinquent in the second.

On the basis of such a table, therefore, a judge in determining whether to sentence a young man to a Reformatory would know immediately that the man with a non-delinquency score of 175 or more has an excellent chance for permanent reformation; while the man with a score of less than 150 has very little chance for reformation if sent to a Reformatory, or, as later researches may indicate, if sent to any penal institution, or regardless of the kind of treatment to which he is subjected. It is not possible, of course, to go as far as this in the use of such a table, for the reason that our knowledge of the effectiveness of the various types of peno-correctional treatment is as yet very limited. Nor is it possible in this study, due to the smallness of the number of reformed offenders, to take into consideration the very important factor of the *age span* during which different types of offenders are most likely to reform. This significant feature of the prediction device will, we expect, be included in another follow-up study now under way concerning the careers of a thousand juvenile delinquents during a fifteen-year span subsequent to their appearance before a juvenile court.

Table 32 is a still further contraction of the one just analyzed. From this table it is clear that a man having a non-delinquency score of 175 or more has 8 out of 10 chances of becoming a non-delinquent, and 2 out of 10 chances of continuing to be delinquent within a ten-year span; while the man with a non-delinquency score of 150 to 175 has a little over 5 out of 10 chances of being non-delinquent, 3 out of 10 of continuing to recidivate, and 1½ chances out of 10 of eventually becoming non-delinquent, so that he really has a 7 to 10 chance of immediate or subsequent reformation. Finally, the man with a non-delinquency score of less than 150 has only 1½ chances out of 10 of becoming immediately non-delinquent and remaining so, one out of 10 chances of becoming a non-delinquent during the second half of the ten-year span; and 7 out of 10 chances of continuing to recidivate throughout.

Conclusion

It has been shown that certain factors in the careers of offenders who were sentenced to a reformatory are of considerable value in forecasting their future behavior over a ten-year span beyond the expiration of their sentences. If reformatories are to reform they ought reasonably to be expected so to build up resistances to wrongdoing as to give assurance of law-abiding behavior after the end of supervision. It is one thing for ex-prisoners to meet the conditions imposed by parole, when their conduct is supervised and when the threat of return to a reformatory or prison to complete the unexpired portion of their indeterminate sentences hangs like the sword of Damocles over their heads. It is quite another for them to continue to satisfy the normal requirements of life in a legally ordered society once the supervision and threat are removed.

Hence careful selection of offenders for different types of treatment in the light of a reasonable forecast of their conduct thereafter becomes of the utmost importance. Herein lies the value of predictive instruments. As we have stressed in previous studies concerning the use of prognostic tables in the administration of criminal justice, it is not suggested that the mechanical application of such tables to individual cases should entirely supersede the reflection and professional experience of those who at various stages exercise discretion in this field—judges, penal administrators, and parole boards. The value of predictive instruments lies in their aid to a more efficient exercise of discretion than we have at present. By the use of such tables, the disposition of each case is made in the light of objectified and organized experience with hundreds of similar cases. This seems to be the only realistic meaning in the widely prevalent demand to "individualize justice." A sentencing and paroling practice that purports to provide an absolutely *unique* prescription for each offender's ills is on its face illusory. On the other hand, one that is founded on the classification of offenders into types, to the members of each of which can be assigned that form of corrective treatment which experience has shown to be most fruitful of desired results, is a realistic and scientific one.

Furthermore, by carefully noting similarities and differences between hundreds of offenders who have passed through the various chambers of the mills of justice, and then comparing the different types thereby established in the light of their behavior after they have been treated by some specific correctional device, the door is opened to a more effective design of correctional instruments suitable to different classes of offenders. For if prediction tables covering each of the major forms of *existing* peno-correctional practice (e.g., probation, short-term imprisonment, imprisonment in a long-term penal institution, release on parole, release without parole, release under police supervision, and the like) should demonstrate that *none* of the existing methods produce sufficiently satisfactory results for certain types of offenders, other correctional means will have to be developed and experimentally applied.

Chapter XIII

CASES ILLUSTRATING VARIED CRIMINAL CAREERS

I N a research such as this a statistical presentation of the data is required in order to obtain a general picture of a mass of criminals and to arrive at a determination of the influences and conditions which affect a large group of cases. The statistical method serves to break down, assemble, and classify the personal traits, environmental circumstances, and behavior of offenders as a group. The general abstractions emerging from a statistical analysis should be illustrated, however, by specific cases in order that the more subtle interrelationships of traits and forces involved in the evolution and devolution of criminal careers may more clearly be viewed as an organic whole than is possible within the limitations of the statistical method.

Our analysis has shown that the process of maturation through aging plays a more significant role than any other factor in bringing about reformation. In the individual case we see more clearly, however, what are the subinfluences that release the forces of normal maturation. And we see more clearly also what influences block this normal process of growth or maturation.

The following cases are divided into two groups, therefore: those who reformed within the ten-year span, and those who continued to recidivate.

Men Who Reformed

JOSEPH

There are many cases in which the offender passes through a long period of instability—a sort of delayed adolescence—with such accompaniments as a strong Wanderlust *or desire for adventure. The process of maturation in such cases is somewhat delayed.* This pattern of development is illustrated by the following case.

Joseph was the youngest of four children of English-Irish parents and the only one of the four to show any signs of delinquency. His father, however, had been intemperate for many years and was once committed to jail for lewdness, and his only sister had been a mental patient. Joseph's father, a mill hand, was barely able to support his family, and when our youth was sixteen, the father deserted his family and has not been heard from since. From his earliest years in school, Joseph was a truant and ran about the streets with questionable young companions. He left school in the sixth grade and went to work as a mill hand.

Joseph's first arrest occurred when he was sixteen years of age on a charge of "stubbornness" entered by his mother. This was shortly followed by an arrest for larceny for which he was committed to a correctional school. During the following ten years prior to his commitment to the Reformatory on the particular sentence for which he was included in this research, Joseph was arrested on numerous occasions for burglary, larceny, and carrying concealed weapons. He was returned to the correctional school several times, was twice committed to the Massachusetts Reformatory, subsequent to his release from which he joined the army from which he was given a dishonorable discharge.

Between the ages of twenty-four and twenty-seven, Joseph worked off and on in mills and bakeries, frequently going away from his home city for short periods, just barely supporting himself, and only occasionally contributing toward the support of his mother who would often say about him that "he would give you the last ten cents he has but he has no stability." Whenever he lived at home, Joseph would help his mother in the household with dish-washing, running errands, and so on, and she has particularly emphasized the fact that he never spoke a cross word to her in his life.

At the time of his commitment to the Reformatory on the sentence which we have particularly studied, Joseph was already twenty-seven years of age. He had returned home only a short time before this, after one of his frequent absences, and this in response to a telegram from his mother saying that his only sister to whom he was very much attached had to undergo an operation. During the few weeks prior to his arrest, he had loafed about, not doing much of anything and paying frequent visits to the home of a friend of his who had a young daughter. He got into the habit of calling on the girl in the afternoons while her father was away and she was at home alone. The girl soon complained to her father that Joseph indecently assaulted her; and this was the occasion for his arrest and sentence to the Reformatory.

At the time of his admission, mental examination showed him to be of borderline intelligence and to be somewhat suggestible but not suffering from any mental disease or any marked deviations of personality or character. In the institution his conduct was perfect and he was extremely capable in his work in the kitchen, showing great interest and cheerfulness in any extra tasks assigned him. This it should be remembered was already his third commitment to the Reformatory. During the first one he spent twelve months there, during the second eighteen months, and during the present one fifteen months. Each time he behaved equally well.

When Joseph was released on parole he went to live with his mother and sister, and worked a few months as a laborer. But he soon reverted to his habit of idling and wandering about.

During the first five-year follow-up period, Joseph's family heard very little from him. On one of his infrequent returns home he was arrested for burglary and placed on probation, so that clearly he had not yet ceased the commission of serious offenses. As he could find no regular work in his home town, he soon drifted away again. He worked here and there mostly in bakeshops and restaurants through the East and South, and also made frequent trips as a mess boy on freight boats plying to Europe and South America. He managed to get along without assistance from any public agencies and never wrote home for money. He was now and then arrested for vagrancy or disturbing the peace but there is no evi-

dence that after his thirtieth year he committed any further burglaries or larcenies.

Shortly after the death of his mother, which occurred in the
second year of the second five-year follow-up period, Joseph, now
thirty-seven years old, returned home to live with his sister. His
sister, who has remained unmarried, was very happy indeed at his
return and they have been keeping house together ever since. They
have been supported more or less through public relief funds, but
Joseph gets a day's work now and then. He does most of the house-
work for his sister who is not very strong, showing his devotion to
her by accompanying her to the stores in order to carry home the
purchases. He has not shown any initiative about getting work,
tending always to wait until something turns up.

For the last three years Joseph has not been arrested nor has he
committed any offenses other than sex indiscretions "just about
like any man." He does not hang about the streets very much and
shuns all but one or two companions, spending most of his time
about the house with his sister. He says that he does not intend to
marry, has completely gotten over his desire to wander about aimlessly, and is very happy indeed to have a home, simple as it is.

Apparently Joseph has really settled down, at least to the extent
of being no longer a social menace. Relatives and also the police
fully confirm this fact. He has had a very long period of adolescence which, from the time he began truanting from school, has
expressed itself in a strong desire for adventure. This has gradually
diminished with the passing of the years.

LEO

*In some cases the natural process of maturation seems to be
facilitated or hastened by the shock of severe punishment in the
case of an offender who theretofore has done pretty much what he
liked and escaped unscathed. This is especially true when the
offender has a good family background and tradition.* Such an
instance is illustrated by the following brief career of wrong-doing.

Leo is the second youngest of five children of Portuguese parentage. Both his father and mother are of excellent character and Leo is the only one of the five youngsters who has given any real worry to his family. Leo's father had a small barber shop from which a sufficient income was derived to support the growing family without any assistance from outside sources. However, when the boy was five years of age, his father became very ill with tuberculosis and returned to Portugal, leaving the barber shop, which was heavily mortgaged, to the management of Leo's mother. She had to engage several men in turn to carry on the business while she was occupied in caring for her family.

Within a year after his return to Portugal, Leo's father died and his mother lost the shop and was left with a very small insurance. The older children had of necessity to go to work, but what they were able to earn was not sufficient to support the family and for some ten years after the father's death, the mother had to be partly supported by public and private charitable organizations. The mother's reputation has been excellent in her community and her intelligent devotion to her children is manifest in the fact that she saw to it that they all belonged to local boys' clubs.

Leo left school in the sixth grade and worked now and then in stores, but very irregularly and with very little feeling of his responsibility toward assisting his mother or at least partially supporting himself. He was inclined to laziness and great indifference about the family problems and for this reason caused a great deal of worry to his mother, his brothers, and his only sister. The mother, in her conscientiousness about the boy's upbringing, felt that the best way to force him out of his very irresponsible attitude would be to report him to the court. She therefore entered a complaint against him for stubbornness to which he pleaded guilty and for which he was sentenced to the Massachusetts Reformatory. The sentence was suspended, however, and he was placed on probation. The probation was continued for almost two years, during which time Leo failed to report regularly, worked only occasionally, and was arrested on three occasions, once for trespassing, once for violating an automobile law, and once for violating a city ordinance.

Because Leo had been given every chance by the court to behave himself during his probation which had been continued several times, the judge finally felt that it would be necessary to send the lad to the Reformatory. His mother concurred in this idea, for she was under the impression that a Reformatory was "a sort of a school" and that perhaps a brief stay there would bring the boy to his senses. Consequently, at the age of twenty, Leo was committed to the Reformatory on the charge of being a stubborn child. He was there found to be of borderline mentality but not suffering from any mental abnormalities. Both his industrial and conduct record in the Reformatory were perfect. Shortly after his commitment many pleas were made for his early release from the Reformatory, not only by his mother but by the probation officer and by a member of the staff of the boys' club to which Leo had belonged. It was emphasized by those who had known Leo well that he was never "vicious but always lazy and indolent"; "that he is not dishonest or in any way a criminal." These same pleaders pointed out that a long stay in the Reformatory was likely to do the youth a great deal of harm because he would be placed in close contact with serious offenders.

Apparently the parole board of the Reformatory was inclined to agree with this point of view for at the end of five months they released Leo and he returned to his mother's home. Fortunately for him, he found a position as a helper on a truck and was able to earn $20 a week. He contributed steadily to the support of his mother until two and a half years after the expiration of his parole, at which time, at the age of twenty-three, he married a young Portuguese-American girl who was working for the same firm by which Leo was employed. The young couple moved not very far away from Leo's mother and soon had a child.

Leo's good behavior has continued up to the present time. He is thirty-two years old. He is very proud of his wife and she of him. He is still working for the same company, driving a truck and earning $35 a week. He has a good many friends in the neighborhood with whom he goes out occasionally, and has never reverted to the indifferent ways of his childhood. He continues to work for the same firm by which he was engaged at the time of his release on parole. Though he has no savings, he carries an insurance policy.

Apparently the Reformatory had the beneficial effect on Leo of shocking him out of his indifference. This point of view is evidently concurred in by the examiner at the Reformatory, who talked with Leo soon after his admission. At that time he commented that the youth is "rather an undeveloped youngster mentally whom, I think, a good horsewhipping would have benefited more than all his court appearances."

That time itself without the salutary experience of a severe punishment would have straightened Leo out appears to be quite certain in the light of his excellent home background; but it is also probable that his reformation would not have been accomplished so early. Though the risk was run of criminalistic contagion in sending this type of youth to the Reformatory, it seems to have contributed to a mental stock-taking with salutary results.

EDWARD

In some cases a happy marriage facilitates the natural process of maturation. This is illustrated by the following case.

Edward is the third of four children of Canadian-born parents. The family have continuously lived in a small town in western Massachusetts. Edward's father, though something of a drinking man, has rarely lost any time from his work because of this. He has been a cabinet maker and continuously employed by one concern in the town. None of the other three children were delinquents. The parents had always been in extremely modest circumstances, and it was necessary for the children to earn their way as soon as possible.

Edward left school in the fourth grade at the age of thirteen, because he was sentenced to a correctional school for the commission of burglaries. On one occasion previous to this he had been complained of by his parents as a stubborn child, and when twelve years old he was known to have had illicit sex experiences and to have stolen considerably in school.

Edward was kept in the correctional school for three years, and upon his release at the age of sixteen he went to work in a machine shop. However, he did not stay in any one job for any considerable length of time, preferring to loaf about with other boys, often breaking into barns and garages to sleep, but rarely stealing anything.

When he was nineteen years old, Edward was arrested for larceny and ordered committed to the Massachusetts Reformatory; but the sentence was suspended. Despite frequent warnings by the police that he go to work, he did not do so and was finally turned out by his parents. A few months later he was picked up on a vagrancy charge and the original sentence to the Reformatory was imposed. The complaint which led to his arrest was made by several people who informed the police that their barns or garages had been broken into for sleeping purposes.

Upon his admission to the Reformatory, mental examination showed Edward to be of borderline mentality. The examiner said of him that "he has absolutely no realization of the fact that there is anything due from him in this world and up to the present at least he has been contented in getting by as easily as possible. Everything has been tried to get him to change his ways but apparently to no avail."

Edward remained at the Reformatory for eleven months and gave no particular trouble, though he occasionally committed very minor offenses such as talking loudly, being disorderly or "grossly careless," laughing or "fooling." His plea for release on parole was the one frequently made: "I feel that if I was given another chance I could make good." A lawyer from his home town also strongly urged his release on the ground that "he of late has been corresponding with his father and mother . . . to the effect that he has fully comprehended his misdoings and indiscretions, and he feels that he can come now to his home and engage in a lawful pursuit and be a man. . . . He has evidently repented to the fullest degree, something which he has never done before."

When Edward was released on parole he returned to the home of his parents and secured work in a chair factory for which he was quite well fitted because of the fact that he had learned cabinet making at the Reformatory. However, within two months he was laid off because "he was only a fair worker and spent a good deal of time fooling." Thereafter Edward picked up jobs peddling wood, cutting ice, planting trees, cleaning brush, and doing various odd jobs around the town. These were always temporary. Though Edward did not, during his parole period, commit any offenses for which he might have been arrested, he did not settle down into any steady work and had, for the most part, to be aided by his parents.

For three and a half years of the first five-year follow-up period Edward continued to live with his parents, largely depending upon them for support. During this time he was once arrested for larceny from a building in a nearby town. He claimed that it was his companion who actually did the stealing, though the police felt (Edward denying it) that he was implicated in the larceny and ordered him to make restitution to the amount of $35.

Because of his tendency to loaf and to work irregularly his parents finally became very much disgusted with him and turned him out. Edward then went to live with his married sister, but soon she also became impatient with him. He then went off with a companion who said he had a job for him and they loafed around in neighboring towns working in bowling alleys and restaurants.

Toward the end of the first follow-up period Edward fortunately ran across a job on a lunch cart where he continued to be employed into the second five-year period. To this cart often came as a customer a widow seven years Edward's senior. He had frequent sexual relations with her and two months before their baby was born Leo married her. She had a little daughter of six by a former marriage, whose support he was very happy to assume. Before Edward married he took his fiancée to his mother's home and the couple were married there. At this time Edward was twenty-seven years old.

The couple lived with his parents for a few months and then decided to move to a neighboring rural community where they saw an opportunity to establish a lunch cart business of their own. There they have since lived in a small but comfortable single house and have conducted a modest wayside stand in the summers. In the winters Edward has managed to support his growing family (there are now three children) as a community handy man. He works during the winter on construction jobs or cutting and storing ice or making baskets out of evergreens to sell during the Christmas season. In this latter work his wife assists him. The couple are very congenially mated and Edward's wife bears an excellent reputation in the little community in which they live. Although they are of different religions, he being a Roman Catholic and she a Protestant, there has never been a clash over this. Neither of them attends church for the reason that there is no church near enough to their home and they do not have the means of conveyance.

Edward is very proud of the fact that his furniture is all paid for, that he has no debts, and is managing to keep up his insurance policies. He has committed no offenses of any kind since his marriage and has had no illicit relationships with women. Even the chief of police of his home town, who had often complained of him in the past, feels that Edward has settled down to a life of thorough respectability.

JACK

In some cases misbehavior continues despite a happy marriage and parenthood; and it is only or largely the ultimate influence of aging or maturation that brings about a settling down into legiti-

mate activities. This pattern of behavior is typified by the following case.

Jack is the second youngest of five children of American-born parents. He is the only one of the five who has given any real trouble. During Jack's boyhood the family lived in one neighborhood closely bordering on a deteriorating area. From earliest childhood he ran about the streets with a gang of youngsters who taught him how to shop-lift, and by the time he was fourteen he had become quite an adept.

Although Jack never truanted from school, he very much disliked study and when he was fourteen years old and in the fifth grade he insisted upon leaving school to go to work. While still in school he was arrested for larceny and placed on probation and was also occasionally arrested for "crapshooting" or walking railroad tracks. Shortly after leaving school he was again arrested for larceny.

Jack worked for brief periods in shoe factories, earning about $6 a week. Most of his time, however, was spent in the streets with his gang, indulging in stealing and gambling. When he was sixteen years old, he was sent to a correctional school for six months on a charge of larceny. At this time the police reported that Jack had been going about with a tough crowd and doing little or no work. Soon after his release from the correctional school he was again arrested for larceny and this time sentenced to the Massachusetts Reformatory.

Jack was now seventeen years old. Mental examination showed him to be of borderline mentality, and the psychiatrist stated that the youth was extremely egocentric, had little capacity for self-denial, had lived his life without good plans and ambitions, but that he could make a good life plan and stick to it.

Jack's behavior in the Reformatory was rather erratic, for at times he was only a fair worker "inclined to be lazy and indifferent" and at other times he made a very good industrial record. In the Reformatory school he managed to get through the eighth grade and his conduct and work were apparently satisfactory. It was said of him then that he is "a rather intelligent chap but apparently not over ambitious."

Jack was released from the Reformatory after fourteen months, following persistent pleas on his part for "a chance to go out and earn an honest living and help my mother. . . . I have learned to know what the loss of my freedom is." He was allowed to return to the home of his parents and worked very intermittently as a teamster, frequently leaving his employment without permission. Within a year after his release on parole, Jack was arrested for larceny from the person, and his parole was revoked. This time he remained in the Reformatory for seven months, again returned to his mother's home, and shortly thereafter was once more arrested for larceny, returned to the Reformatory, and released after seven months.

During the parole period which followed, Jack again worked very irregularly on what the parole agent considered to be a "political job," because the youth seemed to be drawing a small salary for not doing much of anything and spending most of his time in the promotion of gambling games. He made false reports to the parole agent, and his permit to be at liberty was again revoked and he was returned to the Reformatory. During this last period on parole, Jack had met a young woman to whom he became very much devoted. She became pregnant by him and he expressed a wish to marry her. Meanwhile he had been returned to the Reformatory. He asked for a hearing by the parole board, writing them as follows: "The matter concerns a lady friend. I intended to do what is right by the girl as she is in a family way and I promised to marry her and save her reputation and honor and would have been married to her now if I was not brought back here. The girl has a good reputation and is a good girl and I was willing to marry her but under present circumstances I do not know what to do."

Arrangements were made for the marriage ceremony to be performed in the Reformatory. At this time Jack was twenty-four years old. "As much as I dislike to be married in here it was the only way to save her good name, so you see I still have got respect and manhood," wrote Jack to the Deputy-Commissioner of Corrections in trying to secure his release. "I have a great deal to worry about. Nothing seems bright, as my baby will be born in a short while and I would like to have a chance to support the wife and child as she is living with my folks now. They have all they can do to get along themselves without the extra burden on their shoulders. . . . It is rather hard to understand a prisoner's point of view, but a man is never so bad but he cannot be good."

Four months after his marriage, Jack, now twenty-four years of age, was released on parole for the last time. As soon as he was able to get four or five days' work a week, he and his wife took a small apartment not very far from Jack's parents. By the time his parole expired, which was two years after his release, Jack was the father of three children. The parole officer reported that although the parolee gambled a good deal and hung around the ball parks, prize fights, and horse races, his conduct was otherwise satisfactory. Whatever he earned from his gambling activities he spent on his wife and children.

During the first year of the five-year follow-up period, Jack was arrested on two occasions for gambling. He has not been arrested since, however. He has worked steadily on a delivery truck for a soda-bottling company. Occasionally during the first five-year period, he still gambled and promoted games of chance at fairs, "running as near crookedness as he can and getting away with it." However, as the years have passed, Jack has gotten away more and more from his gambling companions.

By the end of the second five-year follow-up period, Jack is already thirty-six years old. He is the father of five children and devoted to them and his wife. The family now lives in a suburban neighborhood where the influences are not unwholesome. Jack attends church regularly with his wife and children, has some slight savings, carries a considerable insurance policy on which he pays the premium himself. Except for a small decrease in salary, he did not suffer particularly during the period of the industrial depression. He has continued on the trucking job for the same bottling company throughout the second five-year period and is earning on the average of $35 a week.

CHARLES

There are cases in which normal maturation leads to and is further facilitated by congenial employment and a wholesome marital life. Such a combination of favorable influences is illustrated by the case of Charles.

Charles was the youngest of eight children. He was born in a small Canadian town. When he was two years of age his parents brought the younger children to a small manufacturing town in Massachusetts where his father, a moderate drinker, worked for years as a tinsmith. Charles attended a convent school for nine years, his behavior was always good, and he apparently enjoyed his school work. He on no occasion truanted from school. Neither Charles nor any of the other children gave any particular difficulty to their parents.

When the lad was thirteen years old his mother died, and the father together with the younger children went to the home of a married sister of Charles where they remained until the boy was fifteen. During these years Charles had little supervision and ran about the streets freely, getting into bad company. Then the father took Charles to the home of another married sister in Canada, where they lived for two years. During that time the boy worked in a bookbinding shop earning $5 weekly. About this time he began to show some propensities toward burglary. He claims that he learned how to steal while on a freight-riding expedition and in need of clothing. His escapades finally led to his arrest and conviction, at the age of eighteen, for theft.

After serving four months at hard labor, Charles returned to his home town in Massachusetts to live with his married sister because his father thought it well for him to get away from his bad associates. However, he soon left his sister's home to go to an uncle in another city where he stayed only three months and then again went off to find work in a nearby town. He soon became discouraged and returned to his sister's home; but shortly thereafter went off, spending part of his time on freight excursions, breaking into homes here and there, stealing jewelry or money or any small articles that could be converted into cash. On one occasion he stole a suit of clothing for his own use. He carried a revolver which he had taken from the home of a police officer. Following this series of breaks, Charles, at the age of twenty, was committed to the Massachusetts Reformatory on a five-year indeterminate sentence.

At the Reformatory Charles was found to be of normal intelligence. The examiner at the institution said of him that he is "a boy whose manners show good home training," while Charles insisted to the Reformatory authorities that he "would never have landed here had my mother lived." The examiner felt that "the deterrent effect of his imprisonment and his increasing maturity may do much for him."

On this sentence our young offender spent a year and a half at the Reformatory. He was employed in the printing office and was deemed to be steady and painstaking in his work and of even disposition. He also did very well in the Reformatory school and was found to be industrious and intelligent, although reprimanded on occasion for persistent talking and insolence.

Upon being paroled, Charles went to the home of a brother and was given work in his brother's garage. After ten months he was turned out of his brother's home, because he was "bumming around too much" and neglecting to report to the parole authorities. His brother severely warned him that he would have nothing more to do with Charles unless he mended his ways.

Within two months after leaving his brother's home, Charles was arrested in a nearby city for burglary and was again sentenced to the Massachusetts Reformatory. As reflecting the attitude of his brothers and sisters toward him, none of whom were at any time delinquent or criminal, it should be mentioned that during the two years which he spent in the Reformatory following this second commitment they did not once write or visit him. "They say," philosophized Charles, "that blood is thicker than water but in my case it is just the opposite."

During his second stay in the Reformatory Charles misconducted himself on various occasions and was reprimanded for using tobacco, talking, creating a disturbance, having a daily paper, playing cards, misusing state property, laughing and "fooling," as well as other offenses. He was out on parole only two or three days when he disappeared. The police of his home town at that time reported that "his family do not know of his whereabouts and refuse to have anything to do with him, as after what they have done for him in the past they have lost confidence in him and told him they do not want to see him."

Five months after he disappeared from home Charles was arrested in a neighboring state for robbery and committed to jail there for a year. Upon his release, he made his way to a city in another neighboring state where he heard that there was a good deal of work to be had in airplane factories. For a long time he had been interested in machinery and mechanics. Where he acquired the interest first we do not know. Without the knowledge of any members of his family, he fortunately secured a position as an inspector of airplanes at $25 a week. This occurred some two years before the end of the first five-year follow-up period, and at that time Charles was already twenty-nine years old. He apparently did not dare to communicate with his brothers because on the last occasion of his being turned out of the home of one of them he had been distinctly warned by his family that they would not assist him in any way and would not condone his irresponsible behavior. It was only after Charles had been settled for several years that he finally communicated with one of his married sisters.

Throughout the second five-year follow-up period he has continued to make his home in the city in which he is employed. He has boarded steadily with a family whose members have developed a very friendly feeling toward him. He has worked continuously, changing positions only three times during the last seven years and each time doing so only to improve his occupational status. At present, at the age of thirty-eight, Charles is an inspector for a large aircraft corporation earning some $35 a week. An expert machinist, his future is well assured. He has at no time committed any burglaries or other offenses for which he might be arrested.

Soon after the end of the second five-year period Charles married a woman eleven years his junior. Shortly after the marriage he took his wife to meet his sister who even then, because of his past performances, had such a feeling of distrust that she was not at all convinced that the couple were legally married. But the couple have now been married for three years. They have one child and are extremely happy.

Not only Charles's employers, but the family with whom he lived for so many years before his marriage, speak of him in terms of the highest praise. He is well adjusted to neighborhood life and has developed very friendly relationships with his wife's relatives. He and his wife visit among their friends and participate in neighborhood parties and an occasional game of cards. Although they were inclined to be somewhat extravagant in their expenditures when they were first married, they are learning how to save and to provide for the future. Charles finds his wife to be a "good pal" and they have both assumed their family responsibilities.

Here is a case in which growing maturity and an interesting job were followed by marriage to a congenial woman. But in reflecting upon his abandonment of criminal behavior, Charles himself thinks that his brother's rather stern treatment of him when "he laid down the law," has also had something to do with straightening him out.

ALFRED

There are cases in which a simple environment plus the friendly, continuous oversight of a person of whom the offender is fond and whom he respects, are largely accountable for abandonment of criminalistic behavior with the passing of the years. Such a case is illustrated by the simple annals of Alfred.

Alfred's parentage and heredity are shrouded in mystery. When he was only eight months old he was placed by a young woman, who claimed to be his mother, in the home of a foster family in the country where he lived on a farm until he was fourteen. Even his foster home was broken, for when the boy was six years old his foster father died.

Alfred attended school until he was fourteen, leaving in the ninth grade. He was considered an apt, intelligent pupil; he never truanted from school, nor did he give any particular trouble to his foster mother. After leaving school Alfred went to work on nearby farms and it was shortly after this that he began to get into difficulties. In his free time he fell in with bad companions and began to drink somewhat. While drunk he would manifest a very ugly disposition. A brother of Alfred's foster mother, who was very fond of the boy and who had him from time to time as a visitor on his own farm, said of him that "he has many good traits and at heart is not a bad boy. . . . He never knew of the men he worked for to question his honesty." But he pointed out that the first farm on which Alfred worked was not "the proper place for a boy of his age to be."

In one of his early places of employment, where he remained for only six months, the daughter of the family said of him that "he was large for his age and strong and for the most part willing to work when father was with him. Like many boys of that age he was not reliable when out of sight of his employer. . . . He grew to be sly and we could not always depend on what he said for truth." Shortly after Alfred left this place of employment he returned one night and stole a bicycle. His employer did not report him to the police. This proved to be only the beginning of numerous escapades. From then until Alfred was twenty he stole a good deal from neighbors—cigarettes, candy, bicycles, automobiles, horses, anything in fact that he could lay hands on. He was known around the town as a pretty bad character, but it was not until he was twenty that he was actually arrested. For some time, he had not even been suspected of breaks, because he was apparently honest in the places of his employment. Alfred was given a five-year indeterminate sentence to the Massachusetts Reformatory.

The examiner at the Reformatory said of him that this "is a boy representing a class that we seldom see at this institution. . . . His industrial record is good and I am prone to believe that the causative factor of his delinquency is without doubt the use of intoxicating liquors. . . . He has the equipment to succeed industrially if freed from temptation to drink." Alfred worked in the Reformatory kitchen where the officer in charge spoke of him in the highest terms as a youth who always tried to do what was right. "He is an intelligent, capable man with not a lazy bone in his body and can be relied on at all times to do what he is told."

At the end of fourteen months, Alfred was released, but was immediately taken by Federal officers on warrants which had been issued shortly before his commitment to the Reformatory for breaking and entering a post office. As in the Reformatory, his conduct in prison was altogether commendable. When Alfred was finally released at the age of twenty-four, he went to work on a farm. There he proved to be very troublesome because he worked erratically and would go off on sprees "with the boys." He was shortly arrested for burglarizing the barn on the farm of his foster mother's brother who had so often befriended him when he was little. He took a horse, sleigh, robe, harness, and horse blankets, selling the entire outfit in a neighboring town for only $10. (It should be reiterated that Alfred never stole directly from an employer.)

Following two and one-half years in prison for this burglary, Alfred was released. His behavior and conduct record in prison had been excellent. Alfred wandered about rather aimlessly for a month and was then picked up by the police on a charge of vagrancy. He pleaded to be sent to jail as he had no shelter, and claimed to have no means of support. He seemed to have developed a real fear of the antagonism of people and was glad for the protection which commitment offered him.

Upon release from jail after three months, Alfred returned to the rural neighborhood in which he had spent most of his life. Being very fearful of rearrest, he wandered deep into the woods on the edge of a farm and built himself a crude shack where he lived for some months, foraging about for food. He used a rifle to kill wild birds and once turned it on two coon hunters who he thought were police officers on his trail. He became very friendly with the man who had charge of a fire tower nearby, and he was the only companion of Alfred for several months. He developed the reputation in the nearby town of being a dangerous hermit and the neighbors kept scrupulously away from him with the exception of the farmer whose land bordered on the woods where Alfred was making his home.

One day this farmer tactfully approached Alfred and asked him to look after his cows a bit in their summer pasture on the hill. For this the farmer paid him a small amount and told him to help himself to vegetables from the garden. Illustrative of Alfred's great state of fear was the reply that he did not dare to take any vegetables. When asked why not, he answered, "If any officer should catch me taking vegetables from the garden they would say I was stealing and clap me back into prison." The farmer assured Alfred that he need have no fear of this and was able very gradually to win the youth's confidence. He finally got him to come down to work on the farm by the day. After a few weeks, Alfred suggested that it was a pretty long walk back and forth from the farm to his shack so the farmer invited him to come and live on the farm. To this Alfred very readily acquiesced and within a short time both the farmer and his wife became very fond of Alfred. He tremendously enjoyed the work on the farm and was given $7 a week in return for his services.

At the end of the first five-year follow-up period, when Alfred was twenty-eight years old, he was living on this farm happy in his work, going down to town occasionally and getting along satisfactorily except that he manifested an ugly mood now and then after a drink "with the boys." The farmer was extremely patient with these occasional lapses, being convinced that his employee was by no means a criminal "but just a childish fellow." He participated very little in the neighborhood life, partly because of his seclusive nature and partly because the community was very scattered and it was not so easy to get into town. At no time did he steal, and his employer had the utmost confidence in him in this regard. In fact, Alfred became very much a member of the farmer's family.

After living on the farm for almost three years, Alfred met a waitress, eleven years his junior, in a restaurant where he happened to take lunch. An immediate friendship was struck up and Alfred began to have illicit sexual relations with this girl, who became pregnant, she claimed, by him. (It was later discovered that the pregnancy actually was brought about by another lover. This girl had had many illicit sexual relationships, and had already served a sentence.) Alfred's employer greatly objected to his companionship with the woman, but was unable to prevent a marriage.

Shortly before the marriage took place Alfred became involved with his fiancée in the larceny of an automobile. Although it was evident that she was the instigator of this crime and that he was merely an accomplice who had been forced into the commission of the larceny, Alfred took the full blame for the offense and was given a four months' jail sentence. Upon his release the marriage took place. Alfred's employer was willing that he and his wife remain on the farm. Alfred's wife, however, had other plans for him. She felt that he would not advance sufficiently on the farm and urged him to go with her to work in a hotel in a nearby state. After three months of this the couple returned and Alfred went back to his former employer. His wife refused to live on the farm and took a position as a waitress nearby.

On two occasions growing out of his unfortunate marriage

Alfred was arrested, once for assault and battery on his wife (while drunk) and once for non-support, on which latter case he was discharged. Alfred's wife claimed that during their brief married life he drank considerably and was very cruel to her when under the influence of liquor. Fortunately for him, his wife soon became involved with a former lover and was committed to jail on the ground of adultery. The couple were never reunited and Alfred procured a divorce shortly after. He was then thirty-two years of age.

In the fifth year of the second follow-up period Alfred reestablished himself on the farm of his former employer and has since continued to live very happily there, very seldom going on a drinking spree and then only with one or two companions. He is contented and looks forward to spending many years on the farm. He has no ambition to change his employment or advance himself in any way, has tremendous regard and affection for his employer and is greatly influenced by him. He has recently refused an offer on a larger farm where he would earn more money.

Continuing Offenders

JOHN

The benign influence of aging on the maturation process may be delayed, blocked, or distorted if a delinquent is burdened by a make-up termed by psychiatrists "psychopathic personality" or "constitutional psychopathic personality."[1]

[1] This is a condition which is admittedly difficult to diagnose, since the pathologic traits and trends that compose it are merely excessive degrees of conditions found among ordinary persons. Rosanoff describes the psychopathic personality types as follows:

"There is a large group of persons who, though not necessarily suffering from epileptic, psychotic, or psycho-neurotic symptoms, alcohol or drug addiction, or subnormal intelligence, are nevertheless incapable of attaining a satisfactory adjustment to the average social environment. This group is very heterogeneous, yet there is much evidence, in family and personal histories and in clinical manifestations, to show that the various conditions comprised in it are in some way related to one another and to other neuropathic conditions.

"The maladjustment in these cases seems to arise on a basis of inherent anomalies of judgment, temperament, character, ethical sense, or sexual make-up. It need hardly be added that both the underlying defect of personality and the social maladjustment vary in

In the following case the difficulties of the adjustment of such an offender to industrial and other demands of the "average social environment," and the deep-rooted trend toward anti-social forms of expression, are illustrated.[2]

John was the second of three children of Irish parents. His father, somewhat intemperate, was a machinist earning barely enough to support his family. John's childhood was spent in a mill town, where the neighborhood influences were rough and unwholesome. When the boy was seven years old, his mother died and his older brother, then ten years of age, did some of the housekeeping with the occasional help of a grandmother. It was not until several years later that John's father remarried, so that the boy, though he attended school until the age of fourteen, where he did not progress beyond the third grade, had practically no supervision. Although John was not outstandingly troublesome in school, he did not like study and insisted on leaving to go to work in factories, chiefly as a mill hand.

It was about this time that the boy began to masturbate excessively, and also to gamble with the neighborhood boys. His father and older brother found him to be extremely restless, changeable, uncontrollable from earliest childhood, and they were never able to guide him. John's father was always very strict with the lad, but to little avail. An older brother was also subjected to

degree and that, moreover, not all social maladjustment rests upon constitutional abnormality of the individual.

"Whatever the basic anomaly may be in a given case, it is likely to become manifest in childhood or early youth, but becomes greatly accentuated with emancipation from parental control and the assumption of the entire burden of social adjustment and responsibility. Thereupon, sooner or later, the individual comes to the attention of the police, courts of law, health officers, charitable organizations, or other public authorities as criminal, prostitute, vagrant, sanitary menace, or dependent." Aaron J. Rosanoff, editor, *Manual of Psychiatry*, 6th ed., New York, John Wiley & Sons, 1927, p. 186.

[2] The different temperament and character types embraced in the concept "constitutional psychopathic personality" present one of the most puzzling problems of modern penology. Special institutions for "psychopathic delinquents" have in recent years been recommended, but the problem goes deeper than the mere provision of separate housing for such offenders. It involves the need of deep-probing research into the hereditary and mental mechanisms involved in the origin and development of psychopathic personalities.

the father's intense discipline, but says that he was able to bear it better than John did, and that as soon as he was old enough he left home. The father always demanded that John turn over his pay envelope to him and the lad was extremely resentful of this.

Despite his stormy boyhood, it was not until he was seventeen that John was arrested. He was charged with "gaming on the Lord's day" and received a small fine. During the months he was given in which to pay the fine John refused to work. He hung about the street corners "with bums and loafers" and the repeated threats of his father and brother seemed to have had no effect upon him. Shortly after this his father reported John to the police. In the company of another boy, John had stolen a pair of shoes and sold them to a cobbler for 85 cents. The father was insistent that the boy be committed to an institution in order that he might be thoroughly punished for his offense. It was on this occasion that John, at the age of seventeen, received a five-year indeterminate sentence to the Massachusetts Reformatory.

For four months before the commission of this crime John had been out of work, and the examiner at the Reformatory, who had a long talk with him, commented that "the bad influence of another boy and the fact of his being out of work would appear to be the causes of his landing here." Mental examination showed John to be of borderline intelligence. It was considered that he was "a neglected boy with fair innate ability, undeveloped," and that he was highly "suggestible." In the Reformatory John was found to be a willing worker but "his disposition was variable . . . occasionally disagreeable." He made very little progress at the institution's school, being entered in the second grade and promoted only to the third. During this first stay in the Reformatory John lost many marks for misconduct, including fighting, carelessness, talking, being out of place.

In his plea for parole, John wrote: "I have a good home and position ready to go to . . . my confinement has taught me a greater lesson than I can express in words . . . if released I will no longer prove a menace to society." And a maternal aunt of John's also begged for his release. "I never seen anything wrong with him, he seemed good and kind and I think bad company had a good deal to do with his misfortune . . . he used to get work but some way it would not last long, I think it was because he was small for his age but if you will give him his liberty I will promise you that he will have work the moment he comes home."

After thirteen months, John was released on parole and went to his father's home. He did not, however, take the position which had been secured for him by his aunt, but found a job in a factory. He worked for only a few days, found another job, dropped that, and finally his father complained to the parole officer that John was proving a burden. He added, however, that he would not like to have the youth returned to the Reformatory. The parole officer tried very hard at this time to keep John at work, but to no avail. The lad began to run around with a tough crowd who hung about the street corners, and even forged his father's name to a permit to patronize a cheap poolroom. Within five months after his release on parole John was arrested for burglary and was given a suspended sentence to jail. Soon after this his parole permit to be at liberty was revoked and he was returned to the Reformatory where he this time remained for a year.

Upon his second release, John went to live in the home of his brother who was now married and comfortably settled. After a short time he became very restless and left his brother's home without permission of the parole authorities. This brought about a second revocation of his permit, and his return to the Reformatory. After nine months, John was again released, this time going to live with a sister. He soon left his sister's home, however, claiming that he could not get along there, and left his place of employment with the comment that "I have a right to leave a job if I don't like it." He was extremely vile in his language to the parole officer, threatening that if he were sent back to the Reformatory again he would upon his release "get somebody," and that if he could not do it alone he would have some of the "gang" help him. Again John had to be returned to the Reformatory.

After seventeen months in the institution he was again released, this time going to the home of his brother, of whom he was fonder than of any other member of his family. He was soon arrested for being involved in a bootlegging enterprise supplying liquor to soldiers and sailors. For this offense he was given a six months' jail sentence and after serving this his parole permit was again revoked and he was returned to the Reformatory, where he once more served seventeen months.

By the time John's original sentence to the Reformatory expired, he was twenty-five years old. It will be remembered that he was first sent there at the age of seventeen. Of these eight years he had spent five behind walls.

The beginning of the first follow-up period found John drifting about in the underworld of a neighboring state. Among his companions were several ex-inmates of the Reformatory. John's brother pleaded with him to return home and avoid these associations and the risk of being sent to prison. John only laughed at this advice and said he did not care if he did go to prison. "I want to go there." Shortly after the beginning of the first five-year period his brother's warning became a reality. John was arrested for burglary and receiving stolen goods, crimes in which he had been involved with several others, and was sentenced to prison for from five to seven years.

Throughout the remainder of the first follow-up period John was in prison. His brother visited him occasionally and felt that John's physical and nervous condition was deteriorating. "He seemed to me then to have become absolutely no good."

In applying for parole, John wrote: "Since I have been here I have found out who my friends are. My family are my only friends . . . in the first place it was my father that sent me to the Reformatory and since then my father would have nothing to do with me but now he is willing to take me back home . . . I have a good conduct record here . . . if you will give me a chance I will do the right thing, hoping you will believe me sincere in my plea."

Seven months after the beginning of the second follow-up period, and after serving five years and four months, John was released on parole and went to live with his father. His brother had secured a job for him in the mills, where he worked for about six weeks and then became so restless that the brother began to wonder whether John was "mentally all right." No sooner was he settled in his father's home than he wanted to go to live with his brother, and then went back to his father again, and so on, back and forth for a few months, being absolutely unable to settle down to any work. Finally he threw up his job, ran away, and his family were then certain that he went back to the underworld.

With an ex-inmate of the Reformatory, John drifted to a large nearby city in an adjoining state and there worked in a restaurant by day and in his spare hours began to engage in a large bootlegging business. Because he had disappeared from home, his permit to be at liberty was revoked and he was soon traced, arrested, and returned to prison where he was held for thirteen months.

In appealing for his second parole, he wrote: "My job is still open for me—I was doing fine and living a real man's life. . . . I am through with the crooked life. . . . My conduct here is perfect." His employer, who had a small restaurant, promised to give John employment again upon his release from prison, claiming that "he is a very good man—one of the best I ever had." On his release from prison John was allowed to return to his previous place of employment but worked there for less than a month. His employer soon reported that John left because he was dissatisfied and that he was now absolutely useless as a worker. John next drifted to a large city where he acted as a runner for a gang of bootleggers, earning as much as $150 a week. This money he squandered in night-clubs and on chorus girls, spending it just as rapidly as it came in. After a time he returned to his former place of employment, and for several months gave no trouble. His employer now spoke very well of him and trusted him on many occasions to bank the day's receipts.

But when John was again located his parole permit was revoked because of his misbehavior. On his return to prison, he was incarcerated until the expiration of his sentence of seven years. "I was leading a straight and honest life," he complained. "I had planned to be married next month and had saved up some money to start a modest little home." During this stay in prison, however, he attempted to escape.

Upon the expiration of his sentence, John again returned to the city where he claimed he had done so well for several months. Within four months' time he was arrested there for snatching a handbag from a woman in the restaurant where he was working, and given a two months' jail sentence. Soon after his release from jail, he returned to his bootlegging activities with several other Reformatory graduates, from one of whom he learned that large sums of money were being transported to a bank in a neighboring city without any protection. Within a few days he and his associates trailed the car of the bank president, fired at it, and got away with a bag of money containing $20,000. No suspicion fell upon John for some months after this. Meanwhile he was associated in two large holdups of "speakeasies." This led to his arrest and a new sentence to prison for "robbery armed with intent to kill," for which he received sentences totaling eighteen to thirty years, and will not be eligible for parole again for about ten years.

During the months while he was still at liberty, John had gone off with $8,000 of the $20,000 which was his share of the loot. This he spent in night-club life, also living illicitly with women.

At the time of his sentence to prison John was thirty-six years old. He has been diagnosed by the psychiatrist as a "psychopathic personality . . . he has probably inherited some unstable tendencies." He is frank to admit that he had almost never worked and he says "Maybe I've led a wasted life but from earliest times I've felt a man was a fool to work, and me and the ordinary citizen speak a different language."

John is now a "model prisoner." The warden says of him that "he knows how to do time." In speaking of his future plans John says that by the time he comes out of prison he will be almost fifty years old and that he thinks he will settle down somewhere in the country on a farm. He is meanwhile sending to his brother whatever money he earns in prison and this is being saved for him. When asked whether he had ever sent to his relatives any of the money which he had earned illicitly, he said, "No, I wouldn't give five cents to them—that is blood money," meaning that money secured in this way would carry a curse with it if given to his honest relatives. During all of his escapades John had kept in touch with his brother, acknowledging, however, that he bluffed him into thinking that he has worked in legitimate occupations.

John still thinks that he never should have been sent to the Reformatory in the first place and gives the impression that he has nourished a grudge against the state authorities for having given him so severe a sentence for the slight crime of stealing a pair of shoes from his father in order to get a little spending money. What would have happened to John had he not been committed to the Reformatory is of course only a matter of conjecture.

RICHARD

A somewhat different type of psychopathic personality is illustrated by the following case.

Richard is an only child. His parents were married when his mother was nineteen and a thoroughly inexperienced girl, for her parents had raised her very strictly and she was brought up, as she puts it, "on my own front porch." Richard's father, who was six years older than his mother, was "very much a man of the world." Shortly after the marriage, the young wife became severely infected with syphilis and returned to the home of her parents in order that she might receive proper medical care. Here Richard was born. Although Richard's father visited the mother occasionally, by the time the boy was seven a separation was agreed upon because the father had reinfected her with syphilis and she had to undergo a very serious operation. Richard had had practically no oversight from his father and ran about quite freely despite the severity of his grandparents who did not really know how to discipline him.

In order to support herself and the boy, Richard's mother took a course in practical nursing and was away from home a good deal either as a nurse or housekeeper. The boy attended the public schools, where he did not present any particular difficulty and was known to be a rather bright youngster. His mother arranged for him to belong to the Boy Scouts and the local Y.M.C.A., but after a short time Richard took no interest in these activities. The boy was always fond of music, however. He early learned to play the French horn and for a short period also sang in the church choir.

Richard continued in school until he was fourteen years old. By that time his mother was finding the boy to be utterly uncontrollable. On one occasion he even tried to purchase a revolver. His mother was discovering that whenever the boy wanted something, particularly clothes (of which he was extremely fond), he would steal them. She reports that he was very irresponsible in childhood about many things. From the age of five, she recalls, he had been extremely deceitful, and he very early manifested a tendency to pilfer. Whenever he wanted something he would take it unobserved; and as he grew older and began to steal from people outside of the family, his mother would make restitution and keep the matter quiet in order to protect the boy from the police. On one occasion when Richard was fourteen he stole a bicycle and apparently some difficulty arose about restitution. The mother decided to send him away to a farm school so that she could straighten the matter out during his absence. While he was in this school the superintendent said of Richard that he was "a very erratic boy. He was dishonest and many times let his imagination talk beyond what can be accepted." However, he also reported that Richard "was not a hard boy to manage and his school work was passable." While in the school, Richard maintained his interest in music by playing in the school band.

Shortly after his return home, he twice ran away and his mother once more returned him to the farm school where he stayed for a few months. Richard's grandmother was sure that the boy "had inherited something." In this connection, it should be mentioned that Richard's father had been not only promiscuous but also something of a drinker; that the maternal grandmother had in the past had a "nervous breakdown," and that Richard's maternal uncle eventually became a drug addict.

It was not until Richard. came out of the farm school for the second time, at the age of eighteen, that he began to do any work. His first job was as a press-feeder and he has, off and on throughout his career, been interested in the printing business. He himself has admitted that the longest time he ever held a job was seven months. Although he managed to earn about $15 a week when he did work (depending mostly on his mother for support), he never seemed to be able to make this money cover his needs. His fondness for clothes and for other luxuries (jewelry, automobiles) led him more and more deeply into stealing to satisfy his desires.

Richard was not arrested, however, until his eighteenth year. He was on that occasion charged with the larceny of an automobile in a neighboring city while the owner was in a store nearby. He was making his way toward Boston when he was apprehended. The police were already searching for Richard on another charge of larceny from a printing office where he had been employed and to which he had a key. He had stolen a Kodak and sold it for $1. He was also charged with running up board bills in rooming houses. There was also a warrant on file against him for three burglaries in another nearby city, and he was wanted for larceny from a street railway.

Richard's first arrest was brought about by his mother, who had grown extremely fearful of the boy's future and had gone to the local probation officer requesting that the boy be watched and, when arrested, be sent to some institution where he could be observed. She had herself already arranged that the boy be examined in a mental hospital, but when Richard got wind of this he ran away from home.

As a result of the arrest for theft of the automobile, Richard was sentenced to the Massachusetts Reformatory. Mental examination showed him to be of normal intelligence, "impulsive, pleasure-loving, headstrong, and unwilling to assume any obligations." The examiner at the Reformatory felt that Richard would do well under the strictest supervision. This proved to be so in the Reformatory, for his conduct there was perfect. For the eleven months of his incarceration, Richard played in the band and seemed altogether happy.

Upon his parole he went to live with his mother. Almost immediately he was taken to the police court of a neighboring town to answer to a charge of burglary which had been placed against him prior to his commitment to the Reformatory. The case was continued for six months and Richard agreed to make restitution. Meanwhile he joined the navy as a musician and his mother agreed to turn over his allotment of $15 a month to the probation officer. For the remaining five months of his parole period Richard was in the navy, coming home to visit his mother for an occasional weekend.

The beginning of the first follow-up period, when Richard was twenty-one years old, found him still in the navy. But within a few months he was arrested for larceny (this time of the captain's uniform) and was committed to a United States naval prison for five months. He was given a dishonorable discharge, and for a large part of the first follow-up period wandered about from one city to another picking up a job here and there, occasionally as a printer, sometimes as a mill hand, and for a few weeks in an orchestra. He rarely communicated with his mother and then only when he needed money. He moved from one rooming house to another, forging checks to pay his rent.

He finally returned to his mother's home, where he stayed a few months getting a job as a printer, but soon went off to a nearby city, returning home occasionally and telling his mother that he was a chauffeur. Actually he was doing odd jobs, getting an occasional day's work washing windows or cleaning in cheap hotels. In the course of such employment Richard was arrested for stealing a watch from the room of one hotel guest, a suit of clothes from another, and a suitcase from a third. He was at this time also charged with the removal of three telephone coin boxes from a subway station.

As a result of these numerous charges, Richard was committed to jail for two years. This was at the beginning of the second follow-up period, and by this time Richard was twenty-five years old. During the course of the three years of the second follow-up period, between his release from jail and the end of the five-year span, Richard was arrested twice for larcenies and on each occasion was committed to jail. It is noteworthy that during these periods of incarceration his conduct in jail was excellent. He was always known as a model prisoner.

It would be almost impossible to follow Richard through all his numerous escapades between incarcerations. On one occasion, for example, he broke into the rooms of pupils and teachers in a boarding school where he was engaged to wash windows. On several others he gave forged checks in payment for purchases or room rent. He was eventually brought to trial on these charges (subsequent to the second follow-up period).

Twice in his life Richard has shown real interest in a woman but in neither case was this interest followed by marriage. His mother had always hoped that he would marry a decent girl, but

Richard has not shown any strong inclination for matrimony although he has had a great many illicit affairs. He is known to have had a venereal disease.

During one of Richard's jail sentences he was given a thorough psychiatric examination, as a result of which he was found to be "a constitutionally unstable individual. It is unfortunate he has no close relatives to take a hand in this case and give him some firm guidance. . . . He has an excellent opinion of himself. . . . His long history of maladjustment without learning anything from experience, his inability to keep a job or to plan for himself, makes examiner believe he comes under the class of psychopathic personality."

Richard has always been a lone offender, never being associated with others in the commission of his crimes. He admits that he has never felt any pangs of conscience over his great desire for self-indulgence. He buys anything that he wants, whether he can pay for it or not, puts off the settling of a bill as long as possible and then forges checks to meet the payments. He says that he is fully aware of the possibility of arrest and punishment but that this in no way deters him from satisfying his immediate desire for money. What may happen in the future causes him no worry now.

HENRY

The normally-to-be-expected maturing that comes with increasing years does not have scope if there is present a marked tendency toward chronic alcoholism. There are many persons—good workmen when sober—whose alcoholic deterioration outstrips Nature's maturation process. Such a case is illustrated by the following account of the deterioration of an offender whose marked tendency toward alcoholism manifested itself very early in life.

Society still treats chronic alcoholics by the ineffective round of continuous arrest, brief imprisonment, release. The problem of the treatment of such offenders is still unsolved.

Henry is the third of four children of American-born parents of Irish extraction. His two sisters are high-school graduates. His father has been a plumber by trade. From Henry's earliest years his family have been in very poor economic circumstances and have lived in a crowded, tumble-down region of a large manufacturing city in western Massachusetts. The father, like a paternal uncle of Henry's, has been a chronic alcoholic, but this has never interfered with his work. He has always been very strict with the boy, who from early childhood showed signs of stubbornness and disobedience. Henry's mother was always kindly and very much attached to him.

The boy greatly disliked school and began early to truant. He claims that this was due to the fact that he could not keep up with his school work (mental examination at a later time showed him to be of borderline intelligence). Henry's parents remember that even as a small boy he would steal from home occasionally, he lied a great deal, began early to smoke, and was the leader of a street-corner gang. When the boy was twelve, his father brought him into court on a charge of stubbornness. This case was filed after a brief admonition by the court.

It was not until Henry left school at the age of fourteen (having attained only the fifth grade) and began to work first as a plumber's helper (assisting his father) and later in the mills, that he started to drink and have illicit sex experiences. On Saturday nights he would join a group of mill hands (fellow employees) in bars and cheap poolrooms. From the early age of sixteen, therefore, Henry was very much of an alcoholic, and no upbraidings by his parents seemed to have any effect on him.

Despite these habits, however, and although Henry did not keep any of his jobs for a considerable time, he was always considered a capable workman. The crime which resulted in his commitment to the Massachusetts Reformatory on a five-year indeterminate sentence when he was but seventeen years old, was the burglary of a barber shop in the company of several others, and the stealing of cigars, pipes, razors, and other goods. The offenders divided the spoils and were arrested on the following day. There is no indication that Henry was drunk at the time of the burglary. His family were convinced that he had been influenced to the commission of this offense by his associates. And the examiner at the Reformatory concluded that Henry was an easy prey to bad surroundings and companions.

At the Reformatory Henry was a good and willing worker, and his conduct was excellent. In the institution's school, also, his conduct was perfect. In asking for his parole, he wrote to the parole board as follows: "I want to try and make good. I have been used pretty good by my parents. While I was at home I dident apperciate it so I want to show them I mean to do wright. Another reason is that my father can't do very mutch work on account of his back so if I go to work and do wright I'll be making it easy for them."

When Henry was released, after thirteen months at the Reformatory, he returned to the very poorly kept home of his parents and resumed his work as helper to his father. After a few months, however, plumbing work slackened and Henry managed to find a job in a local factory where he remained for about eight months. Then he got work in a railway freight depot as a freight truckman, remaining for about ten months. After being laid off from here he found another job in a machine shop. During all this time Henry was behaving quite well, rarely going off on drinking sprees. He claims that his old associates began to influence him at about this time and that in order to avoid them he decided to go South. This he did without getting permission of the parole board. He remained away for a year, during which he worked as a "jitney" driver, earning $20 a week. Meanwhile a warrant for his arrest had been issued by the parole authorities, and shortly after he returned home from the South he was apprehended following reports from the local police that he was drinking again. Upon recommitment to the Reformatory he stayed one month and was then released on the plea of his mother. "I have only one boy to work for me his father is sick and can't work much and he was the oldest and kept it up now I have to work in a laundry and I am fifty-seven years old."

Henry next secured work in the freight yards again. His former employers were very glad to take him back because he was an able workman. When after two months he was again arrested for drinking and disturbing the peace and his permit to be at liberty was revoked a second time, his mother wrote frantically to the Department of Correction: "The agent took him back again and I could not find out why it was and he was sick with influenza and he was not able to work and got in with some fellows and got drinking . . . it did not take very much to go to his head that is all he done he was in every night at ten o'clock and did not touch a drop after that it is a terrible thing to put him there for that. . . . I have to work in the laundry so hard and he was so good to help me I am asking you to give him one more chance."

During this second revocation and return to the Reformatory, Henry was transferred to the prison camp and hospital for treatment of his alcoholic condition, and following his release after three months he again returned to live with his parents, sometimes working in the freight yards, occasionally assisting his father, and now and then driving a truck. The parole officer said of him at this stage that he was doing fairly well but that when drunk he was very likely to "crank someone's automobile and take a ride." Henry now helped to support his parents, so that at least they were not dependent upon social agencies. Within a few months, however, and close to the end of the expiration of his five-year indeterminate sentence to the Reformatory, he was arrested for breaking into a garage and trying to start away with an automobile. For this he was committed to a house of correction for eighteen months.

The beginning of the first five-year follow-up period found Henry in this institution. He was now twenty-six years old, and thoroughly confirmed in his alcoholic habits. He would occasionally "take the pledge" but to no avail, always promising, when in confinement, that he would stop drinking. During the course of the first follow-up period Henry was arrested twelve times. Ten of these arrests were for drunkenness, one for larceny of an automobile, and one for breaking glass. Four of the arrests were followed by commitments to jail, houses of correction, or state farms. Henry was always a model prisoner and when in the house of correction became quite a favorite of the warden. Of the sixty months of the first five-year period Henry spent forty-two in institutions. During the course of one of these commitments he was examined by a psychiatrist who summarized his findings as follows: "It is evident that he cannot abstain from the use of alcohol without some restraining influences and he cannot improve industrially until abstinence is brought about. An indefinite period of treatment in an institution that would prevent the use of alcohol and provide training and occupation is indicated."

The beginning of the second five-year period found Henry, recently freed from jail, again living with his parents. As might be expected, he was very soon arrested for drunkenness and returned to jail. Paroled after four months, he was again arrested only two days later for drunkenness, returned to jail, and released after five months. A month later he was once more arrested for drunkenness. This was followed by two more arrests within six months, on one of which he was given a suspended sentence to jail and on the other a year's probation.

A month after the last arrest Henry was committed to jail for thirty days. This was soon followed by still another arrest and a suspended sentence, and a few months later the suspension was revoked and he was committed to jail where he remained for three months. Two months after his release, he was once more arrested for drunkenness and also for larceny, and was again committed. In four months he was paroled, and within a month thereafter he was arrested for drunkenness and his permit to be at liberty was revoked. He was released within four months (a month earlier than was due him on the sentence) upon receipt of a telegram that his father had died.

Within two months after his return home, Henry was again committed to jail for drunkenness. In three months he was released and within a month was again returned to jail, was released in four months, returned a month later, and again paroled after four months. The master of the jail wrote to the Board of Parole that "the conduct of Henry . . . has been excellent at this institution."

Following this release, which occurred within two months of the end of the second follow-up period, Henry went to the home of his married sister, for his mother had recently died. By that time he was thirty-five years old. During the course of the five years comprising the second follow-up period, Henry had been arrested twenty-one times, had served nine sentences, and been on probation four times. He had spent a total of thirty-one months out of the sixty in incarceration. During his short periods of freedom, he has worked usually as a plumber's helper, but because of his increasingly frequent drinking sprees he keeps his jobs for shorter and shorter periods, and has now become somewhat dependent on his relatives for support although previously he had not only supported himself but contributed to the income of his parents.

ALPHONSE

The natural maturation process is often delayed by a psychotic condition which may temporarily obscure latent tendencies that ultimately come to the fore. The following case is suggestive of such a pattern of development.

Alphonse is the second child of French-Canadian parents. He has three sisters, one older and two younger than himself. He was born in Canada, but when he was one and a half years old his parents moved to New England, going from one small city to another until the boy was five years old. Alphonse's father was an agent for a large advertising company and the family were in fairly comfortable circumstances. When the boy was nine years old, his mother became ill and had to go to a hospital for a considerable time. The lad had now little supervision and for a period his father sent him away to a convent school.

There had been a good deal of conflict between the parents about the discipline of this boy. His mother, a highly emotional woman, was inclined to be very lenient with him and would constantly criticize the father's strict attitude toward the child, so that after a time Alphonse ceased to have any respect for his father's opinion. The boy had been an habitual school truant from about the time he was twelve years old. He ran about the streets with questionable companions and would not heed the advice of his parents to curb his delinquent behavior. He soon began to steal, and when he was thirteen years old he was placed on probation for six months for stealing a bicycle with several other boys. His father tried to keep the boy home evenings, but whenever the father himself would go out of the house Alphonse would sneak out. On several occasions he ran away from home and was known to be associating with boys older than himself, most of whom were idling about. An old friend of Alphonse's father said of him at about this time, "I came to the conclusion that his irresponsibility is more due to a mental affliction than to criminal inclinations."

A year later, when the lad was fourteen years of age, he was committed to a correctional school on a charge of burglary. "I got in with a bunch of older fellows and went to the bad." From here he escaped several times, going off on freight-riding expeditions.

When he was finally released from the correctional school, Alphonse went to work as an auto mechanic. He soon secured a license to drive a car (giving a false age on his application) and developed a tremendous interest in automobiles. It was his interest in and love of automobiles which caused Alphonse, at the age of sixteen, to be committed to the Massachusetts Reformatory. The offense consisted of his taking the automobile of a neighbor, driving it to a nearby city, and operating a car under the influence of liquor. At this time Alphonse was still on parole from the correctional school. He insisted that he took the car without any intention of stealing it. He claimed that the owner was a friend of his family's and that on previous occasions the car had been loaned him for short rides. In any event the boy was committed to the Reformatory where he complained bitterly about not having received fair treatment by the Court.

Mental examination showed Alphonse to be of borderline intelligence, and the psychiatrist found that the boy had marked ideas of persecution and very grandiose notions about himself, all of which was suggestive of a paranoid condition.

When Alphonse had been in the Reformatory only three months, he and another inmate conceived a plan for escaping. They struck one of the officers, knocking him unconscious and taking his revolver and club away from him, rushed through the yard to the guard room, and turned a revolver on the officer there in an attempt to get through the door. At this point they were captured by another officer. The trial, on a charge of robbery while armed, with intent to murder, resulted for Alphonse and his pal in a six-year sentence to a house of correction. It will be remembered that at this time he was sixteen years of age. Alphonse soon began to plead for his liberty, but was not released until he was twenty-two years old. The sheriff of the house of correction spoke very well of him. "He has had the freedom of the yard and certainly has been a good prisoner and I thoroughly believe he intends to go out and do what is right."

When Alphonse was released on parole he went to the home of his parents, a good-sized comfortable house in the suburbs. He took a position as a marble setter, but did not stay very long, growing very restless. As soon as his parole from the house of correction had expired (this was in the midst of the first five-year follow-up period), Alphonse left home and wandered throughout the East and South earning his living as a barber (which trade he had learned at the house of correction). During this time he was a constant source of anxiety to his family because of his tendency to spend his leisure time with "sporty" friends and to squander all his earnings on night-club life. On the rare occasions when he would visit his father's home, he would refuse to tell about his activities. "If you don't want me to lie to you, why do you ask me questions about myself?"

During the course of the first five-year period Alphonse became very much excited over the possibilities of earning large sums of money in Florida, and drove down there only to discover that there was nothing in his wild dream. When he returned from this expedition, at about the beginning of the second five-year follow-up period, he resumed his work as a marble setter and his family was hopeful that this was some indication that his restlessness had subsided and that he would now settle into normal activities. But although Alphonse worked capably and fairly steadily, he continued to run about with a sporting crowd now and then, drink excessively, and indulge in many illict sexual affairs. Alphonse was, however, considered to be a good workman, capable of earning as much as $35 a week. He was able to support himself and rarely asked for any assistance from his family.

Toward the middle of the second follow-up period, when Alphonse was twenty-nine years of age, he married a young woman whom he had known for several years and who was the daughter of a neighbor's family. Alphonse's father opposed this match because he felt that the girl was selfish, eager for money and a good time. But the son married her despite his father's objections and lived with her for a short time in his father's home, until the young couple established their own home nearby. However, in less than a year they separated. The girl was soon to become a mother, but Alphonse did not seem to feel that he had any responsibility toward her and the baby because "her parents are quite well to do and can take care of her."

After Alphonse separated from his wife he did not return to the home of his parents. He had been tremendously infatuated with his wife for a few months after their marriage, but when his disillusionment came he felt deeply discouraged, began to drink rather heavily, and showed severe signs of emotional upset. He roomed with a friend, and one day, less than a year after his marriage, he was found dead at the wheel of his car, having committed suicide by inhaling carbon-monoxide gas. Shortly before this, Alphonse's wife had visited him in the company of another man who was paying a good deal of attention to her. Whether his suicide was directly precipitated by this occurrence, or whether he had been contemplating it for some time, his family does not know.

It is only a matter of conjecture whether, had Alphonse lived, he would have at any time committed offenses of as serious a character as before his commitment to the house of correction. But since his release from there eight years before his death, he had been arrested on only one occasion, and then only for violating an automobile law. He did not at any time continue his burglarizing nor did he ever attempt to assault anyone. Obviously he was suffering from a mental condition which needed careful watching.

FRANK

The maturation process cannot follow a normal course in the face of an innate (or early conditioned) handicap of extreme instability. An individual so burdened is very likely to lack the stamina necessary for steady work; and if chance throws him in with wrong companions, he falls an easy prey to anti-social suggestion, alcoholism, or drug addiction. Such habits bring about further physical and mental deterioration, so that instead of increasing stability with advancing years, the opposite results. A deteriorating career of this kind is illustrated by the following case.

Frank is an only child. His father, though a capable workman in carpet factories, was a confirmed drinker with a long court record and several jail terms not only for drunkenness but for occasional larcenies when under the influence of liquor. When Frank was only four years old, his mother, whose reputation was excellent, had to apply to a social agency for aid for herself and the boy, because her husband did not support them and was so frequently in jail. Frank's father was abusive not only to his wife but to the child, and the mother, to escape this, would go with Frank from the home of one relative to another. Finally, when Frank was nine years old, his parents separated and nothing was heard of the father until some ten years later, when word was received of his death in a nearby city in a "bums' hotel," followed by a pauper's burial.

After the separation of the parents, Frank's mother had taken a position as a domestic and placed the boy in a farm and trade school for four years. She paid $2 a week for him steadily throughout those years. The school principal reported that Frank was an apt pupil and earned an excellent rating in his studies and behavior. By the age of fourteen the lad had completed the first year of high school. At this time he returned to his mother who had established a little home for him. She was extremely fond of the boy and he was apparently very much attached to her.

Frank now went to work for jobbers in the automobile accessory business. Soon he began to fall in with bad companions, started to drink, steal, lie, and show marked signs of anti-sociality. His mother tried very hard to keep him away from his bad associates, but to no avail. She entirely lost her grip on him and was unable to control his actions. On various occasions he stole from her, taking clothing, valises, and other articles, and when she would ask him what he had done with them he would reply that he had "loaned them to a fellow," but never would reveal who the "fellow" was. In her effort to exercise control over him, his mother tried to keep him away from public dance halls and asked the proprietors of these places not to admit him because he was under eighteen. All these attempts failed because Frank insisted upon frequenting such places with his crowd.

When the youth was sixteen he was arrested and fined for drunkenness. Six months later he was again arrested for drunkenness and disturbing the peace and was placed on probation. Although he had been committing larcenies for some time, he was not actually apprehended until he was seventeen years old. On this occasion he was returning home from a dance hall with several companions. They saw a large touring car parked nearby and decided to go for a ride. After driving a few miles, Frank's companions became frightened and deserted him in the car. As he was unable to drive he was soon apprehended and committed to the Reformatory. On the night previous to this escapade he had broken into a dance hall, stolen a cornet, and pawned it.

Upon his admission to the Reformatory on a two-year indeterminate sentence, Frank was "grouchy in his manner to the verge of being insolent." Mental examination showed him to be of normal intelligence. He was found to be suffering from gonorrhea, and admitted having had illicit sexual experiences from the time he was fifteen. He was in the Reformatory for nine months during which time his conduct on the whole was good and he was an able worker. In pleading for his parole, he said: "I feel that I've had sufficient punishment and it has certainly made a different sort of fellow out of me."

Upon release, Frank returned to his mother's home. After he had worked in a factory for two weeks he and his mother decided to go to the home of a maternal uncle in a neighboring state where more remunerative work was to be had. Soon Frank's mother and uncle decided that the youth ought to have an opportunity to become an electrician, as he was particularly interested in this kind of work; so they urged him to enlist in the navy where he could attend an electrical school. Frank was given the necessary permission by the parole authorities, but after two months he returned home claiming he was on a visit but actually having deserted.

When the naval authorities began to look for him, Frank ran off to a neighboring state. On the way he fell in with a young fellow with whom he was shortly arrested for breaking into a hotel room and stealing a valise full of clothes. They were both sentenced to ninety days in jail. Upon Frank's release, he was turned over to the parole authorities in Massachusetts and sent back to the Reformatory. Again he served for nine months. He now pleaded to be allowed to return to the navy so that he might continue his training in the electrical trade. "Kindly let me go home from here and let the naval authorities take me, so I may be punished there for what I have done . . . that I may be restored to duty there after doing what time they desire me to do. I wish to go back to the navy . . . and learn the electrical trade . . . so that I may help support my dear mother. . . . I love my mother and hope you will kindly do me this favor please for her sake. . . . I am very sorry for what I have done to get myself in this mix-up."

Shortly after the expiration of his parole period, which occurred six months after his second release from the Reformatory, Frank met a young woman with whom he became involved in shoplifting activities. She was the sister of a notorious robber. To his association with this girl, Frank's mother strenuously objected; but the boy insisted upon marrying her. At about this time Frank began to use heroin. It would appear that his wife had something to do with the beginnings of his drug habit. Shortly after his marriage he was arrested for unlawful possession of drugs and a letter was found on his person, signed by himself and his wife, arranging for the purchase of drugs in quantity. Following this arrest Frank defaulted, and in order to escape apprehension he and his wife went off to another state working here and there in hotels. He did not communicate with his mother for fear of arrest and for about two years she had no idea where he was.

During the whole of the first five-year period it is known that Frank not only used heroin but drank habitually and went about with crooks. He and his wife were unable to get along together, and toward the end of the first five-year period she brought divorce proceedings against him on charges of cruelty. At about this time he was again arrested for larceny. He now began to write his mother again saying that he would like to rejoin her, resume his trade, and try to make good. Frank's landlady wrote his mother that she felt very sorry for the young man; that he had gotten in with a crowd that were drinking, and that he commits thefts while under the influence of liquor. By this time Frank was twenty-five years old.

It was not until over a year later, however (shortly after the beginning of the second five-year follow-up period) that Frank actually rejoined his mother, for in the meantime he had again been arrested for larceny and committed to jail on a year's sentence. After his release he went home to his mother, but stayed only a short time. Again he disappeared from view and his mother did not know that he had once more been arrested for drunkenness and placed on probation, had defaulted, had gone off to another state, and was there arrested for drug addiction. On this latter charge he was held in jail for seventeen months.

Meanwhile Frank had again communicated with his mother and she arranged for him to return home following his release. Not long after this (at the age of twenty-nine) Frank was again arrested for larceny and committed to jail for six months. During two of his incarcerations within the last five years he has been treated for drug addiction, but without any effective result. Physicians who have examined him say that he is deteriorating from both drugs and alcohol. A psychiatrist who had occasion to examine Frank before the end of the second five-year follow-up period, reported that "he is decidedly an unstable person who is likely to continue to be a problem and should if possible be permanently segregated. His conduct is the result probably of an inherited lack of stability, a nervous high-strung temperament, and lack of proper discipline and security as a boy due to his father's conduct and desertion of his family. His use of alcohol and drugs, while factors in his arrests, are symptomatic of that inherited weakness of temperament."

BENNETT

Neither Nature's benign process of maturation nor the dogged faithfulness and sacrifice of a devoted wife can prevail against a greatly handicapped hereditary equipment. Physical, mental, and moral deterioration progress tragically in the case of Bennett.

Bennett is one of six children of Canadian-born parents. His three brothers and one sister died of diphtheria while Bennett was still a very young boy. His oldest sister recalls that when two of the boys died (practically at the same time) Bennett's father, who had always been extremely cruel to the children and to his wife and was a very hard drinker, refused to go to the funeral. "Hell, no, I'll go down and have a drink on 'em!"

While Bennett was still very little his mother was once or twice arrested for drunkenness, but she was not nearly so excessively intemperate as the father, who would often severely beat his wife and children when under the influence of liquor. Bennett's sister superstitiously attributes the boy's early propensity for thieving to the fact that when Bennett's mother was pregnant one of her sisters, who paid her a visit, stole a good many things from their home. "From the time Bennett was born he was marked for thievery."

Bennett's first arrest occurred when he was thirteen years old. On this occasion he and a playmate were delivering a bundle of washing to a customer of his mother. On arrival at the house the boys saw some money lying about and took it to go to the movies with. Bennett's father refused to make reimbursement of the theft and insisted that the boy be severely punished. The Court ordered Bennett committed to the care of the state and from then until he was seventeen years of age he was in a foster home, working mainly as a farm hand.

Until the death of his foster parents, to whom he became very much attached, the lad did very well indeed. After their death, however, he was returned to his home and was soon again arrested for larceny (of a watch), as the result of which he was sentenced, at the age of seventeen, to the Massachusetts Reformatory where he remained for fourteen months. This, however, is not the particular sentence to the Reformatory which brought him to our attention. Shortly thereafter he joined the navy for a couple of years. At about this time Bennett began to drink rather heavily.

Not long after his discharge, he was again committed to the Massachusetts Reformatory, this time for larceny of clothing valued at $14. By now Bennett was twenty-two years old. On admission, he was found to be of dull-normal intelligence and already somewhat deteriorated from the use of alcohol for which, he volunteered, he had inherited an appetite. Except for the fact that he was rather inclined to "fooling about," he worked fairly well in the Reformatory for a while as a weaver, then as a tinsmith and as a general cleaner. He was occasionally punished for smoking, talking, being out of place, but was not guilty of any really serious misconduct while in the institution. He was able to give only a very vague account of his life from the time that he left the care of his foster parents. It was obvious, however, that except for the period which he spent in the navy he was mostly idle, doing odd jobs here and there but largely depending on his parents for support.

It should be mentioned at this point that some years later, when Bennett was already thirty-five years of age, and in connection with the treatment of a head injury, he was diagnosed by an experienced psychiatrist as a "psychopathic personality . . . it is possible that his drinking habits may have something to do with some of his misdemeanors but his congenital basis seems to be the most common factor."

After nineteen months in the Reformatory, Bennett was released on parole. He went to the home of his parents to live and, as was characteristic of him, worked very irregularly at odd jobs, rarely holding one for more than a month. Within six months after his release on parole, he was once more arrested for larceny and returned to the Reformatory. In ten months' time he was again paroled, once more returning to the home of his parents.

Shortly thereafter Bennett married a widow of good reputation, some six years older than himself, who was successfully conducting a rooming house. She was very much devoted to him and very anxious that he behave himself properly. As he would not or could not get much of any work, his wife urged him to assist her in the running of the rooming house. He shortly began to steal from the lodgers, his permit to be at liberty was revoked by the parole agent, and he was returned to the Reformatory. On this recommitment, Bennett was held for four months, and upon his release rejoined his wife. Because he was so inclined to steal from the lodgers, Bennett's wife, who remained very loyal to him, gave up her lodging house and she and Bennett went to live in the rooming house of a friend of hers. But here again Bennett stole freely from roomers and was once more returned to the Reformatory where he now stayed for eleven months. Shortly after his release, Bennett was charged with the larceny of lead pipe from empty houses. He admitted that he had been drinking very heavily for a long time and that he wanted the lead pipe to exchange for booze. He was sentenced to a house of correction for two years, and upon his release from this institution, was committed to the Reformatory on a revoke warrant.

It should be mentioned that on several occasions during his previous paroles Bennett had deserted his wife. She was always ready to take him back, however, even after he had thrown a bottle at her, inflicting a severe scalp wound. Although he manifested a certain amount of affection for his wife, Bennett did not hesitate to steal from her, always for the purpose of getting money for liquor. Preceding his last return to the Reformatory, on the revoke warrant, his wife pleaded with the parole authorities that he be permitted to remain at large. "He tells me he is done with drink and crime for life and I am writing this to give him just this one chance for there might be some good in him while he is young. [He was then thirty years of age.] I know it will make him worse to send him away after two years in jail. I do hope that he may be allowed to go in the navy. He would be better dead than from one prison to another."

After his final release from the Reformatory, Bennett, apparently spurred on somewhat by his wife's devotion, worked steadily for two months in an inn. He visited his wife on his day off and turned his money over to her. She wrote the parole authorities: "Bennett never done so well before. I don't think he ever thinks of any wrong now. . . . Bennett is living straight. What is done is done."

His good behavior was very short-lived, however. On the very day on which his parole expired, Bennett was again arrested for larceny and was placed on probation for six months. Two months after the end of his probation he was once more arrested for larceny and committed to jail, where he remained for six months. For two years after his release he lived with his wife off and on, rarely contributing to her support, continually abusing her. She worked in a local department store and he occasionally managed indirectly to get a little money from her for drink. Once he sold a $14-dress of hers for $2 and used the money for liquor. By this time his parents and his sister had long ceased to show any concern in him and would not help him in any way. He was so enslaved to the alcoholic habit that when, on his mother's death, shortly after the beginning of the first follow-up period, he collected $12 among the neighbors for flowers for her funeral, he spent the money on drink.

There is no need to present the details of Bennett's escapades during the first follow-up period. Suffice it to say that during these five years he was arrested on eleven occasions, six times for larceny and five times for drunkenness; he was on two occasions committed to jail; he rarely worked, depending largely on his wife for support.

This situation continued into the second follow-up period, in the midst of which Bennett's wife died of cancer. Her death cut off his last means of support. His father had died a year or two previously and his sister would have nothing whatever to do with him. Indeed, one of her great fears is that when Bennett dies, the authorities will try to locate her and force her to pay his funeral expenses.

Bennett now has to depend upon the welfare agencies of the community for assistance. Within the two years between the death of his wife and the end of the second follow-up period, he has been arrested on four occasions: once for larceny, once for drunkenness, and twice for indecent exposure. Three of these arrests were followed by commitments to jail. Continuing his alcoholic excesses between incarcerations, Bennett manages to pick up a night's lodging here and there, sometimes stealing to pay for it, sometimes wheedling the money out of a social agency. He has no fixed abode and is now, at the age of forty-two, a chronic alcoholic and drifter, rapidly deteriorating both physically and mentally.

Conclusion

In the foregoing case summaries we have presented sketches of some of the personality and behavior types that have entered into the more abstract statistical discussion of our group of ex-inmates of the Massachusetts Reformatory. The cases illustrate the pattern of normal maturation and settling down that comes with aging, and the blocking or distortion of the natural maturation process by innate or early-conditioned defects of personality and temperament.

Had these cases been presented in the early part of this book rather than at the end, the reader might have gained a somewhat distorted impression of the underlying causes for reformation and recidivism, perhaps attributing them to factors which, in the statistical analysis, have been revealed as not of basic significance when the group is taken as a whole. For example, marriage to a decent woman in the case of Edward who reformed, and to a disreputable one in the case of Alphonse who continued to recidivate, does not illustrate, as might at first glance appear, that marriage *per se* brings about reformation or relapse. The statistical analysis has shown that this factor cannot in the mass of cases be held accountable for the results (see Chapter IX), but that apparently in cases in which a natural process of maturation is proceeding or is latent, a happy marriage is more likely to occur, than in cases in which the normal process of personality growth is counteracted by some mental distortion. The same is true in respect to interesting employment and other circumstances apparently favorable to reformation; these are secondary rather than primary phenomena.

Chapter XIV

SUMMARY AND CONCLUSIONS

W E have now completed the presentation of the materials of this book. Several avenues of investigation and more detailed data on certain aspects of the study might have been presented, but they have been reserved for another time because they would not especially contribute to the main line of investigation and discussion.

Major Findings

GENERAL TREND TOWARD IMPROVEMENT IN CONDUCT

It may be well briefly to review the main facts disclosed by this second follow-up study of the ex-inmates of the Massachusetts Reformatory. A comparison of their environment and behavior in this second period as compared with the first five years shows a general improvement in the group as a whole, though greater in some respects than in others. A high relationship was found to exist between non-delinquency during the ten-year span and the favorable aspects of other major factors in the life careers of our men. This finding raised the crucial question of the reasons for the decrease in criminal conduct.

RELATION BETWEEN REFORM AND IMPROVEMENT IN MAJOR ASPECTS OF LIFE
CAREERS

At this point it was emphasized that these high correlations do not necessarily involve any causal relationship between the abandonment of criminal conduct and betterment in other ways. It could only be concluded that a general improvement in behavior and status *accompanies* reformation in criminal behavior. It was suggested that all the improvements which occurred in the second follow-up period as compared with the first may in turn be attributable to one or more influences not yet ascertained. To a determination of these, a later chapter was devoted.

COMPARISON OF REFORMED AND UNREFORMED

Before turning to a consideration of the reasons for this improvement a comparison was made of the characteristics of those who reformed during the first or second five-year follow-up period and those who continued to recidivate. This comparison revealed that there was little difference between the characteristics and conditions of the two groups of men *prior to their commitment* to the Reformatory. The few significant differences that did exist were, as was to be expected, in favor of those who ultimately abandoned their delinquent behavior. In comparison with those who continued to recidivate, a smaller proportion of those who reformed, had left home at an early age; fewer had been unskilled workers during the pre-Reformatory stage; fewer then had poor work habits, and the like. The only very marked difference in the two groups was found to exist in the far greater proportion of those with mental abnormalities (disease, distortion, or serious liabilities of personality) among the men who continued to recidivate than among those who reformed. This difference, it will be recalled, amounted to an incidence of abnormal mental condition in the former of 51.2 per cent compared to but 7.6 per cent among the reformed. It was found, however, that *following the expiration of their Reformatory sentences,* the differences between those who reformed during the first or second five-year period and those who continued to recidivate became much more marked, and increased with the passage of time. As has already been indicated the differences are consistently in favor of those who reformed. For example, a far lower proportion of these moved about excessively than did the men who continued to recidivate, a far lower proportion of the former than of the latter failed to assume their economic responsibilities, a far lower proportion were industrial failures, and the like.

MATURATION THE UNDERLYING INFLUENCE IN REFORM

A basic problem of this research was to determine which of the 63 factors studied were chiefly responsible for the reduction in criminality. This was accomplished by examining each of these factors in turn, comparing the incidence of non-delinquency within each subcategory of the factor with its incidence in the entire group of cases. Such analysis revealed that only within the factor of *Aging* was a significant explanation to be found for the increasing trend away from criminal conduct. This finding made questionable the existence of any causal relationship between the betterment in the major aspects of the life careers of our men, and reformation. It was at this point concluded that improvement in family relationships, assumption of economic responsibilities, industrial status, or use of leisure was not the *cause* of the improved behavior of our men, but an accompaniment of it, being itself in turn due to the factor of maturation through aging.

ACCOMPANIMENTS OF MATURATION PROCESS

The factor of *Aging* having emerged as of such significance in the reformative process, it was then subjected to a detailed analysis in order to determine what its accompaniments actually are. A correlation of the various age groups among our men (at the beginning of the second follow-up period) with the factors of the second five-year period strikingly revealed that, with but two or three exceptions, improvement in all respects progresses and accumulates to roughly the thirty-sixth year, after which a marked decline sets in. Such a pattern of evolution and devolution suggests that the benign process of maturation in large measure ceases by about the thirty-sixth year. This analysis led to the conclusion that the improvement which has occurred in practically all the aspects of the careers of our group is very probably a natural accompaniment of the "settling down" process of growth or maturation, to which is largely attributable such reformation as has occurred with the passing of the years. It seems evident also that those offenders who have not reformed by the thirty-sixth year are much less likely to do so thereafter, although it may be that there will later emerge another period of maximal reformation. Only further follow-up studies of this group will reveal this.

MENTAL ABNORMALITY AS HAMPERING REFORM

Having ascertained the fact that the natural process of maturation largely accounts for the improvement which has occurred in our group, we were next concerned to ascertain why it is that, despite the passing of the years, so many of the men did *not* reform. A comparison of the status of our men prior to their commitment to the Reformatory and during the second five-year follow-up period clearly revealed that although, with the passage of time, a very marked improvement had occurred in the major aspects of their careers, this could not be said of their mental condition which had practically not changed over the years. Side by side with this significant finding is another important piece of evidence, obtained by a comparison of the characteristics of those who reformed and those who continued to recidivate. This revealed that *the most marked difference between the reformed and unreformed lies in the factor of mental or emotional difficulties,* as evidenced by the finding that only 15.2 per cent of those who reformed were burdened with some psychiatric condition as opposed to 89.9 per cent of those who continued to be delinquent or criminal. Moreover, this finding was supported by a preceding, independent case-by-case analysis of the reasons for continued recidivism, which had revealed that the presence of a mental abnormality of the kind noted by psychiatrists was the major impediment to reformation.

Detailed analysis was next made of the characteristics of those with and those without psychiatric abnormalities, this clearly indicating that the presence of mental or emotional difficulties unfavorably affects every aspect of the lives of offenders and therefore seriously blocks the reformative process.

PREDICTING CRIMINAL CONDUCT OVER TEN-YEAR SPAN

In Chapter XII, which precedes the chapter of illustrative case summaries of those who reformed and those who continued to recidivate within the span of time covered by this research, a predictive table is presented which permits the forecasting, over a ten-year span following the expiration of their sentences, of the probable behavior of men committed to a reformatory. This was accomplished by a correlation of the pre-Reformatory factors with the criminal conduct of the men throughout the first and second follow-up periods. The factors found to be most highly predictive of outcomes during the ten-year span were pre-Reformatory work habits, assumption of economic responsibilities, age at first known delinquency, arrests prior to the one for which the men had been committed to the Reformatory, and the presence or absence of mental abnormalities (disease or distortion). The table which was constructed on the basis of these data illustrates an instrument of great potentialities in the more realistic administration of criminal justice.

Conclusions

MATURATION AND THE LIFE CYCLE

The analysis of the data of this research raises several fundamental questions. In the first place, may it not be that certain typical physical and psychologic changes which occur for a more or less definite span of time preceding and following the thirty-fifth year, would tend to explain the occurrence and accumulation of reform up to that age as well as the marked drop in its incidence thereafter? This question is one for wide-flung exploration by the biologist, psychologist, and psychiatrist. In this connection, it is of interest to reproduce a diagram presented in 1917 by Dr. Bernard Glueck in a report of his examination of some six hundred serious offenders consecutively admitted to Sing Sing Prison.[1] In this chart, he "endeavored to present tentatively a number of etiologic factors of maladjustment in their relation to the various epochs in an individual's life. The curve represents an imaginary life cycle divided

1 Bernard Glueck, Types of Delinquent Careers, *Mental Hygiene*, 1:171–195, April, 1917.

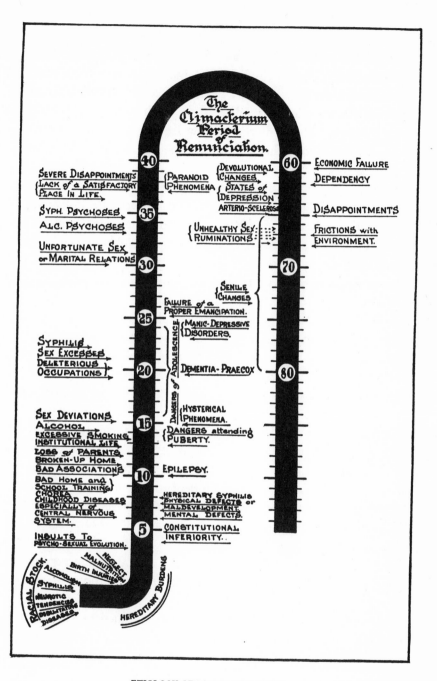

ETIOLOGY OF MALADJUSTMENT

into age periods, the factors enumerated outside the curve consti-
tuting the environmental etiology of maladjustment, those inside
of the curve the constitutional causes. Naturally, this chart represents only schematically the deleterious possibilities in an individual's career but it is remarkable how frequently one or more of
these etiologic possibilities occur in the life histories of adult
criminals."[2]

It will be seen that the "climacterium period of renunciation"
(see chart) immediately follows the span between thirty-five and
forty, within which are said to occur "severe disappointments, lack
of a satisfactory place in life," and "paranoid phenomena." The
span immediately preceding—from thirty to thirty-five years of
age—is typically the period in which unfortunate sex and marital
relations occur, together with the harvesting of such exogenous
mental disorders as syphilitic and alcoholic psychoses from seeds
recklessly sown in the preceding years. The years from about fifteen
to twenty-five are beset with the dangers of adolescence and by the
appearance of such mental disorders as schizophrenia and manic-
depressive psychoses, as well as personality and character distortions
related to the failure of wholesome emancipation from parental
dominance. The crucial years of adolescence are further endangered
by such environmental experiences as sexual excesses, the threat
of venereal diseases, and employment in deleterious occupations.
This chart, therefore, constructed independently some twenty years
ago, might with slight modification serve to describe schematically
the picture that occurs in the careers of many of our offenders.

It seems reasonable to believe that the years from about twenty-
five to thirty-five are the crucial ones for offenders. During these
years a sifting seems to occur which differentiates those offenders
whose delinquency and criminality were essentially conditioned
by adverse environmental and educational influences from those
whose inability to conform to the demands of a complex society is

[2] *Ibid.*, pp. 174–176.

more nearly related to organic or early conditioned mental abnor-malities. With the passage of time the members of the former group experience a normal integration of personality and impulses, and if the environment is at all favorable they settle down to a law-abiding course of life. However, the passage of the years only serves to bring into being or to continue deep-rooted defects of personality and character in the second group of offenders. Normal integration is interfered with and sometimes greatly thwarted. Our research shows how this differentiation proceeds as the men get older, becoming quite marked by the time they are in their late thirties.

Unfortunately, the psychologic and psychiatric examinations of our group at different age levels have not been sufficiently uniform and deep-probing to enable us to do more than speculate about the influences involved. Moreover, to dig more deeply into this crucial problem would require intensive periodic examinations of a com-parable sample of non-criminals. At all events, further exploration of the typical patterning of the lives of criminals should yield scientific and practical results. If it can be definitely established that in a large proportion of the careers of offenders certain physical and mental changes related to criminalistic behavior are to be ex-pected at different age periods, considerable light will be thrown both on causation and on promising methods of control.

CAN MATURATION BE HASTENED?

Another question raised by this research is whether it will be possible to develop and apply artificial substitutes to bring about the favorable results that accompany aging in many cases. Can educators, psychologists, correctional workers, and others devise means of "forcing the plant," as it were, so that *benign maturation* will occur earlier than it seems to at present? There is some evi-dence in our study which might be interpreted as indicating that the process of maturing was accelerated through successful marriage, absorbing employment, and the like. On the other hand, there is also evidence that in some cases, despite a favorable marriage, the settling down of the offender has been indefinitely delayed.

Can improvement in the existing sentencing, supervisory, and treatment practices accomplish the reform of criminals which is now brought about largely by the natural process of maturation? In this connection there is evidence in this study of the difficulties encountered by the parolee and ex-parolee in obtaining a legitimate foothold in society. For the ex-prisoner—even one with good equipment—to obtain a job is not an easy matter, especially when so many non-criminals are out of employment. It is also difficult for him to be accepted in legitimate social, recreational, and even religious circles. Will the provision of a more systematic and sympathetic program for the social reabsorption of ex-prisoners hasten or facilitate the maturation process, perhaps bringing about the reform of some who, under the present unfavorable conditions, continue their delinquencies?

Only carefully directed and recorded experiments can answer these and closely related vital questions.

NEED FOR INDETERMINATE SENTENCE

Another question raised by this research deals with the problem of the indeterminate sentence. Very definite evidence emerges from this study in support of the necessity of either a wholly indeterminate sentence or one affording a very broad zone between minimum and maximum limits. Heretofore, the length of the various indeterminate sentences provided in statutory enactments for the different crimes has been the result of the inexpert views of legislators as to the relative seriousness of various crimes, plus compromises arrived at in legislative committees, or downright guess-work. Now it may be confidently suggested that, regardless of the felony committed, a scientific administration of justice requires either a completely indeterminate sentence or a broad-zoned one to cover all serious offenders. But a correlative requirement is a more scientific parole policy and technique enforced by a trained personnel. There is both waste and danger in providing for either a wholly indeterminate or a long-term indeterminate sentence unless those who deal with offenders originally, or who pass upon their release from prison, are professionally trained in the special disciplines required.

IMPLEMENTING THE INDETERMINATE SENTENCE

From this and similar researches is gradually emerging a body of knowledge about the life careers of offenders which will scientifically implement the use of the wholly indeterminate sentence. What type of offender should be incarcerated, what type placed on probation or subjected to some other form of treatment? How long should a certain type of offender be held in an institution? For how long a period is he likely to need parole supervision? What kind of offender can, with reasonable safety to himself and society, be granted freedom with only occasional or only technical oversight?

The answers to some of these questions are already becoming evident from this research. For example, the chances for the reformation of psychopathic offenders appears to be slight, and they continue to commit their depredations even while under parole supervision. Obviously, therefore, for them, either long-time incarceration or very strict extra-mural supervision is necessary if they are not to continue to be a menace to society.

Numerous other illustrations might be given of the probable behavior of various types of offenders, all of which serve as a guide to the use of the indeterminate sentence. The reader is referred to the previous chapter in which sketches have been given of the life careers of various kinds of offenders, and also to Chapter XII in which it has been shown that it is possible to predict the probable behavior of various kinds of offenders.

Of further value toward the future implementation of the indeterminate sentence is the conviction arising out of this and other researches into the careers of criminals, that new treatment procedures are indicated in certain types of cases. For example, there is a type of offender who, with the passage of time, abandons serious crimes and settles down into a course of petty misbehavior often marked by chronic alcoholism. Such offenders, and those who throughout commit only the offense of drunkenness or petty offenses associated with it, present largely medical and psychiatric problems. Their behavior, though not aggressively dangerous to society, entails great expense by their unbroken round of recidivism, rearrest, retrial, resentence, recommitment to short-term institutions which make no pretense of studying or rehabilitating them. For these malefactors, some non-criminal commitment procedure seems indicated, as in the case of "defective delinquents," treatment of whom is, in a few states, supplemented with the medico-psychiatric régimes of a hospital and farm colony.

There are psychologic types, not only the frankly mentally defective or psychopathic, but, for example, those who consistently do well under supervision but are unable to stand on their own feet when oversight is abandoned, for whom special treatment is necessary.

NEED FOR UNIFICATION OF MACHINERY OF INDETERMINATE SENTENCE

Regarding the machinery necessary to implement the proposed indeterminate sentence, this study reinforces a conviction arrived at in prior investigations: The sentence-imposing or treatment function of the criminal courts ought to be separated from the guilt-determining function. The former should be entrusted to a special tribunal particularly qualified in the interpretation and evaluation of sociologic, psychiatric, and psychologic data. The original sentence and the treatment program arrived at in each case should be modifiable in the light of periodic reports of the offender's progress while in prison and on parole, this report to be submitted to a treatment tribunal by those entrusted with carrying out its mandates. The need for special safeguards of the individual offender against possible arbitrariness or other unlawful action by the proposed tribunal has been considered elsewhere and need not here be re-peated.[3]

At present, the fate of a convicted offender is left to several in-dependent agencies. This results in lack of unity and of consistency in treatment. Each agency is inclined to regard as an end in itself its particular segment of what is in fact a unified problem. The judge who has sentenced the offender is little concerned with what happens to him thereafter; in fact he rarely knows what later tran-spires. The penal institution administrator is interested primarily in seeing that the offender is a "good prisoner." Some of the case histories have illustrated how shortsighted such a view is. The pa-role board takes hold long after the original event and begins anew to consider what to do with the prisoner.

In order to bring about a desirable continuity and consistency of treatment, the proposed treatment tribunal ought to take over the work of the parole board. In this way the same group which originally studies the offender's background, makeup, and re-quirements would follow his response to treatment in the institu-tion, and review the entire history of the offender at later stages when the question comes up of changing the treatment from imprisonment to one or another type of supervision in the com-munity. Equipped with a wholly indeterminate or wide-zone in-determinate sentence, the treatment tribunal would be empow-ered to keep under control, within institutions or on parole, offenders who continue to be a social menace; while those whose maturation has resulted in a settling down and the abandonment of criminalistic tendencies, might be released, at least experi-mentally, after relatively short periods of control. At present, as our findings indicate, many aggressively dangerous offenders must be discharged at the close of the maximum limits of narrow in-determinate sentences, even though all concerned know full well that such prisoners or parolees will forthwith embark once more on

[3] Sheldon Glueck, *Crime and Justice,* Boston, Little, Brown, and Company, 1936, pp. 227–228.

a career of crime. On the other hand, socially harmless prisoners, who give every promise of a successful and law-abiding subsequent career, must often be held in prison for so long a time that, when finally discharged, they are of little use to themselves, their families or society.

We have shown that it is possible to forecast, with sufficient accuracy for practical purposes, the probable behavior of an offender or ex-prisoner over a long span of time. The proposed treatment tribunal might well avail itself of prediction instruments both at the point of sentence and when contemplating release of a prisoner. In the present research the prognostic instrument is based essentially upon analysis of the response of ex-prisoners to the particular form of treatment herein investigated; namely, incarceration in a reformatory followed by parole. In a research now under way the authors plan to develop predictive tables for each of the major forms of treatment undergone by a group of offenders. Such tables, giving expectancies of success or failure as the result of placing certain types of offenders on probation, or committing them to a reformatory or to a prison, and the like, should be of practical value in bringing about more realistic sentencing practices. Because the role of predictive instruments has been consistently misunderstood, it is well to stress that they are not intended to supplant, but rather to supplement, the trained intuition of judges and parole authorities. They supply a scientific framework, based on objectified experience, within which the exercise of discretion can more efficiently function.

The treatment tribunal will also have to be equipped with clinics and laboratories; so that during the interval between conviction and sentence, a thoroughgoing physical, mental, and social investigation of each offender may be made.

The proposed system, with its wholly indeterminate or broad-zone indeterminate sentence, far from reducing whatever deterrent effect there may be in the prospect of punishment, would enhance it. Since the length of incarceration would not be determinable in advance and might in some cases endure throughout life, and since (as is not the case under existing practices) offenders would not be automatically released at the end of a stated time regardless of whether or not they were still a social menace, the proposed régime would probably have a greater deterrent effect than the present one.

It remains to be added that the recommended system would be less expensive than the existing practice. When one reviews the frequent rearrests, retrials, resentences, recommitments, and reparoles of the vast majority of our offenders over the years, and realizes that many of them, under the proposed system, would not have been allowed to continue their depredations for long stretches of time, the saving in expense seems obvious.

CAN CRIMINAL CAREERS BE PREVENTED?

The findings of this research also raise some interesting questions about crime-preventive efforts. We have seen, in comparing the men who reformed with those who continued to commit crimes, that although they were very much alike in traits and background at the origin of their delinquent careers, the passage of time increasingly distinguished them from each other. From this phenomenon we may infer that while unquestionably many children respond favorably to recreational and other "crime-preventive programs," they are likely to be those who, in a fundamental sense, were not criminalistically inclined in the first place. Whether such programs—except perhaps those with a psychiatric or mental hygiene approach—are effective in the case of offenders who, because of mental taint, persist in wrongdoing, or of offenders whose turbulent conduct continues until a certain age span, still remains to be determined.

Existing crime-preventive practices may, however, have some value even in such cases, in reducing the opportunities and occasions for anti-social expression. The great question before those who would attack crime at the root is: Can we (paraphrasing William James's well-known call for moral substitutes for war) discover socially harmless substitutes for crime? Can the impulses of those youths who normally continue in criminality until a certain age span, if not of those who go on committing offenses thereafter, be redirected? Or must crime-preventive programs content themselves with aiding those who, in a fundamental sense, are really accidental offenders rather than persons set to run a continuous course of crime? All such questions raise the vitally important problem of finding means for the early differentiation of the essentially environmental delinquents from the essentially organismal delinquents whose careers, it can be predicted, are very likely to run an anti-social course until a certain age or even thereafter, barring some hastening of the maturation process. Careful investigations into the traits of "problem children" and "pre-delinquents," correlated with their subsequent evolution into criminals or non-criminals, are a crying need of the entire field of criminology.[4]

In closing, it ought to be pointed out that in the present research we have presented only a segment, albeit a large one, of the life cycle of a group of offenders.[5] Further follow-up investigations are necessary and contemplated; so that ultimately we may have at least an outline picture of the vicissitudes of offenders from the cradle to the grave.

[4] The authors are making plans for one such investigation.

[5] Compare one of the conclusions in respect to female offenders: "The anti-sociality of the up-grade delinquents and of the non-delinquents is not so deep-rooted as of the delinquents and is to a far greater extent an adolescent manifestation, having its beginnings principally between the ages of thirteen and seventeen rather than earlier."—Glueck, S. and E. T., *500 Delinquent Women*, p. 277.

Appendix A

NOTE ON METHOD

IN view of the fact that the method utilized in the pursuit of the second follow-up investigation of the 510 inmates of the Massachusetts Reformatory for Men is essentially the same as that already reported in *500 Criminal Careers* (Chapter V) and in *500 Delinquent Women* (Appendix A), it is not necessary to describe in detail the methodology of the present investigation beyond briefly stating the additions to or departures from that already recorded in the above-mentioned works. Brief attention will be given to those aspects of the preparation of the schedule for this research, to the making of definitions, to the categorization of factors, to the investigation precedent to field work, and to the analysis and tabulation of the materials for statistical uses that differ from or represent modifications of the methods utilized in the other researches.

For the definition of any factors mentioned here, the reader is referred to Appendix B.

Schedule

In the preparation of the schedule for this research, account had to be taken not only of the factors previously assembled for the first follow-up study (see *500 Criminal Careers*, p. 347, for schedule covering the first five-year follow-up period) but of those comprising the first five-year follow-up investigation into the careers of the *500 Delinquent Women* (see p. 375 for schedule). This was necessitated by our desire to make the data of the new investigation comparable with those of the two mentioned above.

In view of the fact that when the first follow-up study of the 510 men was in process the idea for the continued five-year follow-up studies had not yet been crystallized, the materials of the first study were not in the best possible form for comparative purposes. It now became necessary, therefore, to consider all the possible amplifications of the data of the first five-year period in order to make it comparable with the more detailed information desired for the

---

MEN'S REFORMATORY STUDY
POST PAROLE HISTORY — SECOND FIVE YEAR PERIOD

Interview with   Date of investigation

True name	Aliases		Number
M. R. name	Period studied		Age
Whereabouts (at end of prd)		with	
Present whereabouts		with	

Attitude of O to investigation

Marital History: Date	Term.	Age difference	Bthpl. of wife	Mrtl. status of wfe
Manner of meeting	Time known bef. marr.			Marr. forced
Mixed color marr.	Ctzship of wife	Mixed relgn. marr.		Time wife in U. S.
Occup. of wife	Education	Illness	M. Defect	M. Disease

I. Health of O   V. D.   Partial incapacity   Total incapacity

Chronic illness   Cause of death

Emotional stability   Psychoneurotic traits

How indicated   Mental disease

II. Inst. Exper.   No. penal   Non-penal   Time in penal   In non-penal   Mos. in comm.

F. M.   M. D.   Chronic physical   Penal   Other

List

	5 yr. period	5th year			5 yr. period	5th year
III. Environmental	☐	☐	**IV. Economic Responsibility**		☐	☐
House (Type)			Savings			
Home (Physical)			Insurance	Premium pd. by		
Neighb. (Type)			Property			
Neighb. influ.			Econ. Cond.			
Mobility (Nature of)			Dependents			
Reason for			Disp. of earnings			
Moral standards			No. of S. S. Agencies			
			Type of S. S.			
			Depression victim			
V. Family Relationships	☐	☐	**VI. Industrial History**		☐	☐
Household stability			Usual occup.			
Rel. to nearest rels			Skill			
Attit. of rels to O			Stead.			
Marital status			Wk. hab.			
Conj. rels			No. of diff. occup.			
Att. of O to marr. resp.			Av. wage			
Att. of wife to marr. resp.			Highest wage			
Marital hist. judgment			Av. prd. emp.			
Comp. of wife as homkr.			Long prd. emp.			
No. of chn. (leg. illeg.)	Total (lvg)		Used M. R. occup.			
Att. to chn.			Why not			
Rsdnce. of chn.			Illeg. occup.			
Delinq. of chn.			Diff. sec. wk.			
Delinq. of wife			Rsns. for leaving			
VII. Leisure and Habits	☐	☐	**VIII. Delinquencies**		☐	☐
Society member			Predom. offense			
Church attend			Princ. comp.			
Educ'l activities			Unoff. misc.			
Companionships			No. of arrests			
M. R. associates			No. of conv.			
Haunts			Freq. of arrests			
Habits			Freq. of conv.			
Gang life			Associates in crime			
Street life			Summary of ct. offenses			
Sex irreg.						
Modes of recreation			Summary of dispositions			

IX. Social Service Needs Not Met

EXHIBIT A. SCHEDULE COVERING THE SECOND FIVE-YEAR PERIOD (FACE)

second five-year follow-up study, which latter had in turn been engendered by the more detailed investigation into the careers of the 500 *Delinquent Women*. Although in this book no compari-

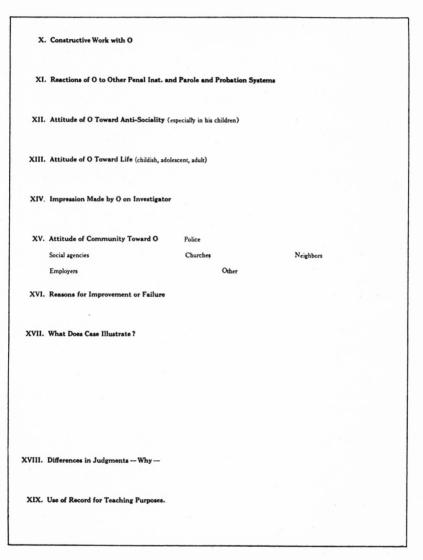

X. Constructive Work with O

XI. Reactions of O to Other Penal Inst. and Parole and Probation Systems

XII. Attitude of O Toward Anti-Sociality (especially in his children)

XIII. Attitude of O Toward Life (childish, adolescent, adult)

XIV. Impression Made by O on Investigator

XV. Attitude of Community Toward O   Police

Social agencies   Churches   Neighbors

Employers   Other

XVI. Reasons for Improvement or Failure

XVII. What Does Case Illustrate?

XVIII. Differences in Judgments — Why —

XIX. Use of Record for Teaching Purposes.

EXHIBIT A. SCHEDULE COVERING THE SECOND FIVE-YEAR PERIOD (BACK)

sons are made with the women delinquents, such comparisons will be made elsewhere. In the preparation of the schedule for the research, therefore, account had to be taken of such future uses of the materials.

In the included schedule (Exhibit A) are integrated the various considerations to which we had to give attention if the materials to be gathered in connection with the second follow-up study of the 510 ex-inmates of the Massachusetts Reformatory for Men were to be of use for the present and future purposes of our researches.

The following factors are entirely comparable with those already gathered in the first follow-up study (listed in the order of their appearance on the above schedule):

Interview with	Number of children
Present whereabouts	Attitude to children
Health	Leisure and habits
Cause of death	Church attendance
Time in penal institution	Companionships
Economic responsibility	Habits
Economic condition	Type of social service agencies
Dependents	Industrial history
Disposition of earnings	Usual occupation
Number of social service agencies	Skill
Months in community	Work habits
Institutional experience—hospital	Highest wages
for mental disease	Delinquencies
Institutional experience—penal	Principal component of miscon-
Home, physical condition of	duct
Neighborhood influences	Unofficial misconduct
Mobility, reason for	Number of arrests
Family relationships	Number of convictions
Marital status	Frequency of arrests
Conjugal relations	Summary of court offenses
Attitude of offender to marital re-	Summary of dispositions
sponsibility	

The following factors were made comparable with the first five-year follow-up study by reediting and retabulating data already gathered for the first follow-up study:

Number of penal experiences
Married during period
Non-penal experiences, number of
Non-penal institutions, length of time in
Feebleminded, number of times in institutions for
Chronic physical, number of times in institutions for
Neighborhood, type
Relation to nearest relatives
Haunts

Savings
Insurance
Property
Steadiness of employment
Average wage
Average period of employment
Longest period of employment
Society member
Educational activities
Illegitimate occupation
Reasons for leaving work

The following factors, though not comparable with the factors of the first five-year follow-up study, were included on the schedule for the purposes of comparability with the factors already gathered in the study of *500 Delinquent Women:*

Whereabouts at end of period (where living and with whom)
Date of end of five-year period
Aliases
Age
Present age
Date of marriage
Termination of marriage—reason for
Manner of meeting
Time known before marriage
Marriage forced
Color of mate
Birthplace of wife
Citizenship of wife
Religion of wife
Time wife in U.S.
Education of wife
Diseases (physical) of wife
Defect (mental) of wife
Mental disease of wife
Venereal disease of offender
Environmental judgment

House, type
Moral standards of home
Household stability
Residence of children
Attitude of wife to marital responsibility
Competency of wife as homemaker
Delinquency of children
Delinquency of wife
Street life of offender
Sex irregularity of offender
Used Massachusetts Reformatory occupation
Difficulty securing work
Predominant offense
Frequency of convictions
Seriousness of offense
Social service needs not met
Constructive work with offender
Attitude of community toward offender
Reason for improvement or failure
What does case illustrate

The entire schedule is comparable with the first five-year follow-up study of *500 Delinquent Women* except for the following factors which are unique to the present investigation:

Attitude to investigation
Mixed color marriage
Occupation of wife
Massachusetts Reformatory as-
    sociates
Gang life
Insurance—premium paid by
Number of different occupations
Mixed religion marriage
Partial incapacity
Total incapacity
Chronic illness

Emotional stability
Mental disease
Depression victim
Associates in crime
Reactions to other penal institu-
    tions, parole and probation
    systems
Attitude toward life
Attitude toward anti-sociality
Impressions made by offender on
    investigator

Definitions

Because of the need for making the factors of the first and second five-year follow-up periods comparable and for possible comparison with *500 Delinquent Women,* the definitions which had already been utilized for the first five-year study of the men were adopted for the second five-year study; and for those factors utilized in the second follow-up study but not in the first and comparable with those in *500 Delinquent Women,* the definitions from the latter were adopted. In these two previous researches a great deal of time had been spent in the building up of the definitions, in testing them out, in clarifying and refining them. For the present study, however, it was obviously possible very quickly to assemble them.

Some further clarification and refinement of definition was possible, however, as a result of experience gained in the prior researches. For example, the original definition of *Neighborhood Influences* as utilized in *500 Criminal Careers* was as follows:

> *Favourable:* fairly good houses, particularly in an open neighbour-
> hood; no gangs, no quarrelling, no extremely noisy neighbours;
> opportunities for good wholesome recreation near at hand.

Fair: average tenement neighbourhood; clean; not too noisy; disturbing conditions not too prominent.

Unfavourable: noisy, crowded, unclean streets; in or near disturbing conditions, such as corner gangs, immoral surroundings, bootlegging centres; places affording little chance for wholesome recreation.

But for the second five-year study the definition of *Neighborhood Influences* utilized in *500 Delinquent Women* was adopted because experience had shown its utility:

> *Good:* no street gangs, no centers of vice or crime within a radius of two square blocks in the city or a mile in the country; opportunity for constructive recreation within easy walking distance—as public playgrounds, school or community centers, parks, and so on.
> *Fair:* no street gangs, no centers of vice or crime within a radius of two square blocks in the city, or a mile in the country, but no opportunities for constructive recreation within walking distance.
> *Poor:* corner gangs, centers of vice or crime within a radius of two square blocks in the city or a mile in the country regardless of whether facilities for constructive recreation exist within walking distance or not.

And again, the definition of *Economic Responsibility* utilized in the first five-year study was further clarified and rephrased for use in the present study. The original definition was as follows:

> *Meets responsibility:* a person who is supporting himself or dependents comfortably; or one who is maintaining himself in marginal economic circumstances, if single, or his wife if married, or other near dependents, to the best of his ability without more than occasional public or private aid (including sporadic assistance from relatives when he should be absolutely self-supporting).
> *Fails to meet responsibility:* one who does not support himself or dependents, or who is contracting avoidable debts or receiving frequent aid from social agencies or from his family when he should be self-supporting.

But the definition of *Economic Responsibility* adopted for the second five-year study, modified somewhat from the one utilized in *500 Delinquent Women* is as follows:

Meets responsibility: if single, separated, widowed, or divorced and is without legal dependents (wife, children or parents) supports self even if by illegitimate employment and at least in *marginal* circumstances with only occasional public or private aid or sporadic assistance from relatives; if he has dependents (wife, children or parents) makes every reasonable effort to support them at least in *marginal circumstances.*

Fails to meet responsibility: does not meet the above standard through his own fault or contracts avoidable debts or receives frequent aid from social agencies or relatives when should be self-supporting.

Anyone interested in the re-formulation of definitions is referred to the volume *500 Criminal Careers* where definitions appear both in the text and in footnotes; to *500 Delinquent Women* (Appendix C, *Definition of Terms*); and to the present volume (Appendix B, *Definition of Terms*).

Categorization of Factors

In the categorization of factors utilized in the second follow-up study the basic principle was again comparability with the factors of the first five-year study and with the study of *500 Delinquent Women,* provided of course that the data already gathered in the first five-year follow-up study of the 510 men could be retabulated to meet the need for conformity. Those factors not comparable with the first study of the men but comparable with the first study of the women were modified in their categorization to meet the needs of the new study and to profit from the experience gained in the study of the women offenders. For example, in *500 Delinquent Women,* the following categorization of the factor *Disposition of Earnings* had been used:

Inapplicable
Self, or husband and children
Self, has dependents
Contributes to support of others
No earnings
Unknown

But for the second follow-up study of the men, the exigencies of the research were better met by the following categorization of this factor:

Inapplicable
Self only
Wife and children, no others
Wife and children and others
Others, has no wife or children

As further illustrating necessary modifications of categories because of present exigencies (without however destroying their value for comparative purposes) is the category *Chronic illness or for other legitimate reasons dependent,* of the factor *Economic Responsibility* used in the study of *500 Delinquent Women.* Because of the effect on dependency of the industrial depression of 1929–1933 (which entered into the midst of the second five-year study of the men), the above category was split in two as follows:

Unable to meet responsibility because of chronic illness
Unable to meet responsibility completely though manifests willingness to do so (largely because of industrial depression)

Likewise in the categorization of *Economic Condition,* it had previously been sufficient to use the simple category *dependent.* But in the present research in order to take account of the industrial depression it seemed better to subdivide this into three categories as follows:

Dependent on agencies or persons outside of immediate family (not because of depression)
Dependent entirely or partially upon relatives (not because of depression)
Dependent entirely or partially on agencies or relatives (because of depression)

Certain changes in categorization were made, however, not because of the exigencies of the present situation but because experience with the factors indicated that further refinement of categories would be clarifying and would better convey the meaning of the factor. For example, in the prior researches the combined category *Relief and family welfare agencies* had been utilized. This has now been split into two categories:

Relief agencies
Family welfare agencies

Likewise in the factor *Used Reformatory Occupation*, the categories employed in the study of *500 Delinquent Women* were:

Used Reformatory occupation
Did not use Reformatory occupation

For the present purpose it seemed more clarifying to divide the first category into two parts:

Used same occupation
Used same technique but different occupation

Anyone interested in the detail of categorization of factors and the changes made from one of our already reported investigations to another will find it helpful to consult *500 Criminal Careers* and *500 Delinquent Women,* in addition to the present volume.

Investigation Preceding Field Work

It will be recalled that for the purposes of the first follow-up study identification cards were prepared (see *500 Criminal Careers,* p. 348) on which were entered any data or clues necessary to the locating of the ex-inmates of the Reformatory. For the purposes of the second follow-up investigation new identification cards were prepared containing information that had been gathered in the course of the first follow-up study, helpful in now tracing the men and their relatives. There were added any tracing clues revealed in clearing the cases through the Massachusetts Board of Probation[1] and the fingerprint files of the Massachusetts Bureau of Criminal Identification. From this point on, the usual procedures relating to

[1] A central clearing house for court records.

the assembling of data prior to actual field investigation were pursued. There is on file in our office a record of the investigations made in each case showing step by step how the data were gathered and verified. These records are called *Diary Cards* (for illustration see *500 Delinquent Women*, pp. 364–369).

Field Work

In the personal field investigation the only unique feature was the problem of interviewing the men and/or their relatives for a second time and smoothing out any resistances they might have to this continuing pursuit of them. Because of the very friendly relationship which had been established by the field worker in the course of the first follow-up study, it was possible with very little difficulty to revisit the men and/or their relatives.

The other aspects of the field investigations—interviews with police, probation officers, employers, social workers, and others— did not differ in the problems presented from those of the first investigation. Actually in 49.6 per cent of cases, the men were personally seen by the field worker (as compared with 37.8 per cent in the first follow-up study). In 32.4 per cent of the cases, although the men themselves were for various reasons not interviewed, near relatives were seen. In the remaining 18 per cent, sufficient data about their activities were available from records or could be gathered by correspondence, to make unnecessary a personal interview. A record which we kept of those men and/or their relatives who were personally interviewed shows that in 90.2 per cent of the cases the field worker had a friendly reception after explaining his purpose; in 4.9 per cent of the cases those interviewed, though not positively friendly, were, however, not hostile and did not block the investigation; and in only 4.9 per cent of cases was there real hostility to the inquiries, which the field worker usually succeeded in breaking down, however.

The following cases are illustrative of the reception accorded the field worker on his second visit to the men or their relatives after an interval of five years. Where there was an attitude of hostility, it will be noted how it was dissipated.

Case I. This man had not been personally interviewed during the course of the first five-year follow-up study. His present whereabouts were unknown. A brother, married and successful, had very inadequately told us A's story but without revealing his whereabouts (although he knew them) nor telling us anything definite on the basis of which we could trace him. He told A of our interest, however. A was overtimid because when on parole he had gone West without giving a forwarding address and his parole had been revoked. So now he suspected that the field worker was playing into the hands of the parole board and might make trouble for him.

So A consulted his lawyer who got in touch with us. Through him, after much delay, an interview was arranged with A at the lawyer's office. As the field worker was able to assure him that the revoke warrant had been canceled years ago, A frankly reviewed his history which gave us a fairly adequate story. His attitude became entirely friendly and trusting. Of course we promised to do nothing to arouse the suspicions of his wife or neighbors who know nothing about his early criminal history.

Case II. When visited at the time of the second study, B's wife, who came to the door, did not recognize the field worker; and as he mispronounced the family name so that she did not recognize it, she was about to dismiss him, saying, "There's no such person living here," when B, who was inside, sprang up and said; "I know this man. Come right in, Mr. — ." He identified the field worker to his wife and after that they were entirely frank and friendly.

This desirable attitude occurred in spite of a suspicious hostility on the part of the wife at the time of the previous investigation, which unless it had been persistently overcome would have wrecked our whole relationship with the family. What had "made us solid" with her was the fact that about midway between the two studies B had come to us in desperation to learn how he could get a doctor for his young child sick with pneumonia. (He was without funds or a steady job.) We telephoned the appropriate social service agency and the matter was attended to. The gratitude of the couple to us for this led to their very friendly attitude when the second follow-up investigation was made some three years later.

When the visit was over the wife accompanied the investigator to the door and told him he would be welcome to come at any time.

CASE III. C had settled down on a remote farm in a small country town inaccessible by public transportation, and distant from any accessible center on the western borderline of Massachusetts and Connecticut. Some general but not completely adequate information had been secured about him from a relative-in-law. Later he was traced and interviewed in Springfield, Massachusetts, where we heard he was living temporarily. The situation was delicate as C was living with his wife at her mother's home and neither the wife nor her people knew anything about his Reformatory history. He took the field worker (whom he had never seen before) into a front room and closed the door. When he understood the purpose of the call, he looked very glum and angry and said, "I have not got anything I can say about that." He said he looked on all this as "hounding." He referred to letters from us that he had received. He said he thought it over; concluded that he "wasn't required to answer them," and so had ignored them. "You know I don't like the idea of being followed up until perhaps I am sixty years old." Then he said that a letter (quite innocent of any reference to past imprisonment or criminal conduct) sent by us to a farmer for whom he used to work had caused him trouble. He said that at that time he was planning to run for the office of selectman in that town. The former employer was opposed to his candidacy and used the letter against him among the townspeople, suggesting to them that there must be something sinister in C's history, else why the investigation? C, naturally supersensitive, was so afraid that someone hostile to him would dig out the real reason for the inquiry that he dropped all plans for seeking office.

The field worker thanked him for telling about the letter; explained to him the caution with which we make such inquiries from past employers which generally are entirely harmless, and told him that this incident was valuable to us in showing the dangers to be guarded against and would be kept in mind in future inquiries, and so forth. Gradually he became interested and fairly responsive and told his story and discussed matters pleasantly. He followed the field worker to the door and expressed the intention of looking him up and calling on him should he sometime come to Boston.

CASE IV. At the time of the first follow-up study, an interview with parents in Newark, New Jersey, seemed adequate enough to make it unnecessary to go to New Brunswick, New Jersey, solely to interview D personally. The field worker found that the apparently friendly attitude of the parents at the time of the first study had changed to coolness and even hostility when he visited them in connection with the second follow-up study.

In spite of the fact that the mother is undoubtedly a good woman and the family has a good reputation she deliberately lied to prevent us from learning that D lived in a nearby suburb and worked in Newark. She said it would be "dreadful" for the field worker to visit D, even though his wife already knew him when he was sent to the Reformatory. She was certain that the bare mention of the old Reformatory experience would be "awfully upsetting to him."

After a good deal of wasted time, the field worker finally learned, very indirectly, where D worked. He did not wish to embarrass him by talking before his employers, so he called shortly before noon at his place of business to invite him out to lunch. It so happened that he was out on business and was lunching at his home, but was due to relieve another salesman shortly. The field worker came back and met him and was received in a most friendly fashion. D took him into a private office and showed great and intelligent interest in our work, and expressed gratification at the call. He laughed at his mother's fears. He was even franker and went further into the details of his life and family relations than he was asked to do.

CASE V. In connection with the first follow-up investigation, E had sought out the field worker when he learned he was being looked for. At that time, being on probation for bootlegging, he was eager to discover how much the field worker already knew, particularly as the probation officer and officials had not understood how deeply he was involved in the bootlegging game.

At the time of the second follow-up study, prohibition having been repealed, E had "arrived" as a successful manager of a legitimate night club.

He finally consented (by telephone) to meet the field worker at a downtown hotel. He was extremely suspicious and brought with him a well-dressed stranger whom he introduced as his "lawyer," who tried (most unsuccessfully) to listen in on the conversation.

Although hostile, suspicious, and alert, E did tell truthfully the full outline of his story at least in its outward aspects, and we were able from other sources to fill in and verify his illegitimate as well as his legitimate activities and mode of life.

CASE VI. At the time of the first study, the field worker had seen F at his mother's house in South Boston to which he had recently come from a seafaring life. At present his only known address was General Delivery at an east side post office in New York City. The field worker was able to locate him through his mother, and when in New York City he invited F to supper with him. F responded eagerly but deliberately refused to go to the place chosen as being too aristocratic and "expensive" (although the expense would not be his).

He accepted the investigation as being to his mind very well worth while, and tried to give suggestions that he thought would be helpful to us growing out of his own varied experiences and his intimate knowledge of the "shady" sections of great cities in this country and in Europe. He frankly covered his own history in all aspects not denying but explaining one or two minor arrests we had discovered in distant states, and adding one or two others that we knew nothing about so that we should have a complete record.

He was so interested in the work that he volunteered to show the field worker around on a later day on a special tour of the lower east side. He showed keen observation and considerable ability at analysis, the significance of which was noted by the investigator. All this in spite of the fact that he is extremely sensitive and has never fully taken his own family into his confidence.

CASE VII. At the time of the first study the interview with G's mother was accepted as adequate because of the difficulty of tracing him on Staten Island. At the time of the second study cautious interviewing of his parents-in-law led to locating him. He was acting as janitor of an apartment and lodging house in Georgetown, Staten Island. As he was doing ERA work daytimes he had to be seen in the evening. Both he and his wife (who, to our surprise, knew all about his Reformatory history) took the visit as a courtesy. Both were frank and willing to tell their whole history to the extent that his rather erratic memory could give it.

After the interview they insisted on taking the investigator for an auto ride of about thirty miles over the most interesting parts of Staten Island, G telling stories of his life all the way. The auto belonged to his employer who was in the habit of letting him use it. Of course the field worker provided a good supply of gas and paid for the "treats" so that the entertainment would not come out of the welfare funds. At the end of the trip they drove him to the New York ferry and parted from him like old friends, telling him to be sure to visit them again.

Case Analysis and Coding

The materials gathered by correspondence and from the field were analyzed and entered on to the schedule card in accordance with the definitions, largely by one of the authors, over the period of three years that the investigation was actively under way. Several checks on these entries were made by two other persons who from time to time analyzed several cases comparing the results with those of the chief analyst. This was done mostly in the early stages of the research in order that reasons for discrepancies in analysis might be discovered and if possible eliminated. It was found that such discrepancies were due either to lack of clarity in the definition or to insufficient data on which to make a judgment. Errors in the categorization of qualitative data were reduced by the use of double and triple rather than more detailed categories of factors (see discussion on this point in 500 Delinquent Women, pp. 342, 343).

In view of the fact that the materials of 500 Criminal Careers had been tabulated by hand and that for this study the machine tabulation method was used, it was necessary to prepare a code not only for the second five-year follow-up period but for the materials of the first study, and to enter on punch cards those facts from 500 Criminal Careers which would have to be correlated with the facts of the present study. To this end it was necessary very early in the investigation to arrive at decisions regarding the details of the entire research particularly about comparisons and correlations of factors. Codes and code cards were prepared and data from the pre-Reformatory period, the Reformatory and parole period, and the first follow-up period were all coded, this being done at the same time that the materials of the second follow-up study were

coded. By this simultaneous coding we believe that any inconsisten-
cies in the data of the various periods were resolved. As it had been
possible in the course of the second follow-up investigation to
secure additional data covering the first five-year follow-up period,
the *unknown* categories of the first period were filled in and previously missing data reduced.

First Five Year Follow-up Period. 1-35
Some Factors for Correlation from Second Five Year Period. 35-73

K 7 — M. R. STUDY — PRE-CODING CARD

M. R. Name   John   Jones   M. R. No.   —   No. —

1	1	¹=26	3-12	54
2	12	²27	1-7-70	55
3	3	²28	3 - 9	56
4	2	29	3	¹57
²5	3 - 8	30	9	58
²6	3 - 7	²31	2 - 12	59
²7	5 - 70 8	=32	3	60
8	3	33	12	61
9	12	34	2	62
10	12	35		²63
11	11	36		²64
12	11	37		²65
13	2	38		²66
²14	4 - 10	39		67
15	11	40		²68
²16	2 - 8 7	41		69
17	4	42		70
18	3	43		71
19	4	44		72
20	8	45		73
²21	3 - 9	46		74
22	4	47		75
23	4	48		76
²24	2 - 7	49		77
25	2	50		78
		51		79
		²52		80
		²53		

EXHIBIT B. PRE-CODING CARD USED IN
SECOND FIVE-YEAR PERIOD

Exhibit B shows a code card filled out before additional data had
been gathered in the course of the second investigation for the first

five-year period and corrected after the additional data had been gathered, thus illustrating the extent to which it was possible in certain cases to reduce the *unknown* category or even to amplify previously incomplete data. The numbers printed on the card represent the factors listed in the *Code-Table Index*, Appendix C, Section B, but special numbers have been assigned to them for purposes of coding. The numbers entered on the card by hand represent the categories and correspond with those given the categories under the corresponding factor in the *Code-Table Index*. Category numbers have been crossed out and replaced by others when more intensive investigation in the second follow-up period made it necessary to change the findings.

The case presented on the card reproduced here is rather an extreme one, but it well illustrates the fact that *unknown* categories of the first five-year period were reduced and some data amplified as a result of further follow-up in connection with the present investigation.

There are, of course, innumerable details in the carrying out of this research and in the preparation of materials for analysis, tabulation, and writing, but this is not the place to present them. There is considerable material in our files which would be extremely useful in teaching others the methods developed for our investigations, but the gaining of this knowledge beyond a certain point necessitates an actual feel of the materials by first-hand experience with them. Beyond the description, therefore, which we have already given in our previous works and in this one there can be no particular value in any more detailed presentation of the methodology of the research.

Appendix B

DEFINITION OF TERMS

ALL the factors included in this research are listed alphabetically. The number or numbers appearing immediately below each factor are its designations in the Code-Table Index (Appendix C), in which are listed all the categories of each factor, together with their incidence. Where no definition or explanation of a factor or its categories appears, the factor is sufficiently explained by its title and its subclasses (Appendix C).[1]

The numerical designations of the factors are as follows:

1 through 17 refers to the Family Background of the 510 Offenders
18 through 59 refers to their Personal History prior to Commitment to the Reformatory
60 through 83 refers to their History in the Reformatory
84 through 103 refers to their History during Parole from the Reformatory
1-1 through 1-58 refers to their History during the First Five-Year Follow-up Period
2-1 through 2-H139 refers to their History during the Second Five-Year Follow-up Period

ACTUAL LENGTH OF PAROLE SUPERVISION
99

Theoretical parole period—the time from the date of release on parole to the official date of expiration of parole.

Actual parole period—theoretical parole period minus the portions thereof during which the offender was not technically under the supervision of the parole officer, as, for instance, offender deported or was outside Massachusetts by permission of the parole department, and not required to make reports; offender committed to a State Hospital, or a penal institution, and therefore, according to the rules of the Massachusetts Parole Department, no longer supervised by the parole agent. If, however, offender disappeared while on parole, or was excused from reporting by virtue of good behavior, or

[1] The definitions of terms are largely adapted from those used in *500 Criminal Careers* and *500 Delinquent Women*.

though in another State or country was required to report by letter, he was in all such instances considered to be technically under parole supervision.

For details, see *500 Criminal Careers,* p. 176, note 31.

AGE AT END OF PERIOD

2–2

That is, at end of second five-year period. If dead, age at time of death.

AGE AT FIRST ARREST

50

AGE AT FIRST COMMITMENT TO PENO-CORRECTIONAL INSTITUTION

55

Includes age at commitment to Reformatory on sentence studied if there had been no previous commitment.

AGE AT FIRST ILLICIT HETEROSEXUAL EXPERIENCE

24

AGE AT FIRST KNOWN DELINQUENCY

49

Refers to official or unofficial delinquency. See PRINCIPAL COMPONENT OF MISCONDUCT for definition of *official* and *unofficial.*

AGE AT LEAVING SCHOOL

37

AGE AT TIME OF COMMITMENT

65

AGE BEGAN WORK

38

AGE FIRST LEFT HOME

20

Refers to the first departure of the offender from the home in which he was reared that signifies a serious breach in his family ties. It denotes, usually, a separation of six months or more from the family, or repeated brief separations.

AGE OF OFFENDER AT FIRST BREAK IN HOME

9

ALIASES

1–21, 2–1a

The purpose of this is to indicate not what aliases were used, but whether any were used.

ARRESTS
46

ASSOCIATES IN CRIME
64, 2–57a

ATTITUDE OF COMMUNITY
2–H133

Friendly—community knows that he is an ex-prisoner, yet accepts him into its activities, as church, club, and so on.

Indifferent—community does not know that offender is an ex-prisoner; or though aware of this fact makes no discrimination against him either because its own moral standards are low or because no attention has been directed toward him.

Hostile—community, as police, church, club, neighbors, know offender is an ex-prisoner and discriminate against him because of it.

ATTITUDE OF OFFENDER TO MARITAL RESPONSIBILITY
2–23

If more than one marriage occurred during the period, refers to the more recent marriage.

Assumes—does not neglect or desert wife or children; not unfaithful; not physically or mentally abusive to wife or children. Assumes economic responsibilities toward them. See ECONOMIC RESPONSIBILITY.

Neglects—fails to meet the above standard.

Inapplicable—offender is single, or separated, or divorced from wife prior to beginning of period judged and has no children.

ATTITUDE OF RELATIVES TO OFFENDER
2–18b

Friendly—fond of him and keep in touch.

Indifferent—do not make effort to keep in touch but are not openly hostile.

Hostile—show definite dislike or disapproval of him.

ATTITUDE OF WIFE TO MARITAL RESPONSIBILITY
2–24

If more than one marriage occurred during the period, refers to the more recent marriage.

Assumes—does not neglect or desert husband or children; not unfaithful; not physically or mentally abusive to mate or children. Carries on her household duties and meets her economic responsibilities. See definition of ECONOMIC RESPONSIBILITY.

Neglects—fails to meet the above standard.

Inapplicable—wife separated or divorced from offender prior to beginning of the period studied. Included here even though she has the custody of offender's children.

ATTITUDE TO CHILDREN

2–29a

This includes illegitimate children and stepchildren.

Good—fond of, cares for.

Fair—casual toward; or fond of but neglectful.

Poor—no affection, or no supervision, or is abusive.

If children not living with offender, i.e. have been placed out or in institution or with wife:

Good—if he maintains an interest in them to the greatest extent possible within the limits of the particular situation.

Fair—if he at least keeps in touch with them even only casually.

Poor—if he is entirely out of touch with children.

Inapplicable—if offender is in an institution throughout the period.

ATTITUDE TO INVESTIGATION

2–H82

The purpose of this is to guide the field investigators in these continuing five-year follow-ups. If offender is found to be very hostile, for example, every attempt will be made in the next follow-up to get the information needed without seeing offender personally.

AVERAGE FREQUENCY OF PERSONAL CONTACT WITH CASE BY PAROLE AGENT

103

AVERAGE FREQUENCY OF VISITS TO PAROLEES BY AGENTS

102

AVERAGE PERIOD OF TIME HELD JOB

96, 1–23, 2–43

Refers to employment in legitimate occupation.

AVERAGE WAGE—WEEKLY

1–29, 2–41

Refers to wage in legitimate employment. In a maintenance position $5 a week is added to wage to cover board and room.

BROKEN AND INADEQUATE HOMES

10

Broken homes are those from which one or both parents are absent because of death, desertion, separation, or divorce or absent for a year or longer as a result of imprisonment, illness, or emigration.

Homes *otherwise inadequate* are those which, though not broken are unsuited to the wholesome rearing of children because of intemperance, immorality, delinquency of parents, neglect or improper oversight by parents, constant quarreling between parents, and so on.

BY WHOM FIRST PAROLE JOB SECURED

91

CAUSE OF FIRST BREACH WITH HOME

21

See AGE FIRST LEFT HOME, for definition.

CAUSES OF DEATH

1–4, 2–H105

CHURCH ATTENDANCE

34, 1–50, 2–47a

Regular means attending every Sunday.

Irregular means attending occasionally.

CITIZENSHIP

19

COLOR OF OFFENDER

18a

COMPANIONSHIPS

27, 1–51a, 2–48a

Harmful—any with whom association might lead to delinquency, as street-corner loafers, cheap poolroom habitués, youths who live by their wits, habitual drinkers, professional gamblers, and so on.

Harmless—those whose influence, though not necessarily wholesome, is at least not harmful.

COMPETENCE OF WIFE AS HOMEMAKER

2–26

If more than one marriage occurred during the period, refers to the more recent marriage.

Good—systematic, economical, clean, neat.

Fair—some of the qualifications of the good homemaker, but because of low mentality or temperamental difficulties or other reasons, at times a poor homemaker.

Poor—wasteful, indifferent, careless.

Inapplicable—wife not living with offender since beginning of period studied.

CONDUCT IN REFORMATORY

72

CONJUGAL RELATIONS

32, 1–37, 2–22

Refers to legal and common law marriages. If more than one marriage, the conjugal relations of offender and his most recent wife are judged.

Good—living together compatibly without undue quarreling.

Fair—living together but grossly incompatibile. Indifferent or hostile to each other but no open breach.

Poor—separation, desertion, divorce, or occasional desertion or separation during period studied.

Inapplicable—not living with wife at least since beginning of period studied.

DATE OF EXPIRATION OF SENTENCE

83

DELINQUENCIES

48a, 89a, 1–19a, 2–51a

See SERIOUSNESS OF DELINQUENCY.

Non-delinquent—no police or court record, or dishonorable discharge or desertion from army or navy, or unofficial misconduct for which he might be arrested, as drinking, abuse of family, stealing, and so on. See OFFICIAL RECOGNITION OF DELINQUENCY for definition. Technical automobile violations in the absence of any other misconduct are allowable in this category.

Delinquent—official or unofficial misconduct except technical auto violations in the absence of other delinquencies.

For differentiation between *serious* and *minor* delinquents, see SERIOUSNESS OF OFFICIALLY RECOGNIZED OFFENSES.

DELINQUENCY IN FIFTH YEAR

1–22, 2–57b

See DELINQUENCIES

DELINQUENCY IN FIRST FIVE-YEAR PERIOD

1–18

The categorization of delinquency utilized in *500 Criminal Careers,* pp. 188–189, has been discarded for the purposes of the second follow-up study.

Non-delinquent—no police or court record and no unofficial misconduct, as drinking to point of intoxication, abuse of family, stealing, and so on. See OFFICIAL RECOGNITION OF DELINQUENCY for definition.

Delinquent—*official* or *unofficial* misconduct.

Inapplicable—in institution or chronically ill during most of period.

DELINQUENCY IN FIVE-YEAR PERIOD AND FIFTH YEAR IN COMBINATION

1–22, 2–61, 2–62

See PRINCIPAL COMPONENT OF MISCONDUCT for definition of *official* and *unofficial* misconduct.

DELINQUENCY OF CHILDREN

2–29b

DELINQUENCY OF WIFE

2–30

See OFFICIAL RECOGNITION OF DELINQUENCY for definition of *official* and *unofficial*. If more than one wife, refers to the last one and is concerned with delinquency only *since* the marriage.

DEPENDENTS

1–39, 2–33b

Refers to wife, children (including illegitimate children), and parents (if they need his aid).

DEPRESSION VICTIM

2–H116

Because of the fact that the financial depression that began in 1929 entered into the midst of this second five-year period, it was necessary to take account of the effect of it on our group. This tabulation purports to indicate whether offender's employment has been seriously affected or not, directly because of the depression.

DISPOSITION OF EARNINGS

1–41, 2–34a

DRINK

26

Use of liquor to point of intoxication

DRUG ADDICTION

22

ECONOMIC CONDITION

2, 1–40, 2–33a

Comfortable—means having accumulated resources sufficient to maintain self and family for at least four months.

Marginal—means living on daily earnings and accumulating little or nothing; being on the border between self-support and dependency. Here are included instances in which temporary aid is resorted to occasionally in order to tide over a critical situation; for example, in case of illness or seasonal unemployment. Aid may have been given for a few days or even a month, and with this little assistance the offender was able to manage his own problem.

Dependent—receiving aid continuously from public funds or from persons outside the immediate family. This means chronic dependency. Aid may have been given in the form of money, clothing, food, coal, or medical assistance. As here applied, dependency is due to reasons other than the economic depression of 1929–1933.

Dependent on relatives—receiving considerable or continuous aid from relatives, *not because of the depression of 1929–1933.*

Dependent on agencies or relatives—receiving considerable or continuous aid *solely because of the economic depression.* This applies to men who would otherwise be self-supporting.

ECONOMIC RESPONSIBILITY

45a, 1–42, 2–31a

In history prior to commitment to Reformatory and in first five-year follow-up period, a three-fold classification was used. For the purposes of categorization in the second five-year period, the good and fair group are merged in the one category *meets responsibility.* See *500 Criminal Careers,* p. 200.

Meets responsibility—if single, separated, widowed, or divorced and is without legal dependents (wife, children, or parents) supports self even if by illegitimate employment and at least in *marginal* circumstances with only occasional public or private aid or sporadic assistance from relatives; if he has dependents (wife, children, or parents) makes every reasonable effort to support them at least in *marginal* circumstances. See ECONOMIC CONDITION, for definition.

Fails to meet responsibility—does not meet the above standard through his own fault, or contracts avoidable debts or receives frequent aid from social agencies or relatives when should be self-supporting.

Inapplicable—unable to meet his responsibilities through no fault of his own, as chronic physical or mental illness or defect, depression victim, and so on.

ECONOMIC RESPONSIBILITY IN FIFTH YEAR

2–64

See ECONOMIC RESPONSIBILITY

EDUCATION OF PARENTS

8

This refers to the highest educational achievement of either parent.

EDUCATIONAL ACTIVITIES

1–53, 2–47b

As attendance at evening school, vocational classes, and so on.

EMOTIONAL STABILITY OF OFFENDER

2–4b

This refers to normality of emotional control. Though we have no way of measuring this we can indicate whether lack of control is present as gleaned from nature of offenses, from temper outbursts, irresponsible leaving of jobs, quarreling with wife or children, and so on.

ENVIRONMENTAL HISTORY IN FIFTH YEAR

2–65a

See ENVIRONMENTAL JUDGMENT

ENVIRONMENTAL JUDGMENT

2–15b

This is a composite picture of neighborhood influences (see NEIGH-BORHOOD INFLUENCES for definition), physical aspects of the home (see HOME—PHYSICAL for definition), and moral standards (see MORAL STANDARDS OF HOME for definition).

If a person has been assigned to the *good* class in all three of these factors, he is here assigned to the *good* class.

If *fair*—fair.

If *poor*—poor.

If two *good*, one *fair* or *poor*—fair (except if neighborhood influences *fair*)—good.

Two *fair*, one *good*—fair.

Two *fair*, one *poor*—fair.

Two *poor*, one *fair*—poor.

Two *poor*, one *good*—fair.

One *good*, one *fair*, one *poor*—fair.

EXTENT OF RUDIMENTARY OCCUPATIONAL ACQUIREMENTS AT REFORMATORY

78

Acquisition of the rudiments of a trade means to have sufficient knowledge of it to work fairly satisfactorily on the outside. For an estimate of the length of time necessary to learn the rudiments of trades taught in the Reformatory, see *500 Criminal Careers*, p. 161, note 45.

FAMILIES KNOWN TO SOCIAL SERVICE AGENCIES

3

This refers in the pre-Reformatory period to parents and married siblings of offender, or to offender and his wife if he is married.

FAMILY DELINQUENCY

1

Refers to *official* and *unofficial* delinquency of own or step-parents and siblings and of blood relatives (includes intemperance). For definition of official and unofficial delinquency see OFFICIAL RECOGNITION OF DELINQUENCY.

FAMILY RELATIONSHIPS

33a, 1–48, 2–16b

If offender is married, his relation to his wife and children is judged.

If offender is separated, divorced, or widowed, his relation to his children is judged.

If offender has no children, his relation to his parents and siblings is judged.

If offender is single, separated, divorced, or widowed before beginning of period studied and has no children, his relation to his parents and siblings is judged.

If the offender is single, his relation to his parents and siblings is judged.

If offender has a common law wife, his relationship to her is judged as though she were his legal wife.

The standard of *socially acceptable conduct* in regard to family relationships adopted for our purposes is the following: The man must not be harming his family in any way deemed injurious to the institution of the family, that is, if married, he must not neglect or desert his wife or children during period judged, and must not be separated or divorced from his wife during the period judged, not have illicit relations with other women, nor be abusive to his wife or children, nor be continually away in the evening if this is not necessary to his business.

If single, separated, widowed, or divorced before beginning of period and living away from home, he must be in touch with his parents or nearest relatives.

If single, separated, widowed, or divorced, and living at home, he must give evidence that he considers it more than merely a convenient place to sleep and eat in; for example, he must not be continually out in the evening if this is not necessary to his work, or live at home only when he is in need of funds.

A man is a failure in his *family relationships* if he does not meet the above standard.

FAMILY RELATIONSHIPS IN FIFTH YEAR

2–63a

See FAMILY RELATIONSHIPS.

FREQUENCY OF ARRESTS

51, 1–11, 2–55

In calculating the frequency of pre-Reformatory arrests the time spent in penal and other institutions which fell within the period between the first known arrest and the arrest resulting in the sentence to the Reformatory was subtracted from the total period. The number of months remaining after legitimate subtractions had been made were divided by the number of arrests occurring within the period.

Frequency of arrests during the five-year follow-up periods is calculated on the basis of sixty months, from which is subtracted the length of time the offender spent in penal or non-penal institutions during this period. Into the time remaining is divided the number of arrests occurring in the sixty-month period.

FREQUENCY OF COMMISSION OF OFFENSES IN REFORMATORY

73

FREQUENCY OF CONVICTIONS

52, 1–13, 2–56

Calculated in same way as frequency of arrests. See FREQUENCY OF ARRESTS. In the pre-Reformatory period "files" were not tabulated as convictions.

GAMBLING

25

GANG LIFE

2–50a

A *gang* is distinguished from a *crowd* by being organized for a definite anti-social purpose (thieving, malicious mischief, and so on), and having specific leadership.

GRADE ATTAINED IN SCHOOL

36

HABITS

21a, 1–53a, 2–49

This refers to any habits which might lead to conflict with the law, as drink, drugs, gambling, stealing, lying, illicit sexuality.

HAUNTS

1–52, 2–48b

Good—places of recreation that are under strict and constructive supervision as public playgrounds, community centers, school recreation centers.

Fair—places in which there is no constructive supervision but where the influences are not necessarily harmful (as political clubs, bowling alleys, public dance halls, skating rinks, beaches), since the great majority of patrons are not there for illicit purposes.

Poor—places that are distinctly harmful in character in that most of those who frequent them have an illicit purpose as their objective, i.e. houses of ill fame, gambling dens, bootlegging joints.

HEALTH

2–4a

Venereal disease refers to the presence of either gonorrhea or syphilis during the period regardless of when contracted.

Partial handicap—see PARTIAL INCAPACITY.

Total handicap—see TOTAL INCAPACITY.

Chronic illness—see CHRONIC ILLNESS.

HIGHEST WAGE—WEEKLY

44, 97, 1–30, 2–42

Refers to wage in legitimate employment.

In a maintenance position $5 a week is added to wage to cover board and room.

HOME—PHYSICAL

1–43, 2–12

Good—adequate space (not more than two people, excluding infant, to a bedroom), light, ventilation, cleanliness, sufficient furniture.

Fair—more than one of the above advantages plus one unfavorable factor.

Poor—overcrowding, dirt, shabby furnishing, lack of ventilation, and so on. One or more of these factors and no advantages to offset them. Cases of extreme overcrowding belong in this class even if the home is good or fair in other respects.

Varied—here are included those, the character of whose physical home changes from one type to another as described above. The predominant type is indicated however.

HOUSEHOLD STABILITY

1–46, 2–17

This refers to the number of changes in the household experienced by offender during the period studied. For example, if offender lives for a time with his parents, and then goes away to work and lives alone, this is counted as one change; if he then marries and lives with wife, this is two changes; if he leaves his wife to go to a mistress, this is three changes; if he leaves a mistress and returns to the parental home, this is four changes.

In a case in which offender has been living with his parents and marries, and the wife comes to live with offender in his parental home, this is not tabulated as a change, so that any additions to the household are not changes in the sense in which the term is used here. Commitments to institutions are not rated as changes.

ILLEGITIMATE OCCUPATION

1–31, 2–45a

This refers to any occupation, engagement in which is illegal, as prostitution, bootlegging, deriving profits from prostitution, drug selling, disposing of stolen goods.

ILLEGITIMATE OCCUPATION—NATURE OF

1–31

Refers to any illegitimate occupation, whether it is engaged in only occasionally or continuously.

IMPROVEMENT IN OCCUPATIONAL STATUS BY REFORMATORY TRAINING

81

This refers to improvement in skill whether in the same or in a different occupation. See definition of SKILL.

INDUSTRIAL EXPERIENCES—GEOGRAPHICAL SPREAD

1–6a, 2–H107

INDUSTRIAL HISTORY

1–32, 2–34b

Success—work habits *good,* and offender a *regular* worker.

Partial success—work habits *good,* and offender either *fairly regular* or *irregular* worker; or work habits *fair* or *poor,* but offender works *regularly.*

Failure—work habits *poor,* and offender is a *fairly regular* or *irregular* worker or is engaged in illicit occupations to the exclusion of all, or almost all, legitimate work.

INDUSTRIAL HISTORY IN FIFTH YEAR

2–63b

See INDUSTRIAL HISTORY.

INSTITUTIONAL EXPERIENCES—NATURE OF

54, 1–15, 2–H139

INSTITUTIONAL EXPERIENCES—NATURE OF (BY TYPE)

1–6, 2–7

INSURANCE

45, 2–32a

Refers to insurance of any type carried by the offender on himself or on members of his family.

INSURANCE—PREMIUM PAID BY WHOM

45, 2–32b

INTELLIGENCE

69

INTERVIEW WITH

1–2a, 2–H81a

Refers to persons interviewed in connection with field investigation. Categorized in the order indicated in the code.

KIND OF OFFENDER IN REFORMATORY

74

Very frequent—indicates the commission of offenses oftener than once in four months.

Frequent—one offense in four months.

Occasional—less frequently than once in four months.

KIND OF WORKER IN REFORMATORY

82

Good—capable and conduct excellent.

Fair—no special ability, though of good conduct; or industrious but of bad disposition, or lazy, or requiring constant supervision.

Poor—of no ability and disposition bad, or lazy, or requiring continual supervision.

LEGITIMACY OF CHILDREN

2–27

LEISURE

28a, 1–54, 2–46a

Constructive—member of a well-supervised social group as Y.M.C.A.; utilizes leisure to further himself culturally or vocationally (as by attendance at night school).

Negative—at least not engaging in harmful activities, even though not utilizing his time constructively.

Harmful—indulges in forms of recreation which might lead to criminal conduct (such as membership in gangs, association with bootleggers, prostitutes, loafers, drug addicts, drunkards, gamblers).

LEISURE IN FIFTH YEAR

2–65b

See LEISURE.

LENGTH OF OCCUPATIONAL EXPERIENCES IN THE REFORMATORY

79

Refers to skilled and semi-skilled work only.

See EXTENT OF RUDIMENTARY OCCUPATIONAL ACQUIREMENTS AT REFORMATORY, for definition.

LENGTH OF SENTENCE

61

LENGTH OF TIME FIRST PAROLE JOB HELD

92

LONGEST PERIOD OF TIME HELD JOB

41, 95, 1–24, 2–44

Refers to legitimate employment only.

MARITAL HISTORY JUDGMENT

2–25

If more than one marriage occurred during the period, refers to the more recent marriage.

A composite of CONJUGAL RELATIONS and ATTITUDE TO MARITAL RESPONSIBILITY.

Good—husband and wife living together and both assuming their marital responsibilities. See ATTITUDE OF OFFENDER TO MARITAL RESPONSIBILITY and ATTITUDE OF WIFE TO MARITAL RESPONSIBILITY.

Fair—husband and wife living together, but one or both not assuming their marital responsibilities.

Poor—husband and wife not living together during period judged or living together but separating frequently. One or both neglecting their marital responsibilities.

MARITAL—NUMBER OF MARRIAGES OCCURRING DURING FIVE-YEAR PERIOD

2–21

This refers to legal and illegal marriages.

MARITAL STATUS

31, 1–36, 2–19, 2–20

If offender died before the end of the period judged his marital status at the time of his death is referred to.

An illegal marriage means that a ceremony has been performed although one or both of the spouses were not free by law to marry.

MARRIAGES—PERIOD IN WHICH OCCURRED

1–35

MENTAL CONDITION

70, 2–6

This refers to mental balance or mental abnormalities.

Although two or more of the conditions listed may be present, the person is classified once in the order of precedence indicated in the code.

Personality liabilities—unusually strong emotional or conative traits such as impulsiveness, lack of self-control, self-indulgence, egocentricity, fault finding, hypochondria, introspectiveness, jealousy, melodramaty, obscenity, opinionation, profanity, seclusiveness, self-pity, self-justification, vanity, unsociality, lack of foresight, irresponsibility.

MENTAL DISEASE OR DEFECT IN FAMILY

17

Refers to own parents, siblings, and blood relatives.

MILITARY OR NAVAL SERVICE OF PAROLEES

90

MOBILITY—NATURE OF

1–49, 2–15a

Mobility—changes in environment which indicate that the individual does not take root and establish close associations in any one community. This is indicated by excessive moving within a city (more than once a year); or from city to city on the average of once in two years; or by coming from or going to a foreign country.

MOBILITY PRIOR TO COMMITMENT

29

See MOBILITY—NATURE OF.

As used here the term differs from its application in the first and second five-year period in that *excessive mobility* does not include moving about within a city. It does not include mobility prior to thirteen years of age.

MONTHS IN COMMUNITY

1–5, 2–11

Refers to the number of months out of the sixty-month period studied that the offender is not under restraint and therefore freely able to commit crime. From the sixty-month period is deducted the time offender spends in penal or non-penal institutions (including hospitals for mental and physical diseases), or is under the disciplinary restraint of the army, navy, or merchant marine.

MORAL STANDARDS OF HOME

2–16a

Refers to the atmosphere of the home in which offender lives during the period judged. If he lives alone, the standards of his immediate physical environment are taken cognizance of. In making the judgment, the conduct and attitude of the offender himself are excluded.

Good—in offender's immediate environment there are thrift, temperance, wholesome ideals, conformity to sex standards, and no delinquency except for slight automobile violations or violations of license laws.

Fair—in offender's immediate environment although there is no delinquency among those comprising the immediate family, or, if offender living alone, among the persons in his nearest vicinity, there is an absence of thrift, temperance, and wholesome ideals, and there is no positive disapproval of criminal conduct.

Poor—in offender's immediate environment there is criminality, alcoholism, or other delinquency, or though no actual delinquency, such conduct is lightly regarded and even encouraged.

NATIVITY

13, 14, 18

NATURE OF OCCUPATIONAL EXPERIENCES IN REFORMATORY

76

NATURE OF OFFENSES COMMITTED IN REFORMATORY

71

Rebellion against authority—means crookedness, possessing anything brought in from outside, insolence, defiance, disobedience of orders, refusal to work, malicious mischief, vile language, attempt to escape, lying.

Violence against the person—includes fighting, quarreling, assault (other than sex).

Violence against property—means destroying or injuring state property or stealing.

Lack of self-control—is reflected in such offenses as inattention, idleness, laziness, laughing, fooling, talking, shirking.

NATURE OF OFFICIALLY RECORDED DELINQUENCY

1–8

NEIGHBORHOOD INFLUENCES

1–45, 2–14

Good—no street gangs, no centers of vice or crime within a radius of two square blocks in the city or a mile in the country; opportunity for constructive recreation (see LEISURE for definition) within easy walking distance—as public playgrounds, school or community centers, parks, and so on.

Fair—no street gangs, no centers of vice or crime within a radius of two square blocks in the city, or a mile in the country, but no opportunities for constructive recreation within walking distance.

Poor—corner gangs, centers of vice or crime within a radius of two square blocks in the city or a mile in the country regardless of whether facilities for constructive recreation exist within walking distance or not.

NEIGHBORHOOD—TYPE

1–44, 2–13

This refers to the predominant type of neighborhood in which offender is resident during the period judged.

A radius of two square blocks in the urban districts and of one mile in rural from the particular place of residence is judged and characterized as:

Urban partly residential—if it is a business, factory, or lodging house area.

Urban residential—if it is an area of tenements or private houses used mainly as permanent residences and not to house transients, and from which business or factory areas are more than two blocks distant.

Suburban—an outlying residential district of a city in which there are mainly detached houses with considerable open space.

Rural or small town—any town of five thousand population or under is classified here.

Varied—if a person has shifted during the period studied from a neighborhood of one type to another type, he is classified in this group but the type of neighborhood in which he has lived the most during the period studied is indicated.

NUMBER OF ARRESTS

46a, 1–9, 2–53

NUMBER OF CHILDREN

31a, 1–38, 2–28

Refers to legitimate and illegitimate children *living* at the end of the period under consideration.

NUMBER OF CHILDREN IN FAMILY FROM WHICH OFFENDER COMES

15

Refers only to living siblings and includes half and step siblings.

NUMBER OF CONSTRUCTIVE OPPORTUNITIES GIVEN BY COURTS

59

NUMBER OF CONVICTIONS

46b, 1–10, 2–54

NUMBER OF DIFFERENT OCCUPATIONS

2–40a

If change of occupation is within the same branch of employment it is not counted as a change. This does not mean number of different jobs but *different types* of work.

NUMBER OF OCCUPATIONAL EXPERIENCES GIVEN EACH OFFENDER IN REFORMA-TORY

77

NUMBER OF PAROLEES WHOSE PERMITS TO BE AT LIBERTY WERE REVOKED

85

NUMBER OF PENAL EXPERIENCES

1–14, 2–8

NUMBER OF REVOCATIONS AND IN-BETWEEN-SENTENCES TO THE REFORMATORY

86

NUMBER OF SOCIAL SERVICE AGENCIES

3a, 1–57, 2–35

NUMBER OF TIMES 203 PAROLE VIOLATORS WERE RETURNED TO REFORMATORY

89

NUMBER OF TYPES OF SOCIAL SERVICE AGENCIES

5

OCCUPATION OF FATHER

7

Classified as in United States Census of 1920.

OCCUPATION OF MOTHER

11

Refers to the occupation of own mother, step or foster mother, at the time of offender's commitment to the Reformatory. If mother is deceased refers to her occupation at time of death.

OFFENSE FOR WHICH COMMITTED TO REFORMATORY ON SENTENCE STUDIED

60

OFFICIAL RECOGNITION OF DELINQUENCY

89b, 1–7, 2–51b

Official—based on police or court records.

Unofficial—delinquency for which the person has not come to the attention of official agencies of the law.

OPINION OF REFORMATORY OFFICIALS REGARDING EQUIPMENT OF OFFENDER TO EARN LIVELIHOOD ON OUTSIDE

80

PARTIAL INCAPACITY

2–H102

This refers to a physical condition which makes industrial adjustment difficult but not impossible, that is, to the abolition of or serious impairment of certain industrially useful functions as sight, hearing, locomotion.

PERIOD STUDIED—END

2–1b

This refers to the date of the end of the second five-year period.

PHYSICAL CONDITION AT TIME OF COMMITMENT

67

"*Physical condition* considers bodily states including disease conditions and the effects thereof, as contrasted with *physique,* which connotes the effects of growth, development, and approach to type in size, form, frame, proportions, and so on. One having a poor physique might conceivably be in good physical condition—that is, poorly developed or small in size or crippled, yet be free from disease, well nourished and strong. A flabby musculature is an element in physique, to be sure, but it is of more cogent significance in determining physical condition. The two terms are not synonymous; but neither can the one be wholly extricated from the other. To illustrate further, if one is undernourished, his physique might not show it conspicuously, but his classification in physical condition would be modified because of the fact. An impaired heart is of primary importance to physical condition, but affects the physique secondarily if to any extent." (Definition prepared by Dr. Guy Fernald of the Massachusetts Reformatory.)

PHYSIQUE AT TIME OF COMMITMENT

68

See PHYSICAL CONDITION for definition.

PREDOMINANT OFFENSE

59a, 1–20, 2–52

This is a social category of offenses which is based on unofficial as well as official misconduct. See OFFICIAL RECOGNITION OF DELINQUENCY for definition of official and unofficial. The type of offense most characteristic of the offender is the predominant offense.

PRINCIPAL COMPONENT OF MISCONDUCT

48b, 1–19, 2–66

Each offender is categorized once, in the order indicated in the code.

PRIOR COMMITMENTS TO MASSACHUSETTS REFORMATORY

57

RANK OF OFFENDER AMONG SIBLINGS

16

Refers only to living siblings and includes half and step siblings.

REASON FOR DIFFERENCE BETWEEN THEORETICAL AND ACTUAL LENGTH OF PAROLE SUPERVISION

100

Dropped—refers to those cases which are no longer kept under supervision because of migration to a foreign country, failure to report, residence in another state.

REASON FOR LEAVING FIRST PAROLE JOB

93

See USUAL REASON FOR LEAVING WORK.

REASON FOR 280 REVOCATIONS OF PERMIT TO BE AT LIBERTY
87

REASONS FOR FAILURE IN CONDUCT
2–H136
This is usually the opinion of the case analyst but sometimes of the offender or relatives.

REASONS FOR IMPROVEMENT IN CONDUCT
2–H135
This is usually the opinion of the case analyst but sometimes of the offender or relatives.

REASONS FOR LEAVING ALL JOBS
94
See USUAL REASON FOR LEAVING WORK.

RELATION TO NEAREST RELATIVES
1–47, 2–18a
This refers to the ties existing between the offender and his nearest blood relatives, that is, to one or both parents if they are living, or to his siblings if one or both parents are not living.

RELIGION
35

REPRESENTED BY COUNSEL ON OFFENSE FOR WHICH COMMITTED
66

RETURNS TO REFORMATORY FOLLOWING 280 REVOCATIONS OF PERMIT
88

SAVINGS
43, 2–31b
This refers to the savings of the offender if he is single, separated, widowed, or divorced before the beginning of the period judged, and to the joint savings of himself and his wife if he is living with her.

SCHOOLING IN REFORMATORY
75

SERIOUSNESS OF DELINQUENCY
48a, 89a, 1–19a
See SERIOUSNESS OF OFFICIALLY RECOGNIZED OFFENSES for definitions.

SERIOUSNESS OF OFFICIALLY RECOGNIZED OFFENSES
1–17
Serious—refers essentially to felonies (property crimes, pathological

sex offenses and rape, homicide, escape or rescue). See *500 Criminal Careers,* pp. 354, 355, 356 for details.

Minor—refers to such offenses as drunkenness, vagrancy, begging, violation of liquor laws, lewd and lascivious cohabitation, fornication, non-support, assault and battery, disturbing the peace, peddling without license.

SEVEREST PENALTY IMPOSED BY COURTS PRIOR TO COMMITMENT

56

SEX IRREGULARITY

23

SIZE OF COMMUNITY IN WHICH RESIDENT AT TIME OF COMMITMENT

30

SKILL

6, 39, 1–28, 2–38a

This generally refers to the *usual* occupation. If it is difficult to determine the *usual* occupation, the highest degree of skill which the individual reflects in any of the occupations he holds during the period judged, is indicated.

The *unskilled laborer* does any kind of rough work to which he can be sent without any training whatever. Mere strength of hand or keenness of eye, untutored through any course of apprenticeship or training, serves for him.

The *semi-skilled* worker uses tools and processes requiring learning. He cannot take up the kind of work unless he has had a period of experience under guidance or of study. The processes, however, are not greatly complicated and the period of training is likely to be short (three days to three months, perhaps).

The *skilled* worker uses tools and processes which are usable only by one who has given a long period of time, perhaps at least a year, to the acquiring of the skill.

SKILL IN FIFTH YEAR

2–38b

See SKILL for definition.

SOCIAL SERVICE NEEDS NOT MET

1–56, 2–60

Refers to the needs of the offender if he is single and has no dependents, or if he is separated or divorced from his wife before period judged and has no legal responsibility for any children.

Refers to the needs of himself and his wife and children if he is married and living with his wife, or though separated, has legal responsibilities toward her and their children during the period judged.

If he has been separated or divorced from his wife before the beginning of the period judged but his children live with or are dependent upon him for support, the needs in such a total situation are considered here.

The needs indicated are only the glaring ones. For example, those tabulated as *needing vocational guidance* are the men who in the period judged were very poor and irregular workers; those set down as *requiring recreational supervision* were the men who spent their leisure time harmfully and not merely negatively; those *in need of family guidance* are the ones who had serious marital difficulties or in some instances those who though unmarried were getting along poorly with nearest relatives. Those *in need of relief* were men in a state of total dependency. If their relatives were taking care of them they were not tabulated as needing relief.

See TYPES OF SOCIAL SERVICE AGENCIES.

SOCIAL SERVICES RENDERED

1-55

See SOCIAL SERVICE NEEDS NOT MET.

SOCIETY MEMBER

28, 1-51, 2-46b

Refers to any organization of which offender was a member during period, that offers opportunity for constructive use of leisure time, including church societies, lodges, Y.M.C.A., K.C., and so on.

STEADINESS OF EMPLOYMENT

1-26, 2-39a

Regular—very few breaks (not more than an average of two months of unemployment a year) in otherwise continuous employment up to 1929. (Because of the industrial depression it was deemed necessary to characterize employment up to 1929 only, if the man was really a victim of the depression.)

Fairly regular—unemployment in excess of two months a year but compensated for by periods of sustained work (up to 1929).

Irregular—frequent or long protracted periods of unemployment, and none of sustained employment (up to 1929).

STEP OR FOSTER PARENTS

12

STREET LIFE

2–50b

This refers to hanging about on street corners.

SUMMARY OF ARRESTS

47, 1–11a, 2–H125

Refers to arrests as officially recorded.

SUMMARY OF ARRESTS—BY TYPE

2–58

SUMMARY OF DISPOSITIONS—BY TYPE

2–59

SUMMARY OF DISPOSITIONS

53, 1–12, 2–H126

THEORETICAL LENGTH OF PAROLE SUPERVISION

98

Means the period of time from date of parole to the official expiration of the sentence. For further details see *500 Criminal Careers,* p. 176, note 31.

TIME IN PENAL INSTITUTIONS

1–16, 2–9, 2–10

TIME OF DEATH OF 55 OFFENDERS

1–3

TIME SPENT IN INSTITUTIONS PRIOR TO COMMITMENT

58

Refers to penal and non-penal institutions.

TIME SPENT IN REFORMATORY ON SENTENCE STUDIED

62

TOTAL INCAPACITY

2–H103

This refers to any conditions which make for complete disability in industry, that is, such abolition or impairment of a function or functions as to leave no industrial value in the person.

TOTAL NUMBER OF VISITS MADE BY PAROLE AGENTS

101

TRANSFER TO OTHER INSTITUTIONS FROM REFORMATORY

63

TYPES OF SOCIAL SERVICE AGENCIES

4, 1–58, 2–36

This refers in *4* to offender's family, and in *1–58* and *2–36* to offender himself if he has no dependents, is single, widowed, divorced, or separated, and has no legal obligations to a wife or children during period under consideration; and refers to him, his wife, and children if he is married and living with them.

Health, physical—includes free hospital care, free clinic attendance, supervision by a hospital social service department or department of health.

Health, mental—includes free mental hospital or out-patient treatment, and schools for feebleminded.

Relief—includes not only aid in the form of money, but clothing, food, groceries, medicines, and so on.

Family welfare—has to do with adjusting problems of domestic relations, unemployment.

Child or adolescent welfare—includes all agencies of the non-punitive type dealing specifically with problems of childhood and adolescence, as the Society for the Prevention of Cruelty to Children, Children's Aid Society, Judge Baker Guidance Center, Division of Child Guardianship, and so on.

Correctional—any agencies dealing with delinquent minors as state industrial schools, truant schools.

USED MASSACHUSETTS REFORMATORY OCCUPATION

1–34, 2–40b

This refers to the utilization of the vocational training received at the Reformatory, either directly by engaging in the selfsame occupation, or indirectly by using a technique learned at the Reformatory but in a different occupation.

USUAL OCCUPATION

40, 1–33, 2–37

Refers to the type of occupation which is engaged in the longest during the period, or which is returned to the most frequently.

If it is impossible to determine the usual occupation because of the variety of work engaged in, tabulated as *varied*.

USUAL REASON FOR LEAVING WORK

93, 94, 1–27, 2–45b

This refers to the most frequent reason if possible; otherwise the last known.

Fault of worker—arrested; discharged for inefficiency, dishonesty, drink, and so on.

Not fault of worker—laid off because of slack work, left to marry, left because of illness.

VENEREAL DISEASE

68a

See HEALTH.

WHEREABOUTS AT END OF PERIOD

1–1, 2–H81b

WITH WHOM LIVING

33, 1–2, 2–3

WORK HABITS

42, 1–25, 2–39b

Good—refers to the person who is reliable, industrious, commended by employers. Is an asset to them.

Fair—refers to the person who has the qualifications of the good worker but who permits his work to be interrupted by periodic drinking, by the drug habit, by occasional vagabondage, by deliberate choice of irregular occupation such as longshoring, for the chief purpose of having leisure time.

Poor—refers to the worker who is unreliable, loafs, is lazy, dishonest, unstable, a vagabond and floater, ambitionless, wayward, or is engaged in illegitimate work.

YEAR FIRST RELEASED ON PAROLE

84

Appendix C

CODE-TABLE INDEX

For definitions of the factors, see Appendix B, *Definition of Terms,* in which they are arranged alphabetically.

SECTION A. FACTORS IN *500 CRIMINAL CAREERS*

In this section are presented in tabular form the data assembled and studied in *500 Criminal Careers.* The tables are numbered in the order of the appearance of the data in the text of that book, the page reference being made in each instance. A few tables, however, have been placed in a more logical order than they appeared in that book, and some tables which were not utilized in *500 Criminal Careers* (although they had been tabulated), or which state in somewhat different form tabular data already utilized, are now included. These tables are 3a, 18a, 31a, 45a, 46a, 46b, 48a, 59a, 89a, 89b, 1–2a, 1–6a, 1–10a, 1–11a, 1–58a. Other tables which do not appear in the first work at all but which were tabulated in connection with the second follow-up study have been inserted in their proper places: Tables 1–2, 1–6, 1–11, 1–13, 1–14, 1–20, 1–21, 1–22, 1–23, 1–24, 1–26, 1–27, 1–29, 1–31, 1–36, 1–37, 1–39, 1–41, 1–44, 1–46, 1–47, 1–49, 1–51, 1–52, 1–53.

The following tables are in summary form and the reader is referred to the text of *500 Criminal Careers* for further details. All tables total 510 unless otherwise indicated. Wherever a line appears beneath a category (as in Table 1–6, Institutional Experiences, under the category "none") it means that in the categories appearing below the line, each case may have been recorded more than once. This is a *multiple* table and totals to more than 510. The sum of the incidence of the categories "inapplicable," "unknown if any," and "none," if subtracted from the total cases involved, gives the number of cases actually represented by the remaining categories or subclasses of the factor.

The numerical designations of the factors in Section A are as follows:

1 through 17 refers to the Family Background of the 510 Offenders
18 through 59 refers to their Personal History prior to Commitment to the Reformatory
60 through 83 refers to their History in the Reformatory
84 through 103 refers to their History during Parole from the Reformatory
1-1 through 1-58 refers to their History during the First Five-Year Follow-up Period

Family Background (Tables 1 through 17)

1. FAMILY DELINQUENCY   p. 111

Number of cases

61	No delinquency
220	Official delinquency
121	Unofficial delinquency
108	Unknown

2. ECONOMIC CONDITION   p. 113

129	Comfortable
252	Marginal
66	Dependent
63	Unknown

3. FAMILIES KNOWN TO SOCIAL SERVICE AGENCIES   p. 113, 114

189	Not known to social service agencies
254	Known to social service agencies
67	Unknown

3A. NUMBER OF SOCIAL SERVICE AGENCIES

189	None
158	One
58	Two
26	Three
12	Four
67	Number unknown

4. Types of social service agencies dealing with 254 families   p. 114

157 Relief agencies
62 Correctional agencies
86 Child welfare agencies
81 Health agencies
14 Other

5. Number of types of social service agencies dealing with 254 families   p. 114

158 One type
58 Two types
26 Three types
12 Four types

6. Skill of fathers   p. 114

143 Skilled
92 Semi-skilled
157 Unskilled
118 Unknown

7. Occupation of father   p. 115

291 Manufacturing and mechanical industries
53 Commerce
37 Transportation
36 Agriculture, forestry, animal industry
26 Domestic and personal service
11 Public service and professions
9 Extraction of minerals
47 Unknown

8. Education of parents   p. 115

44 Both parents illiterate
103 One parent reads and/or writes
266 Both parents read and write
18 One parent attended common school
44 Both parents attended common school
3 One or both parents attended high school

4 One parent attended college
28 Unknown

9. AGE OF OFFENDER AT FIRST BREAK IN HOME   p. 116

84 Under five years
61 5 to 10
69 10 to 15
85 15 to 20
2 20 to 25
5 Age unknown
204 Home not broken

10. BROKEN AND INADEQUATE HOMES   p. 117

306 Broken homes
123 Homes not broken but otherwise inadequate
81 Homes not broken or inadequate

11. OCCUPATION OF MOTHER   p. 117

328 Housewife
128 Worked out (part or full time)
54 Unknown

12. STEP OR FOSTER PARENTS   p. 117

36 Stepmother
45 Stepfather
2 Stepmother and stepfather
12 Foster parent
415 No step or foster parents or unknown

13. NATIVITY OF PARENTS   p. 118

127 Both parents native
278 Both parents foreign
72 One parent native, other foreign
33 Unknown

14. NATIVITY OF PARENTS AND OFFENDER   p. 118

259 One or both parents foreign, offender native
132 Parents and offender native

98 Parents and offender foreign
21 Unknown

15. NUMBER OF CHILDREN IN FAMILY FROM
WHICH OFFENDER COMES   p. 120
35 One
54 Two
72 Three
76 Four
78 Five
63 Six
53 Seven
71 Eight or more
 8 Unknown

16. RANK OF OFFENDER AMONG SIBLINGS   p. 120
138 First
103 Second
120 Third
57 Fourth
29 Fifth
29 Sixth or more
34 Unknown

17. MENTAL DISEASE OR DEFECT IN FAMILY   p. 121
27 One parent mentally diseased or defective
10 One or both parents and one or more siblings
36 One or more siblings
16 No mental disease or defect in immediate family but among blood
    relations
421 None or unknown

Personal History Prior to Commitment to the Reformatory
(Tables 18 through 59a)

18. NATIVITY OF OFFENDER   p. 123
402 Native born
107 Foreign born
  1 Unknown

18A. Color of offender

23 Negro
487 White

19. Citizenship of 107 foreign-born offenders   p. 124

22 Naturalized
76 Alien
4 First papers
5 Unknown

20. Age first left home   p. 125

94 Did not leave home prior to commitment to Reformatory
8 Age unknown
25 6 years and under
38 7–10 years
133 11–14 years
162 15–18 years
50 19 years and over

21. Cause of first breach with home   p. 125

94 Did not leave home
148 Sentenced to peno-correctional institution
71 Break-up of household
56 Went away to work
35 Migration to the United States
26 Ran away from home for six months or more or for frequent brief periods
24 Committed to non-penal institution
20 Enlisted in Army or Navy
13 Committed to care of State
5 Quarreled with family
13 Various other reasons, such as to escape authorities
5 Reasons unknown

21A. Habits—summary of   p. 126

397 Illicit sex
200 Drink
17 Drugs
225 Gambling

22. DRUG ADDICTION   p. 126

17 Yes
11 Doubtful
470 No
12 Unknown

23. SEX IRREGULARITY   p. 126

397 Illicit sexual relations
98 None
13 Doubtful
2   Unknown

24. AGE AT FIRST ILLICIT HETEROSEXUAL EXPERIENCE   p. 126

20 Under 14 years
112 14 to 16 years
163 16 to 18 years
72 18 to 20 years
17 20 to 22 years
3   22 years and over
10 Age unknown
113 None or unknown if any

25. GAMBLING   p. 127

225 Yes
283 No
2   Unknown

26. DRINK   p. 127

200 Yes
308 No
2   Unknown

27. COMPANIONSHIPS   p. 127

481 Harmful
27 Harmless
2   Unknown

28. SOCIETY MEMBER ANY TIME PRIOR TO COMMITMENT   p. 128

429 No
81 Yes

28A. LEISURE AND HABITS   p. 210
o Constructive
18 Negative
487 Harmful
5 Unknown

29. MOBILITY   p. 129
233 Excessive mobility
277 No mobility

30. SIZE OF COMMUNITY IN WHICH RESIDENT AT TIME OF COMMITMENT   p. 130, 131
30 Under 2500 population
8 2500–5000
23 5000–10,000
113 10,000–50,000
92 50,000–100,000
81 100,000–500,000
127 500,000–1,000,000
14 Over 1,000,000
13 No fixed habitat
9 Unknown

31. MARITAL STATUS AT TIME OF COMMITMENT   p. 131
48 Married
462 Single

31A. NUMBER OF CHILDREN IN MARRIED GROUP
16 None
18 One
3 Two
10 Three
1 Four or more

32. CONJUGAL RELATIONS OF 48 MARRIED OFFENDERS   p. 131
29 Good
6 Fair
13 Poor

33. With whom living at time of commitment   p. 131

339 With one or both own parents
  4 With a step or foster parent
 25 With siblings
 30 With other near relatives
 28 With wife
 70 Alone
  1 Army
 13 Unknown

33A. Family relationships   p. 206

137 Succeed
296 Fail
 77 Unknown or inapplicable

34. Church attendance   p. 131

 39 Regular
407 Irregular
 14 None
 50 Unknown

35. Religion   p. 132

335 Catholic
145 Protestant
 20 Hebrew
  6 Other
  4 Unknown

36. Grade attained in school   p. 132

 11 Never attended school
 54 Grade attained unknown
195 Fifth grade or less
208 Sixth to ninth grade
 21 Ninth grade
 18 Entered but did not complete high school
  2 Completed high school
  1 Entered college

37. AGE AT LEAVING SCHOOL   p. 133

11   Did not attend school
38   Under 14 years
143 14 years
88   15, 16 years
11   17 years and over
219 Unknown

38. AGE BEGAN WORK   p. 134

35   Under 14 years
145 14 years
155 15, 16 years
35   17, 18 years
8   19 years and over
130 Unknown
2   Never worked

39. SKILL   p. 134

232 Semi-skilled or skilled
273 Unskilled
2   Never worked
3   Unknown

40. USUAL OCCUPATION   p. 135

2   Never worked
101 Rough labor and odd jobs
62   Trucking and chauffeuring
112 Factory hands
54   Skilled trade
33   Farming
31   Salesmen and store clerks
31   Bellhops and messengers
25   Restaurant work
59   Miscellaneous

41. LONGEST PERIOD OF TIME HELD JOB   p. 135

47   Indefinite, unknown, or did not work
71   Less than 3 months

90 3–6 months
45 6–9 months
65 9–12 months
59 12–18 months
51 18–24 months
46 24–36 months
36 36 months and more

42. WORK HABITS   p. 135

75 Good
105 Fair
198 Poor
132 Unknown

43. SAVINGS   p. 136

19 Savings
479 No savings
12 Unknown

44. HIGHEST WAGE—WEEKLY   p. 136

420 Unknown
2 Never worked
6 Under $5
25 $5–$10
17 $10–$15
17 $15–$20
13 $20–$25
10 $25 or more

45. INSURANCE—PREMIUM PAID BY   p. 136

243 Insurance
   14 Premium paid by self
  210 Premium paid by relatives
   19 Unknown by whom premium paid
252 No insurance
15 Unknown

45A. ECONOMIC RESPONSIBILITY

70 Meet responsibility

326 Fail to meet responsibility
114 Unknown

46. ARRESTS   p. 140

433 Arrested
 47 Never arrested
 30 Unknown

46A. NUMBER OF ARRESTS

 47 No arrests
 68 One
 67 Two
124 Three, four
 90 Five, six
 84 Seven and over
 30 Unknown or unknown if arrested

46B. NUMBER OF CONVICTIONS

 19 None (though arrested)
 99 One
 82 Two
 71 Three
 57 Four
 36 Five
 20 Six
 13 Seven
 36 Eight and over
 30 Number unknown or unknown if any
 47 No arrests

47. SUMMARY OF (1944) ARRESTS   p. 140, 141

950 Against property
 18 Against chastity
 14 Against family and children
495 Against public health (except drink and drugs)
279 Drunkenness
 10 Drug addiction
107 Against the person
 61 Other
 10 Unknown

270 *LATER CRIMINAL CAREERS*

48. Official recognition of delinquency p. 142

434 Based on official record
23 Unofficial
4 Non-delinquent
49 Unknown

48a. Seriousness of delinquency

4 Non-delinquent
62 Minor delinquent
395 Serious delinquent
49 Unknown or seriousness unknown

48b. Principal component of misconduct p. 359, 360

4 Non-delinquent
49 Unknown
368 Conviction for serious offense
3 Warrant out for serious offense
8 Dishonorable discharge or desertion from army or navy
15 Unofficial serious
1 Arrest for serious, not followed by conviction
50 Conviction for minor offense
8 Unofficial minor
4 Arrest for minor, not followed by conviction

49. Age at first known delinquency p. 143

4 Under 7 years
11 7, 8 years
36 9, 10 years
86 11, 12 years
139 13, 14 years
117 15, 16 years
78 17, 18 years
28 19, 20 years
10 21 years and over
1 Unknown

50. Age at first arrest p. 143

1 Under 7 years
10 7, 8 years

34 9, 10 years
76 11, 12 years
91 13, 14 years
85 15, 16 years
88 17, 18 years
55 19, 20 years
69 21 years and over
 1 Unknown

51. FREQUENCY OF ARRESTS   p. 144

83 Incalculable as only one arrest or frequency unknown
47 No arrests
30 Unknown if arrested
14 Arrested once in three months or less
55 Once in 3–6 months
84 Once in 6–9 months
52 Once in 9–12 months
35 Once in 12–15 months
31 Once in 15–18 months
23 Once in 18–21 months
18 Once in 21–24 months
38 Once in 24 months and over

52. FREQUENCY OF CONVICTIONS   p. 145

 30 Unknown if arrested
139 Incalculable (no convictions or one conviction)
  6 Once in less than 3 months
 38 Once in 3–6 months
 55 Once in 6–9 months
 48 Once in 9–12 months
 42 Once in 12–15 months
 29 Once in 15–18 months
 22 Once in 18–21 months
 17 Once in 21–24 months
 84 Once in 24 or more months

53. SUMMARY OF (1944) DISPOSITIONS   p. 145

604 Commitments
549 Probations

221 Fines
59 Commitments for non-payment of fine
237 Files
18 Other convictions (restitution, orders to leave the state, lashings)
245 R.P.O., nol prossed, no bill, not guilty, released
11 Disposition unknown, or other, or awaiting disposition

54. Institutional experiences—nature of (604)   p. 145

11 Schools for feebleminded
6 Children's protectorates
50 Truant schools
209 Industrial schools
76 Reformatories
216 Jails, houses of correction, state farms, workhouses
22 Prisons
14 Unknown or other

55. Age at first commitment to peno-correctional institution   p. 145

48 12 years and under
59 13, 14 years
69 15, 16 years
137 17, 18 years
88 19, 20 years
109 21 years and over

56. Severest penalty imposed by courts prior to commitment   p. 146

268 Commitment to penal institutions
124 Probation
10 Commitment for non-payment of fine
12 Fine
19 Arrested but not convicted
47 Never arrested or convicted
30 Unknown whether arrested

57. Prior commitments to Massachusetts reformatory   p. 146

451 None
49 One
8 Two

1 Three
1 Four

58. TIME SPENT IN INSTITUTIONS PRIOR TO COMMITMENT   p. 146

162 None
77 10 months or less
73 11–20 months
66 21–40 months
62 41 months and over
70 Unknown

59. NUMBER OF CONSTRUCTIVE OPPORTUNITIES GIVEN
BY COURTS PRIOR TO COMMITMENT TO
MASSACHUSETTS REFORMATORY   p. 147

167 None
156 One
60 Two
29 Three
15 Four
6 Five or more
47 No arrests
30 Unknown if arrested

59A. PREDOMINANT OFFENSE

53 Inapplicable, unknown, not determinable
279 Against property
15 Against chastity
2 Against family and children
33 Against public health, safety, and policy
44 Drink
4 Drugs
8 Against person
72 Varied

History in the Reformatory (Tables 60 through 83)

60. OFFENSE FOR WHICH COMMITTED TO REFORMATORY
ON SENTENCE STUDIED   p. 150

416 Against property
34 Against chastity

  1 Against family and children
 14 Against public health, safety, and policy (except drink and drugs)
  1 Drunkenness
  1 Drug addiction
 24 Against person
 15 Juvenile delinquency
  4 Unknown

61. LENGTH OF SENTENCE p. 150

375 5-year indeterminate
 54 2-year indeterminate
  6 Other indeterminate
 31 3- to 6-year determinate
 31 1- to 3-year determinate
 12 Less than 1-year determinate
  1 During minority

62. TIME SPENT IN REFORMATORY ON SENTENCE STUDIED p. 151

 19 Less than 6 months
 72 6 to 12 months
184 12 to 18 months
 94 18 to 24 months
 34 24 to 30 months
 43 30 to 36 months
 24 36 to 42 months
 40 42 months and over

63. TRANSFER TO OTHER INSTITUTIONS FROM REFORMATORY p. 152

456 Not transferred to other institution
 47 Transferred to other institution and not returned to Reformatory
  7 Transferred to other institution but returned to Reformatory

64. ASSOCIATES IN CRIME FOR WHICH COMMITTED TO REFORMATORY p. 152

202 Alone
173 With one other
 72 With two others
 48 With three or more others
 15 Unknown

65. Age at time of commitment   p. 153

20	Under 17
153	17, 18
133	19, 20
81	21, 22
40	23, 24
36	25, 26
12	27, 28
18	29, 30
13	31 and over
4	Unknown

66. Represented by counsel on offense for which committed   p. 153

101	Yes
338	No
71	Unknown

67. Physical condition at time of commitment   p. 153

412	Good or fair
32	Poor
66	Unknown

68. Physique at time of commitment   p. 154

66	Good
369	Fair
33	Poor
42	Unknown

68a. Venereal disease at time of commitment   p. 154

118	Yes
328	No
64	Unknown

69. Intelligence   p. 156

154	Normal
112	Dull
104	Borderline
93	Feebleminded

3 Imbecile
44 Unknown

70. Mental condition p. 157

105 No known mental disease, distortion, or personality liabilities
160 No known mental disease or distortion but personality liabilities
68 Psychopathic personality
9 Epilepsy
13 Sex perversion
2 Congenital syphilis
12 Psychosis
12 Alcoholic deterioration
3 Drug deterioration
126 Unknown

71. Nature of offenses (3135) committed
in reformatory p. 158, 159

1496 Serious
   1055 Rebellion against authority
   345 Violence against person
   92 Violence against property
   4 Sex offenses
1639 Minor
   1552 Lack of self-control
   46 Personal disorderliness
   41 Miscellaneous

72. Conduct in reformatory p. 159

88 Non-offenders
422 Offenders

73. Frequency of commission of offenses
in reformatory p. 159

9 Unknown
88 Non-offender
2 One offense in two weeks
69 One offense a month
80 One offense in two months
66 One offense in three months

48 One offense in four months
23 One offense in five months
24 One offense in six months
49 One offense in over six to twelve months
52 One offense in twelve months and over

74. KIND OF OFFENDER IN REFORMATORY p. 159

88 Non-offender
219 Very frequent
48 Frequent
143 Occasional
12 Unknown

75. SCHOOLING IN REFORMATORY p. 160

367 Required to attend school
    41 Attained 3rd grade or less
    68 Attained 4th grade
    73 Attained 5th grade
    72 Attained 6th grade
    40 Attained 7th grade
    41 Attained 8th grade
    32 Graduated 8th grade
97 Not required to attend school
4 Attendance required but impossible because of illness or brief stay at Reformatory
42 Unknown

76. NATURE OF (1317) OCCUPATIONAL EXPERIENCES IN REFORMATORY p. 160

267 Weaving, spinning, cloth finishing, other mill work
240 Farm work
76 Care of grounds, work in yard
74 Plumbing
67 Sloyd
49 Furniture or cabinet making, finishing, chair caning
48 Clerical, bookkeeping
38 General cleaning
38 Dining room
38 Cow barn, horse barn, stockade

35 Laundry
32 Engineers' department
31 Tailor
27 Carpentry
26 Band
26 Mechanical drawing
21 Engraving
20 Blacksmith
18 Painting
18 Freight handler
17 Compositor
14 Shoe repairing
14 Kitchen work
10 Cooking
10 Masonry
10 Sawyer
9 Tinsmith
6 Hospital attendant
5 Janitor
4 Barber
29 Other

77. NUMBER OF OCCUPATIONAL EXPERIENCES GIVEN EACH
OFFENDER IN REFORMATORY   p. 160

4 None
100 One
162 Two
141 Three
68 Four
28 Five
0 Six
6 Seven
1 Unknown

78. EXTENT OF RUDIMENTARY OCCUPATIONAL
ACQUIREMENTS AT REFORMATORY   p. 161

397 Engaged in an occupation sufficiently long to learn the rudiments
83 Not engaged in an occupation sufficiently long to learn the rudiments
30 Unknown or inapplicable

85. Number of parolees whose permits to be at
liberty were revoked   p. 167

203 Revocation as result of violation of rules of parole or arrest
 59 No revocation even though misbehaved
    20 Arrested or wanted by police
    14 Arrested and sentenced to other institutions
     3 Dishonorable discharge or desertion from army or navy
    22 Other violation of parole
212 No misbehavior, unknown, or inapplicable

86. Number of revocations and in-between sentences
(329) to the reformatory   p. 168

280 Revocation of permit, without new sentence
 49 Revocation of permit and new sentence

87. Reason for 280 revocations of permit to be at liberty p. 168

125 Charge of crime by police
 70 Sentence to other institution
 85 Violation of rules of parole

88. Returns to reformatory following 280
revocations of permit   p. 168

198 Returned to Reformatory
 82 Not returned to Reformatory

89. Number of times 203 parole violators were
returned to reformatory   p. 168

 46 Not returned
 96 Returned once
 40 Returned twice
 13 Returned three times
  7 Returned four times
  1 Returned five times

89a. Seriousness of delinquency

126 Non-delinquent
 77 Minor delinquent
210 Serious delinquent

36 Inapplicable as no parole period
61 Unknown

89B. Official recognition of delinquency

36 Inapplicable
126 No delinquency
251 Based on official record
36 On unofficial only
61 Unknown

90. Military or naval service of parolees   p. 169

160 Yes
285 No
29 Unknown if any

91. By whom first parole job secured   p. 170

22 Did not have job on release or went directly into army
92 By parolee
171 By family
40 By parole agent
6 By Reformatory official
5 By politician
2 By minister
4 By friend
4 Other
128 Unknown by whom secured

92. Length of time first parole job held   p. 171

53 Not at all
125 Less than one month
60 One month
52 Two months
32 Three months
18 Four months
18 Five months
23 Six to nine months
13 Nine to twelve months
10 Twelve months or longer

48 Unknown
22 Inapplicable

93. Reason for leaving first parole job   p. 171

70 Laid off immediately or shortly as work only temporary
70 Left voluntarily
37 Entered military service
30 Wanted by police or parole authorities
27 Illness or injury
17 Left as dissatisfied
12 Discharged as unsatisfactory
 8 Did not leave
203 Unknown or inapplicable

94. Reasons for leaving all jobs (1096)   p. 172

298 Laid off
185 Left voluntarily
110 Entered military service
149 Wanted by police or parole authorities
93 Illness or injury
93 Left as dissatisfied
168 Other reasons or unknown

95. Longest period of time held job   p. 172

 6 Did not work
23 Less than one month
75 One to three months
72 Four to six months
71 Seven to nine months
30 Ten to twelve months
45 Over a year
152 Unknown or inapplicable

96. Average period of time held job   p. 173

52 Less than one month
104 One to two months
87 Two to three months
63 Three to four months

67 Four to six months
32 Six to twelve months
 9 Over twelve months
60 Unknown or inapplicable

97. Highest wage—weekly p. 173

 11 Less than $10
 53 $10 to $15
 97 $15 to $20
 56 $20 to $25
 39 $25 to $30
 19 $30 to $35
 14 $35 to $40
  9 $40 and over
176 Unknown or inapplicable

98. Theoretical length of parole supervision p. 176

 53 9 months or less
 45 10–20 months
 18 20–30 months
 60 30–40 months
216 40–50 months
 82 50 months or more

99. Actual length of parole supervision p. 176

 54 None
159 9 months or less
 93 10–20 months
 30 20–30 months
 42 30–40 months
 65 40–50 months
 31 50 months or more

100. Reason for difference between theoretical and actual length of parole supervision p. 177

241 No difference
 19 Parolee in another state by permission
 53 Parolee disappeared
 57 Parolee excused from reporting

60 Parolee dropped
44 Parolee not supervised after release from army or navy

101. Total number of visits made by parole agents (4120)   p. 177

533 Parolees seen personally
2202 Relatives and others seen
1385 Visits made but no one seen

102. Average frequency of visits to parolees by agents   p. 178

215 Parolee not seen
3 Parolee seen once a month
50 Parolee seen once in over 1 to 6 months
62 Parolee seen once in 6 to 12 months
44 Parolee seen once in 12 to 18 months
27 Parolee seen once in 18 months and over
73 Unknown or inapplicable

103. Average frequency of personal contact with case by parole agent   p. 178

27 No contact with case
55 Case contacted once a month
185 Case contacted once in over 1 to 3 months
38 Case contacted once in 3 to 6 months
26 Case contacted once in 6 to 12 months
11 Case contacted once in 12 to 18 months
8 Case contacted once in 18 months and over
124 Incalculable or unknown or inapplicable

History During First Five-Year Follow-Up Period
(Tables 1–1 through 1–58)

1–1. Whereabouts at end of period   p. 183

68 Boston and environs
111 Other cities in Massachusetts
81 Other states
85 Penal institution
31 Fugitive from justice
6 Hospital for mental disease

1 Hospital for physical disease
6 Army or navy
7 Foreign country
6 Wandering about
6 At sea
55 Dead
20 Known for part of period but not at end
27 Entirely unknown

1–2. WITH WHOM LIVING AT END OF PERIOD

52 Parents (one or both or step)
16 Sibling or siblings (no parents)
4   Other relatives
156 Wife and children
0   Children (no wife)
13 Sweetheart
3   Employer
72 Alone
88 Institution
1   Other (army)
55 Dead
50 Unknown

1–2A. INTERVIEW WITH

193 Offender
179 Near relatives
105 Others or record data
33 Inapplicable or died before beginning of period

1–3. TIME OF DEATH OF 55 OFFENDERS   p. 183

11 While in Reformatory
22 During parole
22 During first five-year period

1–4. CAUSE OF DEATH (55)   p. 183

13 Tuberculosis
13 Pneumonia or influenza
5   Heart disease
13 Accident
11 Other

1–5. Months in community   p. 184

190 60 months
 72 48–60 months
 34 36–48 months
 37 24–36 months
 33 12–24 months
 28 Less than 12 months
 13 Not at all
 33 Died before beginning of period
 70 Unknown

1–6. Institutional experiences—nature of (by type)

 36 Inapplicable
 38 Unknown if any
219 None

_____

  2 School for feebleminded
 17 Hospital for mental disease
 14 Hospital for chronic physical disease
182 Penal institution
 26 Army or navy

1–6a. Institutional experiences—geographical spread of 361

264 Massachusetts
 93 Other states
  1 Canada
  3 Europe

1–7. Official recognition of delinquency   p. 184

 89 No delinquency
307 Based on official record
 26 On unofficial only
 88 Unknown or inapplicable

1–8. Nature of officially recorded delinquency against 307 offenders   p. 185

938 Arrests
 17 Warrants for arrest
  7 Escapes from penal institutions

23 Dishonorable discharges from army or navy
29 Desertions from army or navy

1–9. NUMBER OF ARRESTS   p. 185, 186

99 One
50 Two
55 Three, four
14 Five, six
14 Seven, eight
28 Nine or more
108 No arrests*
142 Unknown

1–10. NUMBER OF CONVICTIONS

27 None (though arrested)
98 One
47 Two
31 Three
16 Four
8 Five
10 Six
23 Seven and over
142 Number unknown or unknown if any
108 No arrests, or inapplicable

1–11. FREQUENCY OF ARRESTS

54 Inapplicable (institution, died before or early in period, ill)
42 Unknown if arrested or number of arrests unknown
236 Incalculable (only one arrest, that is, one in sixty months), or no arrests
13 One arrest in less than 3 months
31 One arrest in 3 to 6 months
25 One arrest in 6 to 9 months
20 One arrest in 9 to 12 months
20 One arrest in 12 to 15 months

---

* 47 Chargeable with criminal conduct but not actually arrested as some were in penal institutions throughout the five-year period or during part thereof on sentence imposed during the parole period, or warrants were out for their arrest, or they were dishonorably discharged or had deserted from the army or navy.

8 One arrest in 15 to 18 months
31 One arrest in 18 to 21 months
4 One arrest in 21 to 24 months
26 One arrest in 24 months and over

I–IIA. SUMMARY OF (938) ARRESTS

244 Against property
60 Against chastity
35 Against family and children
168 Against public health
388 Drink
12 Drugs
13 Against person
18 Other

I–12. SUMMARY OF DISPOSITIONS OF (938) ARRESTS   p. 186

312 Commitment
128 Probation
214 Fine
36 Commitment for non-payment of fine
118 File
3 Restitution
15 Nol pros
6 No bill
106 Not guilty, released, unknown

I–13. FREQUENCY OF CONVICTIONS

54 Inapplicable (institution, dead, or ill)
41 Unknown if arrested
253 Incalculable (only one arrest or no arrests and no convictions or only one conviction)
9 One conviction in less than 3 months
26 One conviction in 3 to 6 months
24 One conviction in 6 to 9 months
11 One conviction in 9 to 12 months
18 One conviction in 12 to 15 months
7 One conviction in 15 to 18 months
17 One conviction in 18 to 21 months

6 One conviction in 21 to 24 months
44 One conviction in 24 months and over

1–14. NUMBER OF PENAL EXPERIENCES

42 Inapplicable (dead, non-penal institution)
242 None
40 Unknown if any
100 One
39 Two
32 3–4
11 5–6
1 7–8
0 9–10
2 11 or more
1 Number unknown

1–15. INSTITUTIONAL EXPERIENCES—NATURE OF (361*)   p. 186

95 Prisons and penitentiaries
38 Reformatories
217 Jails, houses of correction, state farms, workhouses
11 Hospitals for mentally diseased or defective

1–16. TIME SPENT IN PENAL INSTITUTIONS (BY 187 MEN WHO SERVED 397 SENTENCES†)   p. 186

221 None
35 Less than 5 months
26 5 to 10 months
21 11 to 15 months
13 16 to 20 months
13 21 to 25 months
12 26 to 30 months
14 31 to 35 months
7 36 to 40 months
46 Over 40 months
69 Unknown
33 Inapplicable

* Including 49 sentences imposed during parole period and served for part or all of five-year post-parole period. Excludes 36 commitments for non-payment of fine.
† This includes 36 commitments for non-payment of fine.

1–17. Seriousness of (1063*) officially recognized
offenses (committed by 307 men)   p. 187

376 Serious
687 Minor

1–18. Delinquency in first five-year period   p. 188

 89 Non-delinquent
 71 Partial failure
262 Total failure
 88 Unknown or inapplicable

1–19. Principal component of misconduct   p. 189

 89 Non-delinquent
 25 Sentence for serious offense imposed during parole and served for
     part or all of five-year period
144 Conviction for serious offense
 15 Warrant out for serious offense
 22 Dishonorable discharge or desertion from army or navy
  1 Unofficial serious offense
  5 Arrest for serious offense, not followed by conviction
 95 Conviction for minor offense
  1 Arrest for minor offense, not followed by conviction
 25 Unofficial minor offense
 88 Unknown or inapplicable

1–19A. Seriousness of delinquency   p. 189

 89 Non-delinquent
121 Minor delinquent
212 Serious delinquent
 88 Unknown or inapplicable

1–20. Predominant offense

 60 Inapplicable (institution, chronic illness, dead)
 25 Unknown if arrested
 90 Non-delinquent during post-parole period (even though parole
     delinquent and served post-parole sentence)

* Includes 49 offenses committed during parole for which sentence was served for part
or all of post-parole period.

101 Crimes against property
16 Crimes against chastity (including pathological sex offenses)
12 Crimes against family and children
40 Crimes against public health, safety, and policy (except drink and drugs)
78 Drink
5 Drugs
6 Against person
45 Varied
32 Unknown or no outstanding type of misconduct

1–21. ALIASES

95 Used aliases
155 Do not use aliases
75 Unknown
56 Inapplicable (institution, dead)
129 No arrests

1–22. DELINQUENCY IN FIVE-YEAR PERIOD AND FIFTH YEAR IN COMBINATION

90 Non-delinquent
116 Delinquent minor throughout
188 Delinquent serious throughout
16 Delinquent minor upgrade
18 Delinquent serious upgrade
82 Unknown, inapplicable (as in institution, dead)

1–23. AVERAGE PERIOD OF TIME HELD JOB

76 Inapplicable (institution, unable to work, dead)
24 Illegitimate occupation throughout
20 Incalculable (on and off in one place for years, or one long job and others short)
133 Less than 3 months
33 3–6 months
21 6–9 months
16 9–12 months
43 1–2 years
21 2–3 years
2 3–4 years

28 4–5 years
93 Unknown

1–24. Longest period of time held job

76 Inapplicable (institution, dead, never worked, or ill)
18 Incalculable (as on and off in one place)
24 Illegitimate occupation throughout
105 Less than three months ("indefinite" falling in this group)
28 3–6 months
27 6–9 months
22 9–12 months
50 1–2 years
36 2–3 years
14 3–4 years
38 4 years and over
72 Unknown

1–25. Work habits   p. 193

134 Good
98 Fair
167 Poor
111 Unknown or inapplicable

1–26. Steadiness of employment

74 Inapplicable (institution over 55 months, illness, death)
80 Regular
125 Fairly regular
144 Irregular
24 Illegitimate occupation
61 Unknown
2 Army

1–27. Usual reason for leaving work

96 Inapplicable (ill, institution, illegitimate occupation, dead)
52 Steady worker, seldom changes
173 Fault of worker (discharged for inefficiency, dishonesty, laziness, regardless of mental condition)
71 Not fault of worker—seasonality

27   To better self
 2   Other
89   Unknown

1-28. SKILL   p. 194

 76   Skilled
178   Semi-skilled
180   Unskilled
 76   Unknown or inapplicable

1-29. AVERAGE WAGE—WEEKLY

 75   Inapplicable (dead, institution, never worked)
 24   Illegitimate occupation throughout
  0   Less than $5
  5   $5-$10
 20   $10-$15
 31   $15-$20
 50   $20-$25
 42   $25-$30
 34   $30-$35
 15   $35-$40
 18   $40 and over
196   Unknown

1-30. HIGHEST WAGE—WEEKLY   p. 194

 34   Less than $20
 39   $20-$25
 56   $25-$30
 45   $30-$35
 30   $35-$40
 25   $40-$45
 19   $45 and over
262   Unknown or inapplicable

1-31. ILLEGITIMATE OCCUPATION—NATURE OF*

104   Unknown if any
 69   Inapplicable (institution, dead, ill)

* Below the line are presented all the illegitimate occupations in which 75 men engaged.

262 No illegitimate occupation
51 Illegitimate occupation part of time
24 Illegitimate occupation throughout

---

3 Deriving profits from prostitution
29 Bootlegging
2 Receiving stolen goods
43 Other (begging, drug selling, gambling, passing raised bills, lives by crime)
4 Unknown

I–32. INDUSTRIAL HISTORY p. 196

68 Success
112 Partial success
172 Failure
158 Unknown or inapplicable

I–33. USUAL OCCUPATION p. 197

78 Rough labor and odd jobs
51 Trucking, teaming, chauffeuring
55 Factory work
9 Farm work
19 Salesmen and store clerks
74 Skilled trades (electricians, plumbers, carpenters, etc.)
19 Restaurant work
45 Other
160 Unknown or inapplicable

I–34. USED MASSACHUSETTS REFORMATORY OCCUPATION p. 198

131 Used occupational training
233 Did not use occupational training
146 Unknown or inapplicable

I–35. MARRIAGES—PERIOD IN WHICH (234) OCCURRED p. 199

48 Married during pre-Reformatory period
79 Married during parole period
107 Married during first five-year period

1–36. Marital status at end of period

10 Unknown as to status at end of period
30 Unknown if married or single
198 Single
163 Married, living with wife
2 Illegal marriage, living with wife
37 Separated
16 Divorced
7 Widowed
11 Married but confined in institution (not legally separated)
1 Illegally married, separated
34 Dead

1–37. Conjugal relations

15 Inapplicable (separated, divorced, widowed before beginning of period)
30 Unknown whether married or single
198 Single
116 Good
34 Fair
57 Poor
20 Unknown (or marriage too brief to judge)
40 Institution throughout, or dead

1–38. Number of children in married group   p. 204

47 None
71 One
34 Two
17 Three
14 Four
6 Five
1 Six
3 Seven
2 Eight
39 Unknown if any

1–39. Dependents

132 No dependents

272   Dependents
106   Inapplicable or unknown or dead

1-40. Economic condition   p. 199
43   Comfortable
330   Marginal
51   Dependent
86   Unknown or inapplicable

1-41. Disposition of earnings
74   Inapplicable (institution, no earnings, dead)
58   Unknown
204   Self only or mostly
137   Wife and/or children, no dependent parents or unknown as to parents
6   Wife and/or children, dependent parents (not supporting parents)
29   Dependent parents (supporting or helping support)
2   Wife and children and supporting dependent parents

1-42. Economic responsibility   p. 200
242   Meets responsibility
124   Fails to meet responsibility
144   Unknown or inapplicable

1-43. Home—physical   p. 201
72   Good
121   Fair
98   Poor
219   Unknown or inapplicable

1-44. Neighborhood—type
117   Inapplicable, unknown, army, dead, institution 4 of 5 years
307   Urban only
26   Rural only
58   Varied (urban and rural)
2   Army

1-45. Neighborhood influences   p. 201
61   Good

121 Fair
120 Poor
208 Unknown or inapplicable

1–46. HOUSEHOLD STABILITY

 68 One
 22 Two
  7 Three
  0 Four
  0 Five
 12 More than 5
117 Several, but exact number unknown
146 No change
 71 Unknown
 67 Inapplicable (institution, dead)

1–47. RELATION TO NEAREST RELATIVES

 70 Unknown
 69 Inapplicable (no relatives, institution, dead)
201 In touch with—friendly
 83 In touch because or when in need
 87 Rarely in touch

1–48. FAMILY RELATIONSHIPS   p. 205

205 Succeed
172 Fail
133 Unknown or inapplicable

1–49. MOBILITY—NATURE OF*

 68 Inapplicable (institution, chronic illness, dead)
178 No mobility
 53 Excessive moving in one city area, different parts of one city but localities unknown
158 Excessive moving to other cities, states, or countries
 53 Unknown

1–50. CHURCH ATTENDANCE   p. 208

 78 Regular

* Although this factor appears on p. 206, it has been retabulated to separate out *excessive moving within one city,* which was originally included in the category *no mobility.*

68 Irregular
70 None
294 Unknown or inapplicable

1–51. SOCIETY MEMBER

67 Inapplicable (institution, dead, chronic illness)
14 Yes (wholesome)
318 No
82 Unknown
29 Yes (but not particularly wholesome)

1–51A. COMPANIONSHIPS   p. 210

44 Inapplicable
172 Harmless
176 Harmful
118 Unknown

1–52. HAUNTS

68 Inapplicable (ill, dead, institution)
110 Harmless
235 Harmful
97 Unknown

1–53. EDUCATIONAL ACTIVITIES

69 Inapplicable (institution, ill, dead)
14 Yes
347 No
80 Unknown

1–53A. HABITS—SUMMARY   p. 210

At least 40 Illicit sex
At least 126 Drink
At least 10 Drugs
At least 58 Gambling

1–54. LEISURE AND HABITS   p. 210

12 Constructive
119 Negative

212 Harmful
167 Unknown

1–55. SOCIAL SERVICES RENDERED   p. 212

107 No needs present
175 Needs not met
51 Some needs met
30 All needs met
127 Unknown
20 Inapplicable

1–56. SOCIAL SERVICE NEEDS (325) NOT MET (IN 226 CASES)   p. 212

87 Vocational
159 Recreational
56 Family welfare
20 Health—mental
3 Health—physical

1–57. NUMBER OF SOCIAL SERVICE AGENCIES   p. 212

44 Inapplicable
282 None
103 Unknown if any
81 One or more

1–58. TYPE (89) OF SOCIAL SERVICE AGENCIES (IN 81 CASES)

10 Health—physical
15 Health—mental
61 Relief and family welfare
1 Child welfare
2 Other

SECTION B. CODE-TABLE INDEX OF FACTORS IN
SECOND FOLLOW-UP STUDY

In this section the tables refer to the 454 of 510 men who were living at the beginning of the second five-year follow-up period. They total to 454 unless otherwise indicated. It will be recalled that 55 men had died before the end of the first five-year follow-up period. To this number has now been added one man who died a few days after the beginning of the second five-year follow-up period. This leaves 454 of the 510 men with whom the second follow-up study concerns itself.

These tables, covering the second five-year period, are numerically designated from 2–1 through 2–66 and from 2–H81 through 2–H139. As this section of the research (from 2–1 through 2–66) was coded and machine tabulated rather than hand tabulated as the materials of the first follow-up investigation, the numbers immediately to the left of the categories of each factor are their positions on the punch card columns. If the categories are not always in logical order it is because additions were made to the original categories as the study proceeded.

Definitions of the factors will be found in Appendix B, *Definition of Terms.*

2–IA. ALIASES

77	1. Used aliases
116	2. Did not use aliases
64	3. Unknown
34	4. Inapplicable as not in community at all
163	5. No arrests

2–IB. PERIOD STUDIED—END

211	6. 1931
243	7. 1932

2–2. AGE AT END OF PERIOD

0	1. 21–25
62	2. 26–30
213	3. 31–35
116	4. 36–40
45	5. 41–45
15	6. 46–50
3	7. 51–55
0	8. 56 and over

2–3. With whom living at end of period

48	1. Parents (one or both)
20	2. Sibs (no parents)
3	3. Other relations
165	4. Wife and children
3	5. Children (no wife)
7	6. Sweetheart
7	7. Employer
64	8. Alone
70	9. Institution or army or navy
0	10. Other
14	11. Dead
53	12. Unknown

2–4A. Health

17	1. Venereal disease (or evidence of lues)
25	2. Partial handicaps
4	3. Total handicaps
10	4. Chronic illness
78	5. Mental disease (psychosis, drug addiction, alcoholism, epilepsy, other)

202	6. None
129	7. Unknown if any

2–4B. Emotional stability of offender

92	10. Stable
212	11. Unstable
150	12. Unknown

2–6. Mental condition

24	1. Psychosis (manic depressive, dementia praecox, paranoid, sex pervert)
16	2. Constitutional psychopathy
27	3. Psychopathic personality or traits
6	4. Epilepsy (or epileptic characteristics)
55	5. Alcoholism or delirium tremens
11	6. Drug addiction
3	7. Neurasthenia

1   8. Congenital syphilis
4   9. Question of mental disease
75 10. Emotional instability
13 11. Other personality liabilities
219 12. None noted or unknown
          None 123
          Unknown 96

2–7. INSTITUTIONAL EXPERIENCES—NATURE OF (BY TYPE)

0   1. Inapplicable
54 2. Unknown if any
221 3. None

---

0   4. School for feebleminded
20 5. Hospital for mental diseases
11 6. Hospital for chronic physical disease
147 7. Peno-correctional institution
10 8. Army, navy

2–8. NUMBER OF PENAL EXPERIENCES

1   1. Inapplicable
252 2. None
54 3. Unknown if any
66 4. One
29 5. Two
34 6. 3–4
7   7. 5–6
5   8. 7–8
3   9. 9–10
3 10. 11 or more
0 11. Number unknown

2–9. TIME IN PENAL INSTITUTIONS

54 1. Unknown
252 2. None
22 3. Less than 3 months
11 4. 3–6 months
18 5. 6–12 months
13 6. 12–18 months

9	7. 18–24 months
14	8. 24–30 months
6	9. 30–36 months
18	10. 36–48 months
19	11. 48–60 months
18	12. 60 months

2–10. TIME IN PENAL INSTITUTIONS*

252	1. None
30	2. Under five months
17	3. 5–10 months
23	4. 10–20 months
17	5. 20–30 months
14	6. 30–40 months
12	7. 40–50 months
17	8. 50–60 months
18	9. 60 months
54	10. Unknown

2–11. MONTHS IN COMMUNITY

54	1. Unknown
30	2. None
2	3. Less than 3 months
8	4. 3–6 months
12	5. 6–12 months
16	6. 12–18 months
9	7. 18–24 months
10	8. 24–30 months
12	9. 30–36 months
24	10. 36–48 months
56	11. 48–60 months
221	12. 60 months

2–12. HOME—PHYSICAL

45	1. Inapplicable as in institution throughout or in community for less than one year
104	2. Good

* The difference in the groupings of the same factor in tables 2–9 and 2–10 is necessitated by our desire to make these tables comparable with other studies.

104   3. Fair
93   4. Poor
5   5. Varied—good
12   6. Varied—fair
7   7. Varied—poor
84   8. Unknown

2–13. NEIGHBORHOOD—TYPE

45   1. Inapplicable as in institution throughout or in community for less than one year
122   2. Urban partly residential
124   3. Urban residential
4   4. Urban unspecified
26   5. Suburban
30   6. Rural (or semi-rural)
3   7. Small town
29   8. Varied (urban and rural)
71   9. Unknown

2–14. NEIGHBORHOOD INFLUENCES

45   1. Inapplicable as in institution throughout or in community for less than one year
41   2. Good
154   3. Fair
104   4. Poor
5   5. Varied—good
10   6. Varied—fair
10   7. Varied—poor
85   8. Unknown

2–15A. MOBILITY—NATURE OF

40   1. Inapplicable (institution throughout, or no excessive mobility in the less than one year in community)
191   2. Not excessive
49   3. Excessive moving in one city area
4   4. Excessive moving in different parts of one city
0   5. Excessive moving in one city but localities unknown
116   6. Excessive moving to other cities, states, or countries
54   7. Unknown

2–15B. ENVIRONMENTAL JUDGMENT

81 8. Good
140 9. Fair
106 10. Poor
44 11. Inapplicable (in institution throughout or in community for less than one year and environmental judgment not possible)
83 12. Unknown

2–16A. MORAL STANDARDS OF HOME

45 1. Inapplicable (in institution throughout, or in community for less than one year)
132 2. Good
72 3. Fair
113 4. Poor
2 5. Varied—good
4 6. Varied—fair
11 7. Varied—poor
75 8. Unknown

2–16B. FAMILY RELATIONSHIPS

180 9. Succeed
180 10. Fail
52 11. Unknown
42 12. Inapplicable (never in community, or in the less than one year in community, relationship undeterminable)

2–17. HOUSEHOLD STABILITY

29 2. One change
14 3. Two changes
3 4. Three changes
0 5. Four changes
2 6. Five changes
15 7. More than five changes
90 8. Several but exact number unknown
183 9. No change
76 10. Unknown
42 11. Inapplicable (not in community at all, or during the less than one year in community, stability not determinable)

2–18A. Relation to Nearest Relatives

46   1. Unknown
4   2. No relatives
190 3. In touch with—friendly
71   4. In touch when or because in need
103 5. Rarely in touch
40   6. Institution throughout (or if in community less than one year, relationship not determinable)

2–18B. Attitude of Relatives to Offender

39   7. Institution throughout or in community too brief to judge
5   8. No relatives
214 9. Friendly
107 10. Indifferent
25   11. Hostile or disgusted or disapprove
64   12. Unknown

2–19. Marital Status (at beginning of period)

187 1. Single
159 2. Married, living with wife
2   3. Illegally married—living with wife
36   4. Separated
16   5. Divorced
7   6. Widowed
40   7. Unknown, or unknown if married or single
6   8. Married but offender in institution
1   9. Illegally married—separated

2–20. Marital Status (at end of period)

22   1. Unknown
22   2. Unknown if married or single
157 3. Single
164 4. Married, living with wife
4   5. Illegally married—living with wife
42   6. Separated
26   7. Divorced
6   8. Widowed

9 9. Married, wife unfaithful, offender in institution
1 10. Married, wife in institution, no separation prior to this
1 11. Illegally married—separated

2–21. MARITAL—NUMBER OF MARRIAGES OCCURING DURING FIVE-YEAR PERIOD

157 1. Single
37 2. Unknown if married
208 3. None
45 4. One marriage
1 5. Two marriages
0 6. Three marriages
0 7. Four marriages
0 8. Number unknown
6 9. Unknown if any

2–22. CONJUGAL RELATIONS

37 1. Inapplicable (separated, divorced, widowed before beginning of period and not remarried)
37 2. Unknown whether married or single
157 3. Single
122 4. Good
30 5. Fair
49 6. Poor
13 7. Unknown (or marriage too brief to judge)
8 8. Institution throughout or dead
1 9. Wife in institution at least four years

2–23. ATTITUDE OF OFFENDER TO MARITAL RESPONSIBILITY

157 1. Single
37 2. Unknown whether married or single
125 3. Assume
76 4. Neglect
13 5. Unknown (or marriage too brief to judge)
37 6. Inapplicable (as separated, divorced, or widowed before beginning of period and not remarried)
8 7. Institution or dead (over four years)
1 8. Wife in institution four years or more

2–24. ATTITUDE OF WIFE TO MARITAL RESPONSIBILITY

157　1. Single
37　2. Inapplicable (separated before beginning of period and not re-married)
174　3. Assume
20　4. Neglect
20　5. Unknown
8　6. Institution throughout or dead (over 4 of 5 years)
37　7. Unknown whether married or single
1　8. Wife in institution 4 of 5 years

2–25. MARITAL HISTORY JUDGMENT

37　1. Unknown if married or single
157　2. Single
37　3. Inapplicable (separated, divorced, widowed before beginning of period and not remarried)
122　4. Good
32　5. Fair
48　6. Poor
12　7. Unknown
8　8. Institution at least four of five years
1　9. Wife in institution four of five years

2–26. COMPETENCE OF WIFE AS HOMEMAKER

45　1. Inapplicable (as separated, widowed, or divorced before begin-ning of period or offender in institution, or wife in institution four of five years)
157　2. Single
37　3. Unknown whether married or single
128　4. Good
41　5. Fair
14　6. Poor
32　7. Unknown

2–27. LEGITIMACY OF CHILDREN

269　1. No children born during period
87　2. Legitimate children—conceived in wedlock
3　3. Legitimate children—conceived out of wedlock

3   4. Unmarried with illegitimate children
3   5. Married with illegitimate children
6   6. Legitimate and illegitimate children (including children conceived out of wedlock)
83   7. Unknown or inapplicable (dead, institution under strict supervision)

2–28. NUMBER OF CHILDREN

221   1. None
68   2. One
43   3. Two
33   4. Three
19   5. Four
10   6. Five
7   7. Six
2   8. Seven
0   9. Eight
2   10. Nine or more
45   11. Unknown if any
4   12. Number unknown

2–29A. ATTITUDE TO CHILDREN

34   1. Inapplicable (institution throughout or four of five years and no children)
195   2. No children or none living
102   3. Good
31   4. Fair
38   5. Poor
54   6. Attitude unknown or unknown if any children

2–29B. DELINQUENCY OF CHILDREN

70   7. No delinquency
5   8. Official
7   9. Unofficial
67   10. Unknown or unknown if any
305   11. Inapplicable (children too young, or no children)

2–30. DELINQUENCY OF WIFE

157   1. Single

151   2. No delinquency
10   3. Official (except drink)
1   4. Drink only (official or unofficial)
24   5. Unofficial
39   6. Inapplicable (as offender and wife not living together since before beginning of period or wife dead)
35   7. Unknown
37   8. Unknown if married or single

2–31A. Economic responsibility

40   1. Inapplicable (not in community at all, or in the less than one year in community, responsibility not determinable)
183   2. Meets responsibility completely legitimately
122   3. Fails to meet responsibility (through his own fault)
5   4. Unable to meet his responsibility because of chronic illness
7   5. Unable to meet his responsibility completely though manifests willingness to do so
65   6. Unknown
15   7. Meets responsibility illegitimately
17   8. Meets responsibility partly illegitimately

2–31B. Savings

41   9. Inapplicable (not in community at all, or in the less than one year in community, no savings)
76   10. Yes
243   11. No
94   12. Unknown

2–32A. Insurance

36   1. Inapplicable (never in community)
144   2. No insurance
138   3. Insurance
136   4. Unknown

2–32B. Insurance—premium paid by whom

144   5. No insurance
110   6. Paid by self
23   7. Paid by relatives

0 8. Unknown by whom paid
136 9. Unknown if has insurance
36 10. Inapplicable (as never in community)
5 11. Paid by government or employer or social agency

2–33A. ECONOMIC CONDITION

45 1. Inapplicable (institution throughout or in community for less than one year)
34 2. Comfortable
243 3. Marginal
17 4. Dependent on agencies or persons outside of immediate family (not because of depression)
43 5. Dependent entirely or partially on relatives (not because of depression)
64 6. Unknown
8 7. Entirely or partially dependent on agencies or relatives (because of depression)

2–33B. DEPENDENTS

112 9. No dependents
250 10. Dependents
45 11. Inapplicable (never in community or in community less than a year)
47 12. Unknown

2–34A. DISPOSITION OF EARNINGS

188 1. Self only
147 2. Wife and/or children, no dependent parents
6 3. Wife and/or children, dependent parents
11 4. Dependent parents
45 5. Inapplicable (as no earnings either because in institution throughout or most of the time or idle with cause)
57 11. Unknown

2–34B. INDUSTRIAL HISTORY

47 6. Inapplicable (never in community or unable to work for legitimate reasons, or in community too brief to judge)
84 7. Success
128 8. Partial success

126   9. Failure (including illegitimate occupation)
69   10. Unknown

2–35. NUMBER OF SOCIAL SERVICE AGENCIES

35   1. Inapplicable (institution throughout or too brief to judge)
210   2. None
63   3. Unknown if any
68   4. One
34   5. Two
17   6. Three
19   7. Four
4   8. Five
1   9. Six
3   10. Seven and over
0   11. Number unknown

2–36. TYPE OF SOCIAL SERVICE AGENCIES

35   1. Inapplicable (institution throughout or too brief to judge)
210   2. Not known to any agencies
63   3. Unknown whether dealt with by agencies

74   4. Health—physical
14   5. Health—mental
90   6. Relief
11   7. Family welfare
20   8. Child or adolescent welfare
4   9. Correctional
29   10. Other (vocational)

2–37. USUAL OCCUPATION

51   1. Inapplicable (in institution at least four of five years, or did not work for legitimate reasons)
15   2. Mostly idle (able to work but does not)
25   3. Illegitimate occupation
83   4. Rough labor and odd jobs
42   5. Trucking, teaming, chauffeuring
44   6. Factory hand
13   7. Farm hand
31   8. Salesman and store clerks, office work (including own store)

67 9. Trades—electrician, machinist, plumber, carpenter, bricklayer, painter, gardener, barber

21 10. Restaurant or hotel work

49 11. Varied or unknown

13 12. Other (Pullman porter, butler, musician)

2–38A. SKILL

69 1. Inapplicable (institution throughout or in community too brief to judge, or idle, or illegitimate occupation throughout)

125 2. Unskilled

169 3. Semi-skilled

38 4. Skilled

53 5. Unknown

2–38B. SKILL IN FIFTH YEAR

109 6. Inapplicable (institution, chronic illness, idle, illegitimate occupation)

123 7. Unskilled

136 8. Semi-skilled

35 9. Skilled

51 10. Unknown

2–39A. STEADINESS OF EMPLOYMENT

46 1. Inapplicable (never in community, or unable to work for good reason, or in community too brief to judge)

96 2. Regular

116 3. Fairly regular

106 4. Irregular

23 5. Illegitimate occupation

67 6. Unknown

2–39B. WORK HABITS

46 7. Inapplicable (never in community or unable to work for good reason, or in community too brief to judge)

140 8. Good

112 9. Fair

65 10. Poor

23 11. Illegitimate occupation throughout

68 12. Unknown

2-40A. Number of different occupations

69   1. Inapplicable (never in community, idle for cause, illegitimate occupation throughout)

163   2. One

68   3. Two

23   4. Three

5   5. Four

22   6. Five or more

104   7. Unknown

2-40B. Used Massachusetts reformatory occupation

43   8. Inapplicable (never in community, or ill and unable to work, or too brief to judge)

283   9. Did not use Massachusetts Reformatory occupation

51   10. Used same occupation

4   11. Used same technique but different occupation

73   12. Unknown

2-41. Average wage—weekly

50   1. Inapplicable (never in community, or too brief to judge, or idle for good reason, or seldom worked)

23   2. Illegitimate occupation throughout

2   3. Less than $5

11   4. $5–$10

24   5. $10–$15

37   6. $15–$20

40   7. $20–$25

39   8. $25–$30

35   9. $30–$35

15   10. $35–$40

18   11. $40 and over

160   12. Incalculable or unknown

2-42. Highest wage—weekly

166   1. Inapplicable (incalculable, or unknown, or institution throughout)

23   2. Illegitimate occupation throughout

1   3. None

6	4. Under $10
11	5. $10–$15
24	6. $15–$20
46	7. $20–$25
41	8. $25–$30
32	9. $30–$35
35	10. $35–$40
16	11. $40–$45
53	12. $45 and over

2–43. AVERAGE PERIOD OF TIME HELD JOB

46	1. Inapplicable (never in community or too brief to judge, as unable to work)
23	2. Illegitimate occupation throughout
42	3. Incalculable (on and off in one place for years or one long job, others short)
101	4. Less than 3 months
27	5. 3–6 months
6	6. 6–9 months
13	7. 9–12 months
23	8. 1–2 years
28	9. 2–3 years
4	10. 3–4 years
45	11. 4–5 years
96	12. Unknown

2–44. LONGEST PERIOD OF TIME HELD JOB

47	1. Inapplicable (never in community or unable to work or too brief to judge)
28	2. Incalculable (as on and off in one place)
23	3. Illegitimate occupation throughout
76	4. Less than 3 months
21	5. 3–6 months
17	6. 6–9 months
8	7. 9–12 months
30	8. 1–2 years
43	9. 2–3 years
22	10. 3–4 years

47   11. 4 years and over
92   12. Unknown

2–45A. ILLEGITIMATE OCCUPATION

41   1. Inapplicable (never in community, or in community less than one year and not in illegitimate occupation)
23   2. Illegitimate occupation throughout
50   3. Illegitimate occupation part of period
237   4. Illegitimate occupation only
103   5. Unknown

2–45B. USUAL REASON FOR LEAVING WORK

69   6. Inapplicable (never in community, illegitimate occupation throughout, or unavoidably idle throughout)
54   7. Steady worker, seldom changes
129   8. Fault of worker
95   9. Not fault of worker
14   10. To better self
1   11. Other
92   12. Unknown

2–46A. LEISURE

37   1. Inapplicable (never in community, or if in community less than one year, not harmful)
15   2. Constructive
105   3. Negative
231   4. Harmful
66   5. Unknown

2–46B. SOCIETY MEMBER

39   6. Inapplicable (never in community, or if in community less than one year, not a society member)
15   7. Yes (wholesome)
276   8. None at all
95   9. Unknown
29   10. Clubs in which no particularly wholesome activity

2-47A. CHURCH ATTENDANCE

39 1. Inapplicable (never in community, or if in community less than one year, not a church goer)
33 2. Regular
111 3. Irregular
131 4. None
140 5. Unknown

2-47B. EDUCATIONAL ACTIVITIES

39 6. Inapplicable (never in community, or if in community less than one year, no educational activities)
18 7. Yes
303 8. No
94 9. Unknown

2-48A. COMPANIONSHIPS

37 1. Inapplicable (never in community or if in community less than one year, use of leisure harmless)
125 2. Harmless
213 3. Harmful
79 4. Unknown

2-48B. HAUNTS

37 5. Inapplicable (never in community or if in community less than a year, haunts harmless)
27 6. Good
98 7. Fair
200 8. Poor
92 9. Unknown

2-49. HABITS

130 1. Sex
83 2. Stealing
182 3. Drink
16 4. Drugs
53 5. Gambling

15   6. Lying
2   7. Other

107 8. None
64   9. Unknown
35 10. Inapplicable (never in community or too brief to judge)

2–50A. GANG LIFE

38   1. Inapplicable (never in community, or if in community less than one year, no gang life)
20   2. Member of gang
114 3. No gang but crowd
115 4. No gang or crowd
36   5. No gang, but unknown if crowd
131 6. Unknown

2–50B. STREET LIFE

38   9. Inapplicable (never in community, or if in community less than a year, no street life)
131 10. Yes
138 11. No.
147 12. Unknown

2–51A. DELINQUENCIES

118 1. Non-delinquent
125 2. Delinquent—minor
125 3. Delinquent—serious
34   4. Inapplicable (not in community at all or too brief to judge)
52   5. Unknown

2–51B. OFFICIAL RECOGNITION OF DELINQUENCY

34   8. Inapplicable (not in community at all)
118 9. No delinquency
202 10. Based on official record
48 11. On unofficial only
52 12. Unknown

2–52. PREDOMINANT OFFENSE

34	1. Inapplicable (not in community at all or too brief to judge)
16	2. Unknown if arrested
118	3. Non-delinquent
50	4. Crimes against property
14	5. Crimes against chastity
8	6. Crimes against family and children
31	7. Crimes against public health, safety and policy (except drink and drugs)
90	8. Drink
6	9. Drugs
1	10. Against person
42	11. Varied
44	12. Unknown or not determinable or no predominant offense

2–53. NUMBER OF ARRESTS

34	1. Inapplicable (not in community throughout or too brief to judge)
163	2. No arrests
51	3. One
36	4. Two
28	5. Three
18	6. Four
16	7. Five
6	8. Six
8	9. Seven
36	10. Eight and over
1	11. Number unknown
57	12. Unknown if arrested

2–54. NUMBER OF CONVICTIONS

34	1. Inapplicable (not in community throughout or too brief to judge)
182	2. None (though arrested)
56	3. One conviction
30	4. Two
26	5. Three

13 6. Four
15 7. Five
6 8. Six
5 9. Seven
27 10. Eight and over
3 11. Number unknown
57 12. Unknown if arrested

2–55. FREQUENCY OF ARRESTS

34 1. Inapplicable (not in community throughout or too brief to judge)
60 2. Unknown or unknown if arrested
209 3. Incalculable (only one arrest or no arrests, or for other reasons incalculable)
19 4. One arrest in less than 3 months
33 5. One arrest in 3–6 months
15 6. One arrest in 6–9 months
15 7. One arrest in 9–12 months
17 8. One arrest in 12–15 months
5 9. One arrest in 15–18 months
23 10. One arrest in 18–21 months
2 11. One arrest in 21–24 months
22 12. One arrest in 24 and more months

2–56. FREQUENCY OF CONVICTIONS

34 1. Inapplicable (not in community throughout or too brief to judge)
60 2. Unknown or unknown if arrested
214 3. Incalculable (no arrests or only one arrest, or one conviction)
15 4. One conviction in less than 3 months
29 5. One conviction in 3–6 months
15 6. One conviction in 6–9 months
13 7. One conviction in 9–12 months
10 8. One conviction in 12–15 months
5 9. One conviction in 15–18 months
20 10. One conviction in 18–21 months
3 11. One conviction in 21–24 months
36 12. Once conviction in 24 and more months

2–57A. ASSOCIATES IN CRIME

118 1. Non-delinquent
50   2. Unknown if delinquent
82   3. Offenses committed alone
43   4. Offenses committed with one or two others
18   5. Offenses committed with three or more others
104 6. Unknown with whom offenses committed
39   7. Inapplicable (not in community or too brief to judge or delinquency doubtful)

2–57B. DELINQUENCY IN FIFTH YEAR

137 9. Non-delinquent
184 10. Delinquent
62   11. Unknown
71   12. Inapplicable (non-penal institution, dead)

2–58. SUMMARY OF ARRESTS—BY TYPE

34   1. Inapplicable (not in community or too brief to judge)
57   2. Unknown if arrested
163 3. No arrests

---

86   4. Crimes against property
16   5. Crimes against chastity
21   6. Crimes against family and children
88   7. Crimes against public health, safety and policy (except drink or drugs)
101 8. Drink
7   9. Drugs
22   10. Crimes against person
11   11. Other

2–59. SUMMARY OF DISPOSITIONS—BY TYPE

254 1. Inapplicable, or no arrests, or unknown if arrested

---

111 2. Commitment
65   3. Probation
76   4. Fine
18   5. Commitment for non-payment of fine

70   6. File
0   7. Restitution
31   8. Released by probation officer
9   9. Nol pros
6   10. No bill
79   11. Not guilty or released
22   12. Disposition unknown or other, or awaiting disposition

2–60. SOCIAL SERVICE NEEDS NOT MET

104   1. Inapplicable or unknown
30   2. All needs met
77   3. No needs present
108   4. Some needs met

---

121   5. Vocational
189   6. Recreational
68   7. Family welfare
1   8. Relief
81   9. Health—mental
5   10. Health—physical
7   11. Child or adolescent welfare
182   12. Friendly supervision

2–61. DELINQUENCY IN FIVE-YEAR PERIOD AND FIFTH YEAR IN COMBINATION*

118   1. Non-delinquent
235   2. Delinquent throughout
19   3. Delinquent—upgrade
0   4. School for feebleminded throughout
9   5. State hospital throughout
20   6. Penal institution throughout (or for first 4 years, and last year unknown)
1   7. Doubtful delinquency
50   8. Unknown
2   12. Institution throughout (but not entirely penal)

* This is slightly more detailed than 2–62 and more directly comparable to a similar table in *500 Delinquent Women.*

2-62. Delinquency in five-year period and fifth year in combination

118   1. Non-delinquent
235   2. Delinquent throughout
19   3. Delinquent—upgrade
1   4. Doubtful delinquent
20   5. Penal institution throughout or most of time, and time out conduct unknown or too brief to judge
9   6. Non-penal institution throughout, or time out conduct unknown
0   7. Dead (including a few who died after beginning of period but conduct unknown)
50   8. Unknown
2   9. Penal and non-penal

2-63a. Family relationships in fifth year

180   1. Succeed
141   2. Fail
54   3. Unknown
79   4. Inapplicable (institution, dead)

2-63b. Industrial history in fifth year

87   5. Inapplicable (institution, dead, ill)
74   6. Success
91   7. Partial success
93   8. Failure (including illegitimate occupation)
65   9. Unknown
44   11. Depression victim

2-64. Economic responsibility in fifth year

79   1. Inapplicable (dead, institution throughout)
150   2. Meets responsibility legitimately
14   3. Meets responsibility illegitimately
90   4. Fails to meet responsibility
0   5. Self-support not necessary
5   6. Chronic illness
0   7. Dependent for other good reasons
60   8. Unknown

44   9. Depression victim
12   10. Meets responsibility partly illegitimately

2–65A. ENVIRONMENTAL HISTORY IN FIFTH YEAR

93   1. Good
123   2. Fair
84   3. Poor
79   4. Inapplicable (institution or dead or too brief to judge)
75   5. Unknown

2–65B. LEISURE AND HABITS IN FIFTH YEAR

79   8. Inapplicable (institution, dead)
16   9. Constructive
117   10. Negative
174   11. Harmful
68   12. Unknown

2–66. PRINCIPAL COMPONENT OF MISCONDUCT

118   1. Non-delinquent
10   2. Non-penal institution throughout
24   3. Penal institution at least 55 months (or part of time and then mental hospital totalling 55 months) or sentence imposed during first 5-year period and effective for part of second 5-year period, and then non-delinquent
96   4. Conviction for serious offense
4   5. Warrant out for serious offense
3   6. Dishonorable discharge or desertion from army or navy
15   7. Unofficial serious
5   8. Arrest for serious, not followed by conviction
75   9. Conviction for minor offense
40   10. Unofficial minor, or warrant out for minor
12   11. Arrest for minor not followed by conviction, or disposition unknown
52   12. Unknown, or delinquency doubtful

2–H81A. INTERVIEW WITH

225   Offender
147   Near relatives (wife, in-laws, sibs, aunts, cousins)

12 Others (police, probation officers, employers, social agencies)
70 Record data or correspondence only

2–H81B. Whereabouts at end of period

55 Penal institution
14 Non-penal institution
92 Boston and vicinity
99 Other cities in Massachusetts
108 Other states
6 Foreign countries
3 Fugitive from justice
12 Drifting around
15 Dead
14 Unknown but known for part of period
33 Completely unknown
3 Army or navy
0 At sea

2–H82. Attitude to investigation

167 Friendly
9 Indifferent
9 Hostile
269 Inapplicable or unknown

2–H105. Causes of death (14) during period II

5 Accident
1 Suicide
6 Pulmonary diseases
0 Heart diseases
1 Malaria
1 Nephritis

2–H107. Institutional experiences (421)—geographical spread

300 Massachusetts
116 Other states
2 Canada
3 Europe

2–H116. Depression victim

58   Yes
279   No
117   Unknown or inapplicable

2–H125. Summary of (955) arrests

165   Against property
17   Against chastity
39   Against family and children
164   Against public health (except drink and drugs)
488   Drink
11   Drugs
41   Against person
27   Other
3   Unknown

2–H126. Summary of (955) dispositions

282   Commitment
125   Probation
154   Fine
36   Commitment for non-payment of fine
136   File
1   Restitution
50   Released by probation officer
11   Nol pros
6   No bill
119   Not guilty or released
35   Disposition unknown or other or awaiting disposition

2–H133. Attitude of community

218   Not stated
35   Friendly
199   Indifferent
2   Hostile

2–H135. Reasons for improvement in conduct (98 cases)

21   Marriage or other satisfaction of outlet for desire for affection
23   Maturity

8   Vocational adjustment
9   Reformatory experience
5   Close supervision
1   Fear of commitment
17 Wholesome or simple environment
2   Freedom from responsibility
9   Family responsibility
1   Religious conversion
2   Protected environment

2–H136. REASONS FOR FAILURE IN CONDUCT (175 CASES)

50 Alcoholism
12 Mental disease
2   Habit of delinquency
4   Sex perversion
11 Unfortunate marriage
8   Drug addiction
21 Psychopathy
4   Needs custodial care or constant supervision
1   Financial depression
46 Deep seated anti-sociality
7   Defective delinquent
4   Irresponsible make-up
3   Low ethical standards
1   Desire for money
1   Too high wages

2–H139. INSTITUTIONAL EXPERIENCES—NATURE OF (421)

7   Reformatories
98   Prisons
285 Jails, houses of correction, state farms
31   Truant schools, schools for feebleminded, industrial schools, protectorates

Appendix D

PERIOD-COMPARISON TABLES

In the following series of tables (arranged by subject) is presented the status of the 454 ex-inmates of the Massachusetts Reformatory for Men in the first and second five-year periods, who were living at the beginning of the second five-year follow-up period. The comparisons are not only between their status in the first and second five-year periods but, where possible, comparison is made with their status prior to commitment to the Reformatory. In a few instances there are data covering the second five-year follow-up period, but not the first.

All the tables total to 454 or refer to the 454 cases.

From the title of each table it is possible to refer to Appendix B, *Definition of Terms,* for definition of the factor and for reference to the more detailed tables in Appendix C, Section B, from which those here presented have been somewhat contracted.

For the sake of brevity the period prior to commitment to the Reformatory is designated *Prior period;* the first five-year follow-up period, *Period I;* and the second, *Period II.*

With one or two exceptions the tables are numbered in the order in which they are referred to in the text.

Environmental Factors

1. WITH WHOM LIVING

	AT TIME OF COMMITMENT TO REFORMATORY		AT END OF PERIOD I		AT END OF PERIOD II	
	Num- ber	Per cent	Num- ber	Per cent	Num- ber	Per cent
Unknown	12	–	50	–	53	–
Parents	308	69.7	52	12.9	48	12.0
Siblings	22	5.0	16	4.0	20	5.0
Other relatives	27	6.1	4	1.0	3	.7
Wife and children	24	5.4	156	38.6	165	41.2
Children	0	–	0	–	3	.7
Sweetheart or illegal wife	0	–	13	3.3	7	1.7
Employer	0	–	3	.7	7	1.7
Alone	60	13.6	72	17.8	64	16.0
Institution or army	1	.2	87	21.5	70	17.5
Other	0	–	1	.2	0	–
Dead	0	–	0	–	14	3.5

2. WHEREABOUTS AT END OF PERIOD*

	PERIOD I		PERIOD II	
	Num- ber	Per cent	Num- ber	Per cent
Penal institution	85	16.7	55	10.8
Non-penal institution	7	1.4	14	2.7
Boston and vicinity	68	13.3	92	18.0
Other cities in Massachusetts	111	21.8	99	19.4
Other states	81	15.8	108	21.2
Foreign countries	7	1.4	6	1.2
Fugitive from justice	31	6.1	3	.6
Drifting around	6	1.2	12	2.4
Army or navy	6	1.2	3	.6
At sea	6	1.2	0	–
Dead	55	10.8	71	13.9
Unknown, but known for part of period	20	3.9	14	2.7
Completely unknown	27	5.2	33	6.5

* Based on 510 cases. In the text (p. 22) the analysis is on the basis of 454 cases.

3. MONTHS IN COMMUNITY

	PERIOD I		PERIOD II	
	Number	*Per cent*	*Number*	*Per cent*
Unknown	37	–	54	–
None	10	2.4	30	7.5
Less than twelve	29	6.9	22	5.5
Twelve to twenty-four	26	6.2	25	6.3
Twenty-four to thirty-six	36	8.7	22	5.5
Thirty-six to sixty	108	25.9	80	20.0
Sixty	208	49.9	221	55.2
Average number of months in community of those in community at all	45.74 ± .50		47.06 ± .51	

4. INSTITUTIONAL EXPERIENCES (PENAL AND NON-PENAL)*

	PRIOR PERIOD		PERIOD I		PERIOD II	
	Number	*Per cent*	*Number*	*Per cent*	*Number*	*Per cent*
Inapplicable or unknown	0	–	40	–	53	–
No institutional experience	229	50.4	213	51.4	231	57.6
Institutional experience	225	49.6	201	48.6	170	42.4

5. MOBILITY

	PERIOD I		PERIOD II	
	Number	*Per cent*	*Number*	*Per cent*
Inapplicable or unknown	69	–	94	–
No mobility	174	45.2	191	53.1
Mobility	211	54.8	169	46.9

6. HOUSEHOLD STABILITY

	PERIOD I		PERIOD II	
	Number	*Per cent*	*Number*	*Per cent*
Inapplicable or unknown	95	–	118	–
No change	140	39.0	183	54.4
One, two	87	24.3	43	12.8
Three or more	132	36.7	110	32.8

* See Table 47 for *Institutional Experiences—Nature of.*

7. HOME—PHYSICAL

	PERIOD I		PERIOD II	
	Num-ber	Per cent	Num-ber	Per cent
Inapplicable or unknown	126	–	129	–
Good	86	26.2	109	33.5
Fair	123	37.5	116	35.7
Poor	119	36.3	100	30.8

8. NEIGHBORHOOD—TYPE

	PERIOD I		PERIOD II	
	Num-ber	Per cent	Num-ber	Per cent
Inapplicable or unknown	77	–	116	–
Mostly urban	294	78.0	276	81.7
Mostly rural	26	6.9	33	9.8
Varied (urban and rural)	57	15.1	29	8.5

9. NEIGHBORHOOD INFLUENCES

	PERIOD I		PERIOD II	
	Num-ber	Per cent	Num-ber	Per cent
Inapplicable or unknown	122	–	130	–
Good	51	15.3	46	14.2
Fair	145	43.9	164	50.6
Poor	136	40.8	114	35.2

Family Relationships

10. Marital Status

	AT TIME OF COMMITMENT TO REFORMATORY		PERIOD I		PERIOD II	
	Num-ber	Per cent	Num-ber	Per cent	Num-ber	Per cent
Status unknown, unknown if married or single	2	–	40	–	44	–
Single	411	90.9	187	45.2	157	38.2
Married, living with wife	24	5.3	159	38.4	164	39.9
Married, but man in institution	0	–	6	1.4	9	2.3
Illegally married, living with wife	0	–	2	.5	4	.9
Separated	11	2.4	36	8.7	42	10.2
Illegally married, separated	0	–	1	.2	1	.3
Divorced	2	.4	16	3.9	26	6.4
Widowed	4	1.0	7	1.7	6	1.5
Other	0	–	0	–	1	.3

11. Number of Children

	AT TIME OF COMMITMENT TO REFORMATORY		PERIOD I		PERIOD II	
	Num-ber	Per cent	Num-ber	Per cent	Num-ber	Per cent
Unknown or unknown if any	0	–	38	–	49	–
None	423	93.2	258	62.0	221	54.6
One	18	4.0	75	18.0	68	16.8
Two	2	.4	39	9.4	43	10.6
Three	10	2.2	20	4.8	33	8.1
Four or more	1	.2	24	5.8	40	9.9
Average number of children among those with children	$2.20 \pm .27$		$2.04 \pm .07$		$2.46 \pm .11$	

12. CONJUGAL RELATIONS

	PRIOR PERIOD		PERIOD I		PERIOD II	
	Num-ber	Per cent	Num-ber	Per cent	Num-ber	Per cent
Inapplicable, unknown, married too brief to judge, unknown whether married or single	2	–	64	–	96	–
Single	411	–	187	–	157	–
Good	24	58.5	114	56.2	122	60.7
Fair	5	12.2	34	16.7	30	14.9
Poor	12	29.3	55	27.1	49	24.4

13. RELATION TO NEAREST RELATIVES

	PERIOD I		PERIOD II	
	Num-ber	Per cent	Num-ber	Per cent
Inapplicable or unknown	94	–	90	–
In touch with, friendly	193	53.6	190	52.2
In touch with because or when in need	80	22.2	71	19.5
Rarely in touch	87	24.2	103	28.3

14. FAMILY RELATIONSHIPS

	PRIOR PERIOD		PERIOD I		PERIOD II	
	Num-ber	Per cent	Num-ber	Per cent	Num-ber	Per cent
Inapplicable or unknown	65	–	86	–	94	–
Succeed	126	32.4	190	51.6	180	50.0
Fail	263	67.6	178	48.4	180	50.0

Economic Responsibility

15. DEPENDENTS

	PERIOD I		PERIOD II	
	Num-ber	Per cent	Num-ber	Per cent
Inapplicable or unknown	63	–	92	–
No dependents	128	32.7	112	30.9
Dependents	263	67.3	250	69.1

16. Disposition of Earnings

	PERIOD I		PERIOD II	
	Number	*Per cent*	*Number*	*Per cent*
Inapplicable or unknown	87	–	102	–
Self only	199	54.3	188	53.4
Wife and/or children, no dependent parents	134	36.5	147	41.8
Wife and/or children, has dependent parents but does not support them	6	1.6	6	1.7
Dependent parents, supporting or helping support	26	7.1	11	3.1
Wife and children and supports dependent parents	2	.5	0	–

17. Economic Condition

	PRIOR PERIOD*		PERIOD I		PERIOD II†	
	Number	*Per cent*	*Number*	*Per cent*	*Number*	*Per cent*
Inapplicable or unknown	49	–	73	–	117	–
Comfortable	117	28.9	32	8.4	34	10.0
Marginal	229	56.5	302	79.2	243	72.1
Dependent	59	14.6	47	12.4	60	17.9

18. Insurance

	PRIOR PERIOD		PERIOD II	
	Number	*Per cent*	*Number*	*Per cent*
Inapplicable or unknown	12	–	172	–
No insurance	227	51.3	144	51.1
Insurance	215	48.7	138	48.9

19. Insurance—Premium Paid by Whom

	PRIOR PERIOD		PERIOD II	
	Number	*Per cent*	*Number*	*Per cent*
Inapplicable or unknown or no insurance	256	–	316	–
Paid by self	11	5.6	110	79.7
Paid by relatives or others	187	94.4	28	20.3

* Prior to commitment to Reformatory refers to status of parental home.

† In second five-year period *inapplicable* includes those dependent because of the depression.

20. Known to social service agencies

	PRIOR PERIOD		PERIOD I		PERIOD II	
	Num-ber	Per cent	Num-ber	Per cent	Num-ber	Per cent
Inapplicable or unknown	53	–	87	–	98	–
Not known to agencies	160	39.9	278	75.7	210	59.0
Known to agencies	241	60.1	89	24.3	146	41.0

21. Economic responsibility toward family

	PRIOR PERIOD		PERIOD I		PERIOD II	
	Num-ber	Per cent	Num-ber	Per cent	Num-ber	Per cent
Inapplicable or unknown	102	–	89	–	117	–
Meets responsibility*	62	17.6	241	66.0	215	60.8
Fails to meet responsibility	290	82.4	124	34.0	122	39.2

Industrial History

22. Usual occupation

	PRIOR PERIOD		PERIOD I		PERIOD II	
	Num-ber	Per cent	Num-ber	Per cent	Num-ber	Per cent
Inapplicable, unknown, other	88	–	77	–	64	–
Mostly idle	0	–	0	–	15	3.8
Illegal occupation	0	–	27	7.2	25	6.4
Rough labor	91	24.9	84	22.3	83	21.3
Trucking, teaming	51	13.9	51	13.5	42	10.8
Factory work	100	27.3	60	15.9	44	11.3
Farmhand	31	8.5	11	2.9	13	3.3
Salesmen, store clerks	28	7.7	30	8.0	31	7.9
Skilled trades	44	12.0	85	22.5	67	17.2
Restaurant or hotel work	21	5.7	17	4.5	21	5.4
Varied	0	–	12	3.2	49	12.6

23. Illegitimate occupation

	PERIOD I		PERIOD II	
	Num-ber	Per cent	Num-ber	Per cent
Inapplicable or unknown	130	–	144	–
No illegitimate occupation	250	77.2	237	76.5
Illegal occupation part of time	51	15.7	50	16.1
Illegal occupation throughout	23	7.1	23	7.4

* Includes meeting responsibility by illicit employment.

24. SKILL

	PRIOR PERIOD		PERIOD I		PERIOD II	
	Number	*Per cent*	*Number*	*Per cent*	*Number*	*Per cent*
Inapplicable or unknown	3	–	97	–	112	–
Skilled	19	6.5	35	9.8	38	11.4
Semi-skilled	179	37.4	184	51.5	169	50.9
Unskilled	253	56.1	138	38.7	125	37.7

25. USED MASSACHUSETTS REFORMATORY OCCUPATION

	PERIOD I		PERIOD II	
	Number	*Per cent*	*Number*	*Per cent*
Inapplicable or unknown	88	–	116	–
No	299	81.7	283	83.7
Yes	64	17.5	51	15.1
Different occupation but same technique	3	.8	4	1.2

26. AVERAGE WAGE—WEEKLY

	PERIOD I		PERIOD II	
	Number	*Per cent*	*Number*	*Per cent*
Inapplicable, unknown, no legitimate work	249	–	233	–
Under $15	23	11.2	37	16.9
$15 to $25	76	37.0	77	34.8
$25 to $35	73	35.7	74	33.4
$35 and over	33	16.1	33	14.9
Average wage—weekly	$26.45 ± .42		$25.25 ± .44	

27. HIGHEST WAGE—WEEKLY

	PRIOR PERIOD		PERIOD I		PERIOD II	
	Number	*Per cent*	*Number*	*Per cent*	*Number*	*Per cent*
Inapplicable, unknown, no legitimate work	375	–	174	–	190	–
Under $15	43	54.4	9	3.2	17	6.5
$15 to $25	27	34.2	77	27.6	70	26.5
$25 to $35	8	10.1	99	35.3	73	27.6
$35 and over	1	1.3	95	33.9	104	39.4
Highest wage—weekly (average)	$14.65 ± .67		$30.75 ± .36		$32.00 ± .47	

28. WORK HABITS

	PRIOR PERIOD		PERIOD I		PERIOD II	
	Number	*Per cent*	*Number*	*Per cent*	*Number*	*Per cent*
Inapplicable or unknown	115	–	117	–	114	–
Good	67	19.8	121	33.6	140	41.2
Fair	95	28.0	109	30.3	112	32.9
Poor*	177	52.2	107	36.1	88	25.9

29. USUAL REASON FOR LEAVING WORK

	PERIOD I		PERIOD II	
	Number	*Per cent*	*Number*	*Per cent*
Inapplicable, unknown, other	141	–	162	–
Steady worker, seldom changes	51	16.3	54	18.5
Not fault of worker, or to better self	169	54.0	129	44.2
Fault of worker	93	29.7	109	37.3

30. STEADINESS OF EMPLOYMENT

	PRIOR PERIOD		PERIOD I		PERIOD II	
	Number	*Per cent*	*Number*	*Per cent*	*Number*	*Per cent*
Inapplicable or unknown	117	–	92	–	113	–
Regular	⎰ 57	⎰ 16.9	79	21.8	96	28.2
Fairly regular	⎱	⎱	120	33.1	116	34.0
Irregular*	280	83.1	163	45.1	129	37.8

31. AVERAGE PERIOD OF TIME HELD JOB

	PERIOD I		PERIOD II	
	Number	*Per cent*	*Number*	*Per cent*
Inapplicable, unknown, incalculable, illegitimate occupation throughout	164	–	207	–
Less than one year	197	68.0	147	59.5
One to two years	42	14.5	23	9.4
Two to four years	23	7.9	32	12.9
Four to five years	28	9.6	45	18.2
Average number of months held job	$21.86 \pm .93$		$19.7 \pm .80$	

* Includes men mostly employed in illegitimate occupations.

32. LONGEST PERIOD OF TIME HELD JOB

	PRIOR PERIOD		PERIOD I		PERIOD II	
	Num-ber	*Per cent*	*Num-ber*	*Per cent*	*Num-ber*	*Per cent*
Inapplicable, unknown, incalculable, illegal occupation throughout	44	–	141	–	190	–
Less than one year	247	60.2	178	56.8	122	46.2
One to two years	97	23.7	48	15.3	30	11.4
Two to four years	66	16.1	49	15.7	65	24.6
Four to five years	0	–	38	12.2	47	17.8
Longest period of months held job (average)	$12.22 \pm .30$		$17.88 \pm .64$		$23.3 \pm .77$	

33. INDUSTRIAL HISTORY

	PERIOD I		PERIOD II	
	Num-ber	*Per cent*	*Num-ber*	*Per cent*
Inapplicable or unknown	93	–	116	–
Good	77	21.3	84	24.8
Fair	122	33.8	128	37.9
Poor	162	44.9	126	37.3

Leisure and Habits

34. COMPANIONSHIPS

	PRIOR PERIOD		PERIOD I		PERIOD II	
	Num-ber	*Per cent*	*Num-ber*	*Per cent*	*Num-ber*	*Per cent*
Inapplicable or unknown	0	–	110	–	116	–
Harmless	25	5.5	108	31.4	125	37.0
Harmful	429	94.5	236	68.6	213	63.0

35. HAUNTS

	PERIOD I		PERIOD II	
	Num-ber	*Per cent*	*Num-ber*	*Per cent*
Inapplicable or unknown	117	–	129	–
Harmless	108	32.0	125	38.5
Harmful	229	68.0	200	61.5

36. SOCIETY MEMBER

	PRIOR PERIOD		PERIOD I		PERIOD II	
	Num-ber	*Per cent*	*Num-ber*	*Per cent*	*Num-ber*	*Per cent*
Inapplicable or unknown	0	–	101	–	134	–
Yes (wholesome)	75	16.5	14	4.0	15	4.7
Yes (not particularly wholesome)	0	–	29	8.2	29	9.1
No	379	83.5	310	87.8	276	86.2

37. CHURCH ATTENDANCE

	PRIOR PERIOD		PERIOD I		PERIOD II	
	Num-ber	*Per cent*	*Num-ber*	*Per cent*	*Num-ber*	*Per cent*
Inapplicable or unknown	12	–	169	–	179	–
Regular attendance	38	8.5	36	12.6	33	12.0
Occasional attendance	{404	{91.5	124	43.5	111	40.4
None			125	43.9	131	47.6

38. EDUCATIONAL ACTIVITIES

	PERIOD I		PERIOD II	
	Num-ber	*Per cent*	*Num-ber*	*Per cent*
Inapplicable or unknown	101	–	133	–
Yes	14	4.0	18	5.6
No	339	96.0	303	94.4

39. LEISURE AND HABITS

	PRIOR PERIOD		PERIOD I		PERIOD II	
	Num-ber	*Per cent*	*Num-ber*	*Per cent*	*Num-ber*	*Per cent*
Inapplicable or unknown	4	–	97	–	103	–
Constructive	0	–	17	4.7	15	4.3
Negative	16	3.6	93	26.0	105	29.9
Harmful	434	96.4	247	69.3	231	65.8

Criminality

40. SUMMARY OF ARRESTS

	PRIOR PERIOD		PERIOD I		PERIOD II	
	Num-ber	Per cent	Num-ber	Per cent	Num-ber	Per cent
Unknown	10	–	0	–	3	–
Against property	950	49.1	244	26.0	165	17.3
Against chastity	18	.9	60	6.3	17	1.8
Against family and children	14	.7	35	3.7	39	4.1
Against public health	495	25.6	168	17.9	164	17.2
Drink	279	14.4	388	41.4	488	51.3
Drugs	10	.5	12	1.3	11	1.2
Against person	107	5.5	13	1.5	41	4.3
Other	61	3.3	18	1.9	27	2.8
Total arrests	1944	–	938	–	955	–

41. FREQUENCY OF ARRESTS

	PRIOR PERIOD		PERIOD I		PERIOD II	
	Num-ber	Per cent	Num-ber	Per cent	Num-ber	Per cent
Unknown, inapplicable, or incalculable as only one arrest	139	–	281	–	303	–
One arrest in less than nine months	135	42.9	67	38.7	67	44.4
One arrest in nine to eighteen months	109	34.6	46	26.6	37	24.5
One arrest in eighteen or more months	71	22.5	60	34.7	47	31.1
Average frequency of arrests of those arrested more than once	$11.5 \pm .30$		$13.52 \pm .40$		$12.5 \pm .45$	

42. PREDOMINANT OFFENSE

	PRIOR PERIOD		PERIOD I		PERIOD II	
	Number	*Per cent*	*Number*	*Per cent*	*Number*	*Per cent*
Inapplicable, unknown, not determinable	49	–	71	–	94	–
Non-delinquent	0	–	90	–	118	–
Crimes against property	250	61.7	97	33.1	50	20.7
Crimes against chastity	13	3.2	15	5.1	14	5.8
Crimes against family and children	2	.5	12	4.1	8	3.3
Crimes against public health, safety, and policy	27	6.7	38	13.0	31	12.8
Drink	33	8.1	76	25.9	90	37.2
Drugs	4	1.0	5	1.7	6	2.5
Crimes against person	6	1.5	5	1.7	1	.4
Varied	70	17.3	45	15.4	42	17.3

43. DRINK

	PRIOR PERIOD		PERIOD I		PERIOD II	
	Number	*Per cent*	*Number*	*Per cent*	*Number*	*Per cent*
Inapplicable or unknown	0	–	117	–	99	–
No drink	282	62.1	148	43.9	173	48.7
Drink	172	37.9	189	56.1	182	51.3

44. SUMMARY OF DISPOSITIONS

	PRIOR PERIOD		PERIOD I		PERIOD II	
	Number	*Per cent*	*Number*	*Per cent*	*Number*	*Per cent*
Commitment	604	31.2	312	33.3	282	30.7
Probation	549	28.4	128	13.6	125	13.6
Fine	221	11.4	214	22.8	154	16.7
Commitment for non-payment of fine	59	3.1	36	3.8	36	3.9
File	237	12.3	118	12.6	136	14.8
Restitution			3	.3	1	.1
R.P.O.			0	–	50	5.4
Nol pros	263	13.6	15	1.6	11	1.2
No bill			6	.6	6	.7
Not guilty or released			106	11.4	119	12.9
Disposition unknown or other or awaiting disposition	11	–	0	–	35	–

45. Frequency of Convictions

	PRIOR PERIOD		PERIOD I		PERIOD II	
	Number	*Per cent*	*Number*	*Per cent*	*Number*	*Per cent*
Inapplicable, unknown, unknown if arrested, incalculable	154	–	296	–	308	–
One conviction in less than six months	38	12.7	35	22.2	44	30.2
One conviction in six to twelve months	92	30.7	34	21.6	28	19.2
One conviction in twelve to eighteen months	67	22.3	24	15.2	15	10.2
One conviction in eighteen to twenty-four months	32	10.7	23	14.5	23	15.8
One conviction in twenty-four months and over	71	23.6	42	26.5	36	24.6
Average frequency of convictions of those convicted more than once	15.14 ± .37		15.05 ± .46		15.65 ± .48	

46. Number of Penal Experiences

	PRIOR PERIOD		PERIOD I		PERIOD II	
	Number	*Per cent*	*Number*	*Per cent*	*Number*	*Per cent*
Inapplicable, unknown if any	29	–	42	–	55	–
No penal experience	179	42.1	235	57.0	252	63.2
Penal experience	246	57.9	177	43.0	147	36.8
One, two	0	–	130	31.6	95	23.8
Three and more	0	–	47	11.4	52	13.0
Average number of penal experiences			3.44 ± .08		2.72 ± .12	

47. Institutional Experiences—Nature of

	PRIOR PERIOD		PERIOD I		PERIOD II	
	Number	*Per cent*	*Number*	*Per cent*	*Number*	*Per cent*
Reformatories	76	12.6	38	10.5	7	1.7
Prisons	22	3.6	95	26.3	98	23.3
Jails, houses of correction, state farms	216	35.8	217	60.1	285	67.7
Other (truant schools, schools for feebleminded, industrial schools, protectorates, other)	290	48.0	11	3.1	31	7.3
Total institutional experiences of 454 men	604	–	361	–	421	–

48. Institutional Experiences—Geographical Spread

	PERIOD I		PERIOD II	
	Number	*Per cent*	*Number*	*Per cent*
Massachusetts	264	73.1	300	71.3
Other states	93	25.8	116	27.6
Canada	1	.3	2	.4
Europe	3	.8	3	.7
Total experiences	361	–	421	–

49. Time in Penal Institution

	PERIOD I		PERIOD II	
	Number	*Per cent*	*Number*	*Per cent*
Unknown	42	–	55	–
None	235	–	252	–
Under twenty months	95	53.7	69	46.9
Twenty to thirty months	24	13.6	17	11.6
Thirty to forty months	22	12.4	14	9.5
Forty to fifty months	13	7.3	12	8.2
Fifty to sixty months	17	9.6	17	11.6
Sixty months	6	3.4	18	12.2
Average number of months in penal institutions	22.30 ± 1.05		24.26 ± 1.05	

50. Principal Component of Misconduct

	PRIOR PERIOD		PERIOD I		PERIOD II	
	Number	*Per cent*	*Number*	*Per cent*	*Number*	*Per cent*
Unknown or too brief in community to judge	48	–	33	–	62	–
Non-delinquent	4	–	89	–	118	–
Inapplicable (penal institution at least 55 months or part of time and then mental hospital totalling 55 months on sentence imposed during previous period, and non-delinquent or delinquent upgrade after release)	0	–	7	–	24	–
Conviction for serious offense	328	81.7	148	45.5	96	38.4
Warrant out for serious offense	3	.7	13	4.0	4	1.6
D.D. or desertion from army or navy	8	2.0	9	2.8	3	1.2
Unofficial serious	15	3.7	11	3.4	15	6.0
Arrest for serious not followed by conviction	0	–	13	4.0	5	2.0
Conviction for minor offense	42	10.5	76	23.4	75	30.0
Unofficial minor or warrant out for minor	3	.7	40	12.3	40	16.0
Arrest for minor not followed by conviction	3	.7	15	4.6	12	4.8

51. Official Recognition of Delinquency

	PRIOR PERIOD		PERIOD I		PERIOD II	
	Number	*Per cent*	*Number*	*Per cent*	*Number*	*Per cent*
Inapplicable or unknown	48	–	40	–	86	–
No delinquency	4	–	89	–	118	–
Based on official record	384	95.5	289	88.9	202	80.8
On unofficial only	18	4.5	36	11.1	48	19.2

52. Aliases

	PERIOD I Number	PERIOD I Per cent	PERIOD II Number	PERIOD II Per cent
Inapplicable, unknown, no arrests	204	–	261	–
Used aliases	95	38.0	77	39.9
Did not use aliases	155	62.0	116	60.1

53. Associates in crime

	PRIOR PERIOD Number	PRIOR PERIOD Per cent	PERIOD II Number	PERIOD II Per cent
Inapplicable or unknown	10	–	311	–
Offenses committed alone	189	42.6	82	57.3
Offenses committed with others	255	57.4	61	42.7

54. Delinquencies

	PRIOR PERIOD Number	PRIOR PERIOD Per cent	DURING PAROLE* Number	DURING PAROLE* Per cent	PERIOD I Number	PERIOD I Per cent	PERIOD II Number	PERIOD II Per cent
Inapplicable or unknown	24	–	67	–	40	–	86	–
Non-delinquent	4	.9	126	32.6	89	21.5	118	32.1
Delinquent, minor	71	16.5	57	14.7	131	31.6	125	33.9
Delinquent, serious	355	82.6	204	52.7	194	46.9	125	34.0

Mental Condition

55. Mental condition

	PRIOR PERIOD Number	PRIOR PERIOD Per cent	PERIOD II Number	PERIOD II Per cent
Unknown	114	–	96	–
Normal	94	27.7	123	34.3
Abnormal	246	72.3	235	65.7

* This is the only table in which a comparison with the parole period is made.

Appendix E

CASE-BY-CASE CORRELATION OF
FACTOR INCIDENCE

In view of the fact that this research concerns itself with the changes which have taken place in the 454 offenders in the second five-year period as compared with the first five-year period, it is well to present this appendix of tables which indicates case by case the changes which have actually occurred. From the title of each table it is possible to refer to Appendix B, *Definition of Terms,* where not only the definition of the factor will be found but also reference to the original detailed tables in Appendix C, upon which these summary correlation tables are based.

Reading from left to right, the percentages total to 100. *Unknown* and *inapplicable* categories either in one or the other or in both periods, though presented, are not included in the percentages.

I. WITH WHOM LIVING AT END OF PERIOD

FIRST FIVE-YEAR PERIOD	SECOND FIVE-YEAR PERIOD																							Total	Un-known	Grand total
	Parents		Siblings		Other relatives		Wife and children		Children		Sweetheart		Employer		Alone		Institution		Other		Dead					
	Num-ber	Per cent	Num-ber	Per cent	Num-ber	Per cent	Num-ber	Per cent	Num-ber	Per cent	Num-ber	Per cent	Num-ber	Per cent	Num-ber	Per cent	Num-ber	Per cent	Num-ber	Per cent	Num-ber	Per cent				
Parents	29	58.0	4	8.0	1	2.0	10	20.0	0	–	0	–	0	–	3	6.0	2	4.0	0	–	1	2.0	50	2	52
Siblings	0	–	8	50.0	1	6.3	3	18.8	0	–	0	–	1	6.2	3	18.7	0	–	0	–	0	–	16	0	16
Other relatives	0	–	0	–	0	–	0	–	1	25.0	0	–	0	–	1	25.0	2	50.0	0	–	0	–	4	0	4
Wife and children	3	1.9	0	–	1	.6	129	83.8	2	1.3	1	.6	0	–	6	3.9	7	4.5	0	–	5	3.4	154	2	156
Sweetheart	4	33.3	0	–	0	–	2	16.7	0	–	3	25.0	1	8.3	0	–	1	8.3	0	–	1	8.4	12	1	13
Employer	0	–	0	–	0	–	0	–	0	–	0	–	3	100.0	0	–	0	–	0	–	0	–	3	0	3
Alone	5	7.1	3	4.3	0	–	17	24.3	0	–	2	2.9	2	2.8	30	42.9	7	10.0	0	–	4	5.7	70	2	72
Institution	7	8.2	5	5.9	0	–	3	3.5	0	–	1	1.2	0	–	18	21.2	49	57.6	0	–	2	2.4	85	2	87
Other	0	–	0	–	0	–	0	–	0	–	0	–	0	–	1	100.0	0	–	0	–	0	–	1	0	1
Unknown	0	–	0	–	0	–	1	–	0	–	0	–	0	–	2	–	2	–	0	–	1	–	6	44	50

347

2. MONTHS IN COMMUNITY

FIRST FIVE-YEAR PERIOD	SECOND FIVE-YEAR PERIOD								
	Never in community		Some time in community		In community throughout		Total	Inapplicable, unknown	Grand total
	Num-ber	Per cent	Num-ber	Per cent	Num-ber	Per cent			
Never in community	6	60.0	4	40.0	0	–	10	0	10
Some time in community	24	13.0	109	59.2	51	27.8	184	15	199
In community throughout	1	.5	33	16.4	167	83.1	201	7	208
Inapplicable, unknown	0	–	3	–	1	–	4	33	37

3. INSTITUTIONAL EXPERIENCES (PENAL AND NON-PENAL)

FIRST FIVE-YEAR PERIOD	SECOND FIVE-YEAR PERIOD								
	No institutional experience		Institutional experience		Inapplicable	Total	Inapplicable	Unknown	Grand total
	Num-ber	Per cent	Num-ber	Per cent					
No institutional experience	173	84.8	31	15.2	0	204	0	9	213
Institutional experience	54	28.7	134	71.3	0	188	0	13	201
Inapplicable	0	–	2	–	0	2	0	0	2
Unknown	4	–	3	–	0	7	0	31	38

4. MOBILITY

FIRST FIVE-YEAR PERIOD	SECOND FIVE-YEAR PERIOD							
	No mobility		Mobility					Grand total
	Number	Per cent	Number	Per cent	Total	Inapplicable	Unknown	
No mobility	148	89.2	18	10.8	166	4	4	174
Mobility	37	20.7	142	79.3	179	21	11	211
Inapplicable	4	–	7	–	11	14	0	25
Unknown	2	–	2	–	4	1	39	44

5. HOUSEHOLD STABILITY

FIRST FIVE-YEAR PERIOD	SECOND FIVE-YEAR PERIOD									
	No change		One or two		Three or more		Total	Inapplicable	Unknown	Grand total
	Number	Per cent	Number	Per cent	Number	Per cent				
No change	102	77.9	17	13.0	12	9.1	131	6	3	140
One or two	52	69.3	9	12.0	14	18.7	75	7	5	87
Three or more	17	15.5	15	13.6	78	70.9	110	10	12	132
Inapplicable	6	–	1	–	3	–	10	14	0	24
Unknown	6	–	1	–	3	–	10	5	56	71

6. HOME—PHYSICAL

	SECOND FIVE-YEAR PERIOD									
	Good		Fair		Poor					
FIRST FIVE-YEAR PERIOD	Number	Per cent	Number	Per cent	Number	Per cent	Total	Inapplicable	Unknown	Grand total
Good	72	88.9	8	9.9	1	1.2	81	1	4	86
Fair	19	16.8	81	71.7	13	11.5	113	5	5	123
Poor	6	5.9	17	16.7	79	77.4	102	8	9	119
Inapplicable	4	–	3	–	3	–	10	20	4	34
Unknown	8	–	7	–	4	–	19	11	62	92

7. NEIGHBORHOOD—TYPE

	SECOND FIVE-YEAR PERIOD									
	Urban		Rural		Varied					
FIRST FIVE-YEAR PERIOD	Number	Per cent	Number	Per cent	Number	Per cent	Total	Inapplicable, unknown	Grand total	
Urban	243	95.3	3	1.2	9	3.5	255	39	294	
Rural	2	8.3	20	83.4	2	8.3	24	2	26	
Varied	18	41.9	8	18.6	17	39.5	43	14	57	
Inapplicable, unknown	13	–	2	–	1	–	16	61	77	

8. NEIGHBORHOOD INFLUENCES

FIRST FIVE-YEAR PERIOD	SECOND FIVE-YEAR PERIOD									
	Good		Fair		Poor		Total	Inapplicable	Unknown	Grand total
	Number	*Per cent*	*Number*	*Per cent*	*Number*	*Per cent*				
Good	28	60.9	15	32.6	3	6.5	46	2	3	51
Fair	9	6.8	108	81.2	16	12.0	133	6	6	145
Poor	4	3.4	25	21.4	88	75.2	117	7	12	136
Inapplicable	3	–	4	–	3	–	10	20	5	35
Unknown	2	–	12	–	4	–	18	10	59	87

9. MARITAL STATUS AT END OF PERIOD

FIRST FIVE-YEAR PERIOD	SECOND FIVE-YEAR PERIOD													Inapplicable, unknown, or unknown if married or single	Grand total
	Single		Married, living with wife		Separated, divorced		Illegally married, living with wife		Illegally married, separated		Widowed		Total		
	Number	Per cent	Number	Per cent	Number	Per cent	Number	Per cent	Number	Per cent	Number	Per cent			
Single	156	84.3	22	11.9	7	3.8	0	–	0	–	0	–	185	2	187
Married, living with wife	0	–	133	86.4	16	10.4	1	.6	1	.6	3	2.0	154	5	159
Separated, divorced	0	–	5	9.6	42	80.8	2	3.8	0	–	1	2.0	50	2	52
Illegally married, living with wife	0	–	0	–	0	–	1	50.0	1	50.0	0	–	2	0	2
Illegally married, separated	0	–	1	100.0	0	–	0	–	0	–	0	–	1	0	1
Widowed	1	–	3	–	0	–	0	–	0	–	2	–	6	1	7
Inapplicable, unknown, or unknown if married or single	0	–	0	–	2	–	0	–	0	–	0	–	2	44	46

352

10. NUMBER OF CHILDREN

FIRST FIVE-YEAR PERIOD	SECOND FIVE-YEAR PERIOD						
	No children		Children			Number unknown, unknown if any	Grand total
	Num-ber	Per cent	Num-ber	Per cent	Total		
No children	215	86.0	35	14.0	250	8	258
Children	6	3.8	153	96.2	159	0	159
Number unknown, unknown if any	0	–	0	–	0	37	37

11. CONJUGAL RELATIONS

FIRST FIVE-YEAR PERIOD	SECOND FIVE-YEAR PERIOD									Inapplicable, unknown, single	Grand total
	Good		Fair		Poor		Total				
	Number	Per cent	Number	Per cent	Number	Per cent					
Good	96	88.1	4	3.7	9	8.2	109			5	114
Fair	2	6.9	17	58.6	10	34.5	29			5	34
Poor	3	11.1	2	7.4	22	81.5	27			28	55
Inapplicable, unknown, single	21	–	7	–	8	–	36			215	251

12. RELATION TO NEAREST RELATIVES

FIRST FIVE-YEAR PERIOD	SECOND FIVE-YEAR PERIOD							Inapplicable, unknown	Grand total
	In touch with, friendly		In touch when in need		Rarely in touch		Total		
	Number	Per cent	Number	Per cent	Number	Per cent			
In touch with, friendly	167	92.3	9	5.0	5	2.7	181	12	193
In touch when in need	12	16.0	50	66.7	13	17.3	75	5	80
Rarely in touch	4	5.1	4	5.1	70	89.8	78	9	87
Inapplicable, unknown	7	–	8	–	15	–	30	64	94

13. FAMILY RELATIONSHIPS

	SECOND FIVE-YEAR PERIOD						
FIRST FIVE-YEAR PERIOD	Succeed		Fail				
	Num-ber	*Per cent*	*Num-ber*	*Per cent*	Total	Inapplicable, unknown	Grand total
Succeed	154	84.2	29	15.8	183	7	190
Fail	23	14.7	133	85.3	156	22	178
Inapplicable, unknown	3	–	18	–	21	65	86

14. DEPENDENTS

	SECOND FIVE-YEAR PERIOD						
FIRST FIVE-YEAR PERIOD	No dependents		Dependents				
	Num-ber	*Per cent*	*Num-ber*	*Per cent*	Total	Inapplicable, unknown	Grand total
No dependents	85	78.7	23	21.3	108	20	128
Dependents	18	7.5	222	92.5	240	23	263
Inapplicable, unknown	9	–	5	–	14	49	63

15. DISPOSITION OF EARNINGS

FIRST FIVE-YEAR PERIOD	SECOND FIVE-YEAR PERIOD											
	Self mostly		Wife and/or children, has no dependent parents		Wife and/or children, has dependent parents		Dependent parents		Total	Inapplicable, unknown	Grand total
	Number	Per cent	Number	Per cent	Number	Per cent	Number	Per cent			
Self mostly	148	84.1	26	14.8	0	–	2	1.1	176	23	199
Wife and/or children, has no dependent parents	13	10.3	108	85.7	5	4.0	0	–	126	8	134
Wife and/or children, has dependent parents	1	16.7	5	83.3	0	–	0	–	6	0	6
Dependent parents	12	50.0	4	16.7	0	–	8	33.3	24	2	26
Inapplicable, unknown	14	–	4	–	1	–	1	–	20	69	89

16. ECONOMIC CONDITION

FIRST FIVE-YEAR PERIOD	SECOND FIVE-YEAR PERIOD								
	Comfortable		Marginal		Dependent		Total	Inapplicable, unknown	Grand total
	Number	Per cent	Number	Per cent	Number	Per cent			
Comfortable	21	67.8	10	32.2	0	–	31	1	32
Marginal	12	4.7	213	84.2	28	11.1	253	49	302
Dependent	0	–	8	20.5	31	79.5	39	8	47
Inapplicable, unknown	1	–	12	–	1	–	14	59	73

17. KNOWN TO SOCIAL SERVICE AGENCIES

	SECOND FIVE-YEAR PERIOD						
FIRST FIVE-YEAR PERIOD	Not known to agencies		Known to agencies				
	Num-ber	*Per cent*	*Num-ber*	*Per cent*	Total	Inapplicable, unknown	Grand total
Not known to agencies	175	68.6	80	31.4	255	23	278
Known to agencies	20	25.3	59	74.7	79	10	89
Inapplicable, unknown	15	–	8	–	23	64	87

18. ECONOMIC RESPONSIBILITY

	SECOND FIVE-YEAR PERIOD						
FIRST FIVE-YEAR PERIOD	Meets responsibility		Does not meet responsibility				
	Num-ber	*Per cent*	*Num-ber*	*Per cent*	Total	Inapplicable, unknown	Grand total
Meets responsibility	188	87.4	27	12.6	215	26	241
Does not meet responsi-bility	17	15.6	92	84.4	109	15	124
Inapplicable, unknown	10	–	3	–	13	76	89

19. USUAL OCCUPATION

FIRST FIVE-YEAR PERIOD	SECOND FIVE-YEAR PERIOD																				
	Idle through own fault		Illegitimate occupation		Rough labor		Trucking, teaming, chauffeuring		Factory hand		Farm hand		Salesmen and store clerks		Skilled trades		Restaurant work		Total	Inapplicable, varied, unknown, other	Grand total
	Number	Per cent	Number	Per cent	Number	Per cent	Number	Per cent	Number	Per cent	Number	Per cent	Number	Per cent	Number	Per cent	Number	Per cent			
Idle through own fault	0	–	0	–	0	–	0	–	0	–	0	–	0	–	0	–	0	–	0	0	0
Illegitimate occupation	1	5.0	15	75.0	1	5.0	2	10.0	0	–	0	–	0	–	0	–	1	5.0	20	7	27
Rough labor	6	8.3	4	5.6	49	68.1	3	4.2	1	1.4	1	1.4	1	1.4	5	6.9	2	2.7	72	12	84
Trucking, teaming, chauffeuring	1	2.2	2	4.3	10	21.7	30	65.3	0	–	0	–	2	4.3	0	–	1	2.2	46	5	51
Factory hand	3	5.8	0	–	5	9.6	1	1.9	39	75.0	0	–	0	–	1	1.9	3	5.8	52	8	60
Farm hand	0	–	0	–	0	–	0	–	0	–	10	100.0	0	–	0	–	0	–	10	1	11
Salesmen and store clerks	2	7.4	0	–	0	–	0	–	0	–	0	–	25	92.6	0	–	0	–	27	3	30
Skilled trades	1	1.3	2	2.7	5	6.8	3	4.1	3	4.1	2	2.7	1	1.3	57	77.0	0	–	74	11	85
Restaurant work	0	–	0	–	5	29.4	0	–	0	–	0	–	0	–	2	11.8	10	58.8	17	0	17
Inapplicable, varied, unknown or other	1	–	2	–	8	–	3	–	1	–	0	–	2	–	2	–	4	–	23	66	89

20. ILLEGITIMATE OCCUPATION

FIRST FIVE-YEAR PERIOD	SECOND FIVE-YEAR PERIOD								
	No illegitimate occupation		Illegitimate occupation part of time		Illegitimate occupation throughout		Total	Inapplicable, unknown	Grand total
	Num-ber	Per cent	Num-ber	Per cent	Num-ber	Per cent			
No illegitimate occupation	217	96.0	9	4.0	0	–	226	24	250
Illegitimate occupation part of time	7	20.0	24	68.6	4	11.4	35	16	51
Illegitimate occupation throughout	1	5.3	3	15.8	15	78.9	19	4	23
Inapplicable, unknown	12	–	14	–	4	–	30	100	130

21. SKILL

FIRST FIVE-YEAR PERIOD	SECOND FIVE-YEAR PERIOD								
	Unskilled		Semi-skilled		Skilled		Total	Inapplicable, unknown	Grand total
	Num-ber	Per cent	Num-ber	Per cent	Num-ber	Per cent			
Unskilled	99	82.5	20	16.7	1	.8	120	18	138
Semi-skilled	17	10.7	136	85.5	6	3.8	159	25	184
Skilled	0	–	3	9.1	30	90.9	33	2	35
Inapplicable, unknown	9	–	9	–	1	–	19	78	97

359

22. USED MASSACHUSETTS REFORMATORY OCCUPATION

FIRST FIVE-YEAR PERIOD	SECOND FIVE-YEAR PERIOD								
	Did not use Massachusetts Reformatory occupation		Used Massachusetts Reformatory occupation		Used same technique but different occupation		Total	Inapplicable, unknown	Grand total
	Number	Per cent	Number	Per cent	Number	Per cent			
Did not use Massachusetts Reformatory occupation	251	96.9	8	3.1	0	–	259	40	299
Used Massachusetts Reformatory occupation	17	28.8	41	69.5	1	1.7	59	5	64
Used same technique but different occupation	0	–	0	–	3	100.0	3	0	3
Inapplicable, unknown	15	–	2	–	0	–	17	71	88

23. AVERAGE WAGE—WEEKLY

FIRST FIVE-YEAR PERIOD	SECOND FIVE-YEAR PERIOD								
	Less than $25		$25–$35		$35 and over		Total	Inapplicable, unknown	Grand total
	Number	Per cent	Number	Per cent	Number	Per cent			
Less than $25	43	55.1	30	38.5	5	6.4	78	21	99
$25–$35	8	13.8	29	50.0	21	36.2	58	15	73
$35 and over	0	–	4	12.5	28	87.5	32	1	33
Inapplicable, unknown	23	–	16	–	14	–	53	196	249

24. HIGHEST WAGE—WEEKLY

FIRST FIVE-YEAR PERIOD	SECOND FIVE-YEAR PERIOD								
	Less than $25		$25–$35		$35 and over		Total	Inapplicable, unknown	Grand total
	Number	Per cent	Number	Per cent	Number	Per cent			
Less than $25	52	73.2	12	16.9	7	9.9	71	15	86
$25–$35	22	29.7	34	45.9	18	24.4	74	25	99
$35 and over	3	3.6	16	19.3	64	77.1	83	12	95
Inapplicable, unknown	10	–	11	–	15	–	36	138	174

25. WORK HABITS

FIRST FIVE-YEAR PERIOD	SECOND FIVE-YEAR PERIOD								
	Good		Fair		Poor*		Total	Inapplicable, unknown	Grand total
	Number	Per cent	Number	Per cent	Number	Per cent			
Good	102	87.9	13	11.2	1	.9	116	5	121
Fair	22	22.0	68	68.0	10	10.0	100	9	109
Poor*	11	10.3	26	24.3	70	65.4	107	23	130
Inapplicable, unknown	5	–	4	–	5	–	14	80	94

* Includes those engaged in *illegitimate occupation* throughout.

26. USUAL REASON FOR LEAVING WORK

FIRST FIVE-YEAR PERIOD	SECOND FIVE-YEAR PERIOD									
	Steady worker, seldom changes		Fault of worker		Not fault of worker or to better self		Total	Inapplicable, unknown	Grand total
	Num- ber	Per cent	Num- ber	Per cent	Num- ber	Per cent			
Steady worker, seldom changes	32	62.7	4	7.8	15	29.5	51	0	51
Fault of worker	5	4.1	101	82.8	16	13.1	122	47	169
Not fault of worker or to better self	10	11.9	11	13.1	63	75.0	84	9	93
Inapplicable, unknown	7	–	13	–	15	–	35	106	141

27. STEADINESS OF EMPLOYMENT

FIRST FIVE-YEAR PERIOD	SECOND FIVE-YEAR PERIOD											
	Regular		Fairly regular		Irregular		Illegitimate		Total	Inapplicable, unknown	Grand total
	Num- ber	Per cent	Num- ber	Per cent	Num- ber	Per cent	Num- ber	Per cent			
Regular	67	87.0	9	11.7	1	1.3	0	–	77	2	79
Fairly regular	20	17.8	75	67.0	17	15.2	0	–	112	8	120
Irregular	5	4.3	22	18.8	85	72.6	5	4.3	117	23	140
Illegitimate	1	5.3	3	15.8	0	–	15	78.9	19	4	23
Inapplicable, unknown	3	–	7	–	3	–	3	–	16	76	92

28. AVERAGE PERIOD OF TIME HELD JOB

FIRST FIVE-YEAR PERIOD	SECOND FIVE-YEAR PERIOD											
	Less than 3 months		3–12 months		12–36 months		36 and more months		Total	Inapplicable, unknown, incalculable	Grand total
	Number	Per cent	Number	Per cent	Number	Per cent	Number	Per cent			
Less than 3 months	78	82.9	12	12.8	1	1.1	3	3.2	94	38	132
3–12 months	7	17.9	20	51.3	9	23.1	3	7.7	39	26	65
12–36 months	3	6.0	6	12.0	25	50.0	16	32.0	50	13	63
36 and more months	0	–	0	–	5	20.8	19	79.2	24	6	30
Inapplicable, unknown, incalculable	13	–	8	–	11	–	8	–	40	124	164

29. LONGEST PERIOD OF TIME HELD JOB

FIRST FIVE-YEAR PERIOD	SECOND FIVE-YEAR PERIOD											
	Less than 3 months		3–12 months		12–36 months		36 months and longer		Total	Inapplicable, unknown	Grand total
	Number	Per cent	Number	Per cent	Number	Per cent	Number	Per cent			
Less than 3 months	51	68.9	13	17.6	8	10.8	2	2.7	74	31	105
3–12 months	12	25.0	20	41.7	11	22.9	5	10.4	48	25	73
12–36 months	3	4.4	7	10.3	37	54.4	21	30.9	68	16	84
36 months and longer	2	4.3	0	–	8	17.0	37	78.7	47	4	51
Inapplicable, unknown	8	–	6	–	9	–	4	–	27	114	141

30. INDUSTRIAL JUDGMENT

FIRST FIVE-YEAR PERIOD	SECOND FIVE-YEAR PERIOD								
	Good		Fair		Poor				
	Num-ber	Per cent	Num-ber	Per cent	Num-ber	Per cent	Total	Inapplicable, unknown	Grand total
Good	64	86.5	9	12.2	1	1.3	74	3	77
Fair	12	10.4	90	78.3	13	11.3	115	7	122
Poor	5	3.8	22	16.7	105	79.5	132	30	162
Inapplicable, unknown	3	–	7	–	7	–	17	76	93

31. COMPANIONS

FIRST FIVE-YEAR PERIOD	SECOND FIVE-YEAR PERIOD						
	Harmless		Harmful				
	Num-ber	Per cent	Num-ber	Per cent	Total	Inapplicable, unknown	Grand total
Harmless	90	88.2	12	11.8	102	6	108
Harmful	22	11.0	178	89.0	200	36	236
Inapplicable, unknown	13	–	23	–	36	74	110

32. HAUNTS

FIRST FIVE-YEAR PERIOD	SECOND FIVE-YEAR PERIOD						
	Harmless		Harmful				
	Num-ber	Per cent	Num-ber	Per cent	Total	Inapplicable, unknown	Grand total
Harmless	90	88.2	12	11.8	102	6	108
Harmful	22	11.6	167	88.4	189	40	229
Inapplicable, unknown	13	–	21	–	34	83	117

33. SOCIETY MEMBER

FIRST FIVE-YEAR PERIOD	Yes (wholesome)		No		Yes (but not wholesome)		Total	Inapplicable, unknown	Grand total
	Number	Per cent	Number	Per cent	Number	Per cent			
Yes (wholesome)	10	76.9	2	15.4	1	7.7	13	1	14
No	5	1.9	249	94.3	10	3.8	264	46	310
Yes (but not wholesome)	0	–	12	42.9	16	57.1	28	1	29
Inapplicable, unknown	0	–	13	–	2	–	15	86	101

SECOND FIVE-YEAR PERIOD

34. CHURCH ATTENDANCE

FIRST FIVE-YEAR PERIOD	Regular		Irregular		None		Total	Inapplicable, unknown	Grand total
	Number	Per cent	Number	Per cent	Number	Per cent			
Regular	20	64.5	8	25.8	3	9.7	31	5	36
Irregular	7	6.9	78	76.5	17	16.6	102	22	124
None	1	.9	9	8.4	97	90.7	107	18	125
Inapplicable, unknown	5	–	16	–	14	–	35	134	169

SECOND FIVE-YEAR PERIOD

35. EDUCATIONAL ACTIVITIES

FIRST FIVE-YEAR PERIOD	SECOND FIVE-YEAR PERIOD						
	Yes		No			Inapplicable,	Grand
	Num-ber	Per cent	Num-ber	Per cent	Total	unknown	total
Yes	7	58.3	5	41.7	12	2	14
No	6	2.1	285	97.9	291	48	339
Inapplicable, unknown	5	–	13	–	18	83	101

36. LEISURE AND HABITS

FIRST FIVE-YEAR PERIOD	SECOND FIVE-YEAR PERIOD								Total	Inapplicable, unknown	Grand total
	Constructive		Negative		Harmful						
	Number	Per cent	Number	Per cent	Number	Per cent					
Constructive	10	58.8	5	29.4	2	11.8			17	0	17
Negative	5	5.6	71	79.8	13	14.6			89	4	93
Harmful	0	–	19	8.8	196	91.2			215	32	247
Inapplicable, unknown	0	–	10	–	20	–			30	67	97

37. FREQUENCY OF ARRESTS

FIRST FIVE-YEAR PERIOD	SECOND FIVE-YEAR PERIOD						Total	Inapplicable, unknown, incalculable	Grand total
	One arrest in less than a year		One arrest in one to two years		One arrest in two years and over				
	Number	Per cent	Number	Per cent	Number	Per cent			
One arrest in less than a year	47	82.5	10	17.5	0	–	57	29	86
One arrest in one to two years	17	42.5	14	35.0	9	22.5	40	22	62
One arrest in two years and over	3	27.3	5	45.5	3	27.2	11	14	25
Inapplicable, unknown, incalculable	15	–	18	–	10	–	43	238	281

38. PREDOMINANT OFFENSE

SECOND FIVE-YEAR PERIOD

FIRST FIVE-YEAR PERIOD	Non-delinquent	Crimes against property Number	Per cent	Crimes against chastity Number	Per cent	Crimes against family and children Number	Per cent	Crimes against public health, safety, and policy Number	Per cent	Drink Number	Per cent	Drugs Number	Per cent	Crimes against person Number	Per cent	Varied Number	Per cent	Total delinquent	Inapplicable, unknown	Grand total
Non-delinquent	77	1	–	1	–	0	–	3	–	4	–	0	–	0	–	1	–	10	3	90
Crimes against property	10	44	74.6	1	1.7	0	–	6	10.2	4	6.8	0	–	0	–	4	6.7	59	28	97
Crimes against chastity	4	0	–	8	80.0	0	–	0	–	0	–	0	–	0	–	2	20.0	10	1	15
Crimes against family and children	2	0	–	0	–	6	75.0	0	–	1	12.5	0	–	0	–	1	12.5	8	2	12
Crimes against public health, safety, and policy	6	0	–	0	–	2	7.1	19	67.9	6	21.4	0	–	0	–	1	3.6	28	4	38
Drink	5	0	–	0	–	0	–	0	–	66	95.7	0	–	0	–	3	4.3	69	2	76
Drugs	0	0	–	0	–	0	–	0	–	0	–	5	100.0	0	–	0	–	5	0	5
Crimes against person	0	0	–	0	–	0	–	1	50.0	0	–	0	–	1	50.0	0	–	2	3	5
Varied	2	3	7.7	1	2.6	0	–	0	–	5	12.8	1	2.6	0	–	29	74.3	39	4	45
Inapplicable, unknown	12	2	–	3	–	0	–	2	–	4	–	0	–	0	–	1	–	12	47	71

39. FREQUENCY OF CONVICTIONS

FIRST FIVE-YEAR PERIOD	SECOND FIVE-YEAR PERIOD									
	One conviction in less than a year		One conviction in one to two years		One conviction in two years and over		Total	Inapplicable, unknown, incalculable	Grand total
	Number	*Per cent*	*Number*	*Per cent*	*Number*	*Per cent*			
One conviction in less than a year	33	70.2	12	25.5	2	4.3	47	22	69
One conviction in one to two years	15	48.4	8	25.8	8	25.8	31	16	47
One conviction in two years and over	9	37.5	4	16.7	11	45.8	24	18	42
Inapplicable, unknown, incalculable	15	–	14	–	15	–	44	252	296

40. NUMBER OF PENAL EXPERIENCES

	SECOND FIVE-YEAR PERIOD						
FIRST FIVE-YEAR PERIOD	None		One or more				
	Num-ber	*Per cent*	*Num-ber*	*Per cent*	Total	Inapplicable, unknown	Grand total
None	195	86.7	30	13.3	225	10	235
One or more	51	31.1	113	68.9	164	12	176
Inapplicable, unknown	6	–	4	–	10	33	43

41. TIME IN PENAL INSTITUTIONS

FIRST FIVE-YEAR PERIOD	SECOND FIVE-YEAR PERIOD								Total	Unknown	Grand total
	None		Less than 20 months		Twenty months and more						
	Number	Per cent	Number	Per cent	Number	Per cent					
None	195	86.7	24	10.7	6	2.6			225	10	235
Less than twenty months	35	39.3	34	38.2	20	22.5			89	8	97
Twenty months and more	17	21.5	10	12.7	52	65.8			79	3	82
Unknown	5	–	2	–	0	–			7	33	40

42. PRINCIPAL COMPONENT OF MISCONDUCT*

SECOND FIVE-YEAR PERIOD

FIRST FIVE-YEAR PERIOD	Non-delinquent	Penal institution throughout	Conviction for serious offense	Warrant out for serious offense	Dishonorable discharge or desertion from army or navy	Unofficial serious	Arrest for serious not followed by conviction	Conviction for minor offense	Unofficial minor	Arrest for minor not followed by conviction	Unknown, inapplicable (non-penal institution throughout)	Grand total
Non-delinquent	76	0	2	0	0	1	0	4	2	1	3	89
Penal institution throughout	1	3	1	0	0	0	1	0	2	0	0	8
Conviction for serious offense	11	20	67	2	2	8	3	17	5	4	9	148
Warrant out for serious offense	2	0	3	2	0	1	0	1	0	0	4	13
Dishonorable discharge or desertion from army or navy	1	0	1	0	0	1	0	2	2	0	2	9
Unofficial serious	0	0	6	0	1	2	0	0	1	0	1	11
Arrest for serious not followed by conviction	1	0	2	0	0	1	1	3	1	0	4	13
Conviction for minor offense	12	1	10	0	0	0	0	36	9	2	6	76
Unofficial minor	4	0	1	0	0	1	0	7	15	3	1	32
Arrest for minor not followed by conviction	6	0	0	0	0	0	0	5	2	1	1	15
Penal institution for part of period on sentence previously imposed	2	0	3	0	0	0	0	0	0	1	1	7
Unknown, inapplicable (non-penal institution throughout)	2	0	0	0	0	0	0	0	1	0	30	33

* In this table, percentages have not been given because the categories are so fine.

43. OFFICIAL RECOGNITION OF DELINQUENCY

FIRST FIVE-YEAR PERIOD	Official		Unofficial		Non-delinquent	Total delinquent	Inapplicable, unknown	Grand total
	Number	Per cent	Number	Per cent				
Official	177	86.8	27	13.2	36	204	49	289
Unofficial	15	48.4	16	51.6	3	31	2	36
Non-delinquent	4	–	3	–	78	7	5	90
Inapplicable, unknown	6	–	2	–	2	8	29	39

SECOND FIVE-YEAR PERIOD

44. ALIASES

FIRST FIVE-YEAR PERIOD	SECOND FIVE-YEAR PERIOD						
	Used aliases		Did not use aliases				
	Num-ber	Per cent	Num-ber	Per cent	Total	Inapplicable, unknown	Grand total
Used aliases	61	96.8	2	3.2	63	32	95
Did not use aliases	5	5.4	88	94.6	93	62	155
Inapplicable, unknown	11	–	27	–	38	166	204

45. DELINQUENCIES

FIRST FIVE-YEAR PERIOD	Non-delinquent		Delinquent minor		Delinquent serious		Total	Inapplicable, unknown	Grand total
	Number	*Per cent*	*Number*	*Per cent*	*Number*	*Per cent*			
Non-delinquent	78	88.6	7	7.9	3	3.5	88	1	89
Delinquent minor	22	19.1	82	71.3	11	9.6	115	16	131
Delinquent serious	16	10.2	33	21.0	108	68.8	157	37	194
Inapplicable, unknown	2	–	3	–	3	–	8	32	40

SECOND FIVE-YEAR PERIOD

Appendix F

FACTOR-BY-FACTOR COMPARISON OF PERCENTAGE
OF NON-DELINQUENCY IN PERIODS I AND II

In this appendix are presented the tables on which the data and conclusions of Chapter IX are based. Because the findings in the chapter are so significant the authors present in full the tables from which the conclusions were drawn.

In the following tables, therefore, are presented the percentages of *non-delinquency* in Period I and Period II for each category of each factor together with the proportional increase in *non-delinquency* in Period II. The percentage of non-delinquency for all the known cases represented in each factor is also presented. It should be noted that, although the percentage of non-delinquency for the entire group of cases studied is 21.5 in Period I and 32.1 in Period II, and the proportional improvement therefore in Period II as compared with Period I is 1.4, this proportion varies a little from factor to factor because the number of known cases differs in each factor, in the majority of cases the ratio being 1.3.

Examination of these tables on the basis of the standard deviation[1] will show that the only factor in which the increase in non-delinquency in Period II as compared with Period I is significantly greater than the average is the factor of *Age*.

For definitions of the factors and their categories, the reader is

[1] The particular formula applied to these data was suggested to us by Professor Carl Doering, statistician of the Harvard School of Public Health, who describes its significance as follows:

"The standard deviation, σ, of a ratio of two proportions, $p_2/p_1 = R =$

$$\sigma_R = R(\sigma^2 p_1/p_1^2 + \sigma^2 p_2/p_2^2 - 2r_{p_1 p_2} \, \sigma p_1/p_1 \, \sigma p_2/p_2)^{\frac{1}{2}}$$

where

$$\sigma p_1^2 = p_1 q_1/n_1 = p_1(1 - p_1)/n_1; \qquad \sigma^2 p_2 = p_2 q_2/n_2 = p_2(1 - p_2)/n_2$$

where n_1 and n_2 are the denominators of the respective proportions p_1 and p_2 and $\sigma^2 p_1$ and

asked to consult Appendix B, in which the factors are presented alphabetically.

$\sigma^2 p_2$ are the standard deviations of a Bernoulian chance distribution. The term r_{p1p2} is the correlation coefficient of the proportions p_1 and p_2 and is unknown.

Several assumptions and reasonable substitutions can be made in order to make the above formula both applicable and more simply evaluated.

1. r_{p1p2} is assumed to be zero although in the above data it is probably positive and greater than zero but less than unity.

2. The value of R of the whole group is substituted for the individual R's of the sub-groups.

3. The values p_1 and p_2 of the whole group are also substituted in like manner and in addition since p_1 and p_2 are nearly equal their average $(p_1 + p_2)/2$ is substituted for each.

4. Since in most subgroups n_1 and n_2 are nearly equal their average $(n_1 + n_2)/2$ is substituted for each.

The formula therefore becomes,

$$\sigma_R = R\left((p_1 + p_2)/2 \, \frac{[1 - (p_1 + p_2)/2]\, 4 \cdot 2 \cdot 2}{(p_1 + p_2)^2 \, (n_1 + n_2)} \right)^{\frac{1}{2}}$$

$$= 1.3 \left(\frac{(2 - .57)\,(4)}{.57\,(n_1 + n_2)} \right)^{\frac{1}{2}} = \frac{4.1}{\sqrt{n_1 + n_2}}$$

The effect of these assumptions and substitutions is both to increase and diminish the estimated value compared with the true value. It is believed that the errors introduced do not entirely cancel each other but that the estimated value is larger than the true value in most cases. It is further regarded that this error is one in the right direction since from experience it is known that the chance variation is small compared with the true variation."

Family Background of Offenders

1. NATIVITY OF PARENTS AND SONS

	NON-DELINQUENTS IN PERIOD I		NON-DELINQUENTS IN PERIOD II		PROPORTIONAL INCREASE IN NON-DELINQUENCY
	Number	*Per cent*	*Number*	*Per cent*	
One or both parents foreign, son native	44	23.2	60	31.6	1.4
All native	21	21.0	23	24.5	1.2
All foreign	21	31.8	30	45.5	1.4
Total	*86*	*24.2*	*113*	*32.3*	*1.3*

2. EDUCATION OF PARENTS

	NON-DELINQUENTS IN PERIOD I		NON-DELINQUENTS IN PERIOD II		PROPORTIONAL INCREASE IN NON-DELINQUENCY
	Number	*Per cent*	*Number*	*Per cent*	
Both parents without formal education	71	24.6	104	36.4	1.5
One or both parents, common school	15	25.4	17	28.8	1.1
Total	*86*	*24.7*	*121*	*35.1*	*1.4*

3. ECONOMIC STATUS OF PARENTS

	NON-DELINQUENTS IN PERIOD I		NON-DELINQUENTS IN PERIOD II		PROPORTIONAL INCREASE IN NON-DELINQUENCY
	Number	*Per cent*	*Number*	*Per cent*	
Dependent	5	10.6	10	21.3	2.0
Marginal	49	25.4	61	31.6	1.2
Comfortable	24	26.1	32	34.8	1.3
Total	*78*	*23.5*	*103*	*31.1*	*1.3*

4. Family delinquency

	NON-DELINQUENTS IN PERIOD I		NON-DELINQUENTS IN PERIOD II		PROPORTIONAL INCREASE IN NON-DELINQUENCY
	Number	Per cent	Number	Per cent	
Yes	39	17.6	52	23.4	1.3
No	30	36.1	40	48.2	1.3
Total	69	22.6	92	30.2	*1.3*

Personal History prior to Reformatory Commitment

5. Nativity of offender

	NON-DELINQUENTS IN PERIOD I		NON-DELINQUENTS IN PERIOD II		PROPORTIONAL INCREASE IN NON-DELINQUENCY
	Number	Per cent	Number	Per cent	
Native born	66	22.5	85	29.0	1.3
Foreign born	22	32.8	31	46.3	1.5
Total	88	24.4	116	32.2	*1.3*

6. Intelligence

	NON-DELINQUENTS IN PERIOD I		NON-DELINQUENTS IN PERIOD II		PROPORTIONAL INCREASE IN NON-DELINQUENCY
	Number	Per cent	Number	Per cent	
Normal	36	31.6	43	37.7	1.2
Dull	24	26.4	28	30.8	1.2
Borderline	13	18.6	22	31.4	1.7
Feebleminded	10	16.1	14	22.6	1.4
Total	83	24.6	107	31.8	*1.3*

7. Mental condition (disease or distortion)

	NON-DELINQUENTS IN PERIOD I		NON-DELINQUENTS IN PERIOD II		PROPORTIONAL INCREASE IN NON-DELINQUENCY
	Number	Per cent	Number	Per cent	
No mental abnormality	67	37.6	91	51.1	1.4
Mental abnormality	4	4.0	9	8.9	2.2
Total	71	25.4	100	35.8	*1.4*

8. Age at leaving home

	NON-DELINQUENTS IN PERIOD I		NON-DELINQUENTS IN PERIOD II		PROPORTIONAL INCREASE IN NON-DELINQUENCY
	Number	Per cent	Number	Per cent	
Under 14	20	16.8	30	25.2	1.5
14 and over	50	31.3	60	37.5	1.2
Total	70	25.1	90	32.3	1.3

9. Mobility

	NON-DELINQUENTS IN PERIOD I		NON-DELINQUENTS IN PERIOD II		PROPORTIONAL INCREASE IN NON-DELINQUENCY
	Number	Per cent	Number	Per cent	
Yes	45	30.0	54	33.8	1.1
No	43	21.5	62	31.0	1.4
Total	88	25.1	116	32.2	1.3

10. Age began work

	NON-DELINQUENTS IN PERIOD I		NON-DELINQUENTS IN PERIOD II		PROPORTIONAL INCREASE IN NON-DELINQUENCY
	Number	Per cent	Number	Per cent	
Under 15	33	21.6	43	28.1	1.3
15 and over	52	26.3	69	33.2	1.3
Total	85	24.2	112	30.6	1.3

11. Work habits

	NON-DELINQUENTS IN PERIOD I		NON-DELINQUENTS IN PERIOD II		PROPORTIONAL INCREASE IN NON-DELINQUENCY
	Number	Per cent	Number	Per cent	
Good	27	50.9	29	54.7	1.1
Fair	16	20.5	25	32.1	1.6
Poor	20	14.3	32	22.9	1.6
Total	63	23.2	86	31.7	1.4

12. SKILL

	NON-DELINQUENTS IN PERIOD I		NON-DELINQUENTS IN PERIOD II		PROPORTIONAL INCREASE IN NON-DELINQUENCY
	Number	Per cent	Number	Per cent	
Skilled	4	26.7	6	40.0	1.5
Semi-skilled	46	31.1	56	37.8	1.2
Unskilled	37	19.0	53	27.2	1.4
Total	*87*	*24.3*	*115*	*32.1*	*1.3*

13. ECONOMIC RESPONSIBILITY

	NON-DELINQUENTS IN PERIOD I		NON-DELINQUENTS IN PERIOD II		PROPORTIONAL INCREASE IN NON-DELINQUENCY
	Number	Per cent	Number	Per cent	
Meets	25	48.1	28	53.8	1.1
Does not meet	41	17.9	64	27.9	1.6
Total	*66*	*23.5*	*92*	*32.7*	*1.4*

14. FAMILY RELATIONSHIPS

	NON-DELINQUENTS IN PERIOD I		NON-DELINQUENTS IN PERIOD II		PROPORTIONAL INCREASE IN NON-DELINQUENCY
	Number	Per cent	Number	Per cent	
Succeed	29	25.9	45	40.2	1.6
Fail	46	23.2	52	26.3	1.1
Total	*75*	*24.2*	*97*	*31.3*	*1.3*

15. USE OF LEISURE

	NON-DELINQUENTS IN PERIOD I		NON-DELINQUENTS IN PERIOD II		PROPORTIONAL INCREASE IN NON-DELINQUENCY
	Number	Per cent	Number	Per cent	
Harmless	5	45.5	9	81.8	1.8
Harmful	115	33.2	106	30.6	.9
Total	*120*	*33.6*	*115*	*32.2*	*1.0*

16. Church attendance

	NON-DELINQUENTS IN PERIOD I		NON-DELINQUENTS IN PERIOD II		PROPORTIONAL INCREASE IN NON-DELINQUENCY
	Number	Per cent	Number	Per cent	
Regular	7	23.3	13	43.3	1.9
Occasional or none	80	24.8	100	31.1	1.3
Total	*87*	*22.2*	*113*	*32.1*	*1.4*

17. Age at first known delinquency

	NON-DELINQUENTS IN PERIOD I		NON-DELINQUENTS IN PERIOD II		PROPORTIONAL INCREASE IN NON-DELINQUENCY
	Number	Per cent	Number	Per cent	
Under 14	21	14.9	34	24.1	1.6
14 and over	67	30.7	82	37.6	1.2
Total	*88*	*24.5*	*116*	*32.3*	*1.3*

18. Prior arrests

	NON-DELINQUENTS IN PERIOD I		NON-DELINQUENTS IN PERIOD II		PROPORTIONAL INCREASE IN NON-DELINQUENCY
	Number	Per cent	Number	Per cent	
No	19	51.4	23	62.2	1.2
Yes	62	20.3	85	27.8	1.4
Total	*81*	*23.6*	*108*	*31.5*	*1.3*

19. Penal experiences

	NON-DELINQUENTS IN PERIOD I		NON-DELINQUENTS IN PERIOD II		PROPORTIONAL INCREASE IN NON-DELINQUENCY
	Number	Per cent	Number	Per cent	
No	59	39.9	82	55.4	1.4
Yes	25	12.6	61	30.7	2.4
Total	*84*	*21.3*	*143*	*41.2*	*1.9*

20. DELINQUENCY

	NON-DELINQUENTS IN PERIOD I		NON-DELINQUENTS IN PERIOD II		PROPORTIONAL INCREASE IN NON-
	Number	Per cent	Number	Per cent	DELINQUENCY
Non-delinquent	2	50.0	2	50.0	1.0
Minor delinquent	19	33.3	25	43.9	1.3
Serious delinquent	60	21.1	66	23.2	1.1
Total	*81*	*23.4*	*93*	*26.9*	*1.1*

Reformatory History

21. AGE AT TIME OF COMMITMENT TO REFORMATORY

	NON-DELINQUENTS IN PERIOD I		NON-DELINQUENTS IN PERIOD II		PROPORTIONAL INCREASE IN NON-
	Number	Per cent	Number	Per cent	DELINQUENCY
14–17	14	22.2	17	27.0	1.2
18–21	47	25.4	67	36.2	1.4
22–36	27	24.1	32	28.6	1.2
Total	*88*	*24.4*	*116*	*32.2*	*1.3*

22. OFFENSE FOR WHICH COMMITTED TO REFORMATORY

	NON-DELINQUENTS IN PERIOD I		NON-DELINQUENTS IN PERIOD II		PROPORTIONAL INCREASE IN NON-
	Number	Per cent	Number	Per cent	DELINQUENCY
Burglary	26	22.4	32	27.6	1.2
Larceny	37	24.2	52	34.0	1.4
Robbery	6	16.7	11	30.6	1.8
Sex offense	7	28.0	7	28.0	1.0
Total	*76*	*23.0*	*102*	*30.9*	*1.3*

23. Commission of offense* alone or with others

	NON-DELINQUENTS IN PERIOD I		NON-DELINQUENTS IN PERIOD II		PROPORTIONAL INCREASE IN NON-DELINQUENCY
	Number	Per cent	Number	Per cent	
Alone	36	25.5	44	31.0	1.2
With others	52	24.1	70	32.4	1.3
Total	*88*	*24.6*	*114*	*31.8*	*1.3*

24. Physical condition on entrance to reformatory

	NON-DELINQUENTS IN PERIOD I		NON-DELINQUENTS IN PERIOD II		PROPORTIONAL INCREASE IN NON-DELINQUENCY
	Number	Per cent	Number	Per cent	
Good	83	26.0	108	33.9	1.3
Fair	3	12.5	5	20.8	1.7
Poor	0	–	0	–	0
Total	*86*	*24.5*	*113*	*32.2*	*1.3*

25. Kind of worker in reformatory

	NON-DELINQUENTS IN PERIOD I		NON-DELINQUENTS IN PERIOD II		PROPORTIONAL INCREASE IN NON-DELINQUENCY
	Number	Per cent	Number	Per cent	
Good	52	30.4	69	40.4	1.3
Fair or poor	15	22.4	19	28.4	1.3
Total	*67*	*28.2*	*88*	*37.0*	*1.3*

26. Number of occupational experiences in reformatory

	NON-DELINQUENTS IN PERIOD I		NON-DELINQUENTS IN PERIOD II		PROPORTIONAL INCREASE IN NON-DELINQUENCY
	Number	Per cent	Number	Per cent	
One	13	20.3	20	31.3	1.5
Two or three	63	28.1	75	33.5	1.2
Four or more	12	16.9	21	29.6	1.8
Total	*88*	*24.5*	*116*	*32.3*	*1.3*

* This refers to the offense for which man was sent to Reformatory.

27. Conduct in reformatory

	NON-DELINQUENTS IN PERIOD I		NON-DELINQUENTS IN PERIOD II		PROPORTIONAL INCREASE IN NON-DELINQUENCY
	Number	Per cent	Number	Per cent	
Offender	61	20.9	85	29.1	1.4
Non-offender	27	41.5	31	47.7	1.1
Total	88	24.7	116	33.0	1.3

28. Frequency of commission of offenses in reformatory

	NON-DELINQUENTS IN PERIOD I		NON-DELINQUENTS IN PERIOD II		PROPORTIONAL INCREASE IN NON-DELINQUENCY
	Number	Per cent	Number	Per cent	
Very frequent or frequent	32	17.7	49	27.1	1.5
Occasional or none	56	31.6	67	37.9	1.2
Total	88	24.0	116	32.4	1.4

Parole History

29. Supervision during parole

	NON-DELINQUENTS IN PERIOD I		NON-DELINQUENTS IN PERIOD II		PROPORTIONAL INCREASE IN NON-DELINQUENCY
	Number	Per cent	Number	Per cent	
Yes	71	23.9	94	31.6	1.3
No	15	36.6	17	41.4	1.1
Total	86	25.4	111	32.8	1.3

30. Delinquency during parole

	NON-DELINQUENTS IN PERIOD I		NON-DELINQUENTS IN PERIOD II		PROPORTIONAL INCREASE IN NON-DELINQUENCY
	Number	Per cent	Number	Per cent	
Non-delinquent	51	45.9	59	53.2	1.2
Delinquent	30	14.3	45	21.5	1.5
Total	81	25.3	104	32.5	1.3

Follow-up Period—Environmental Factors

31. HOUSEHOLD STABILITY

	NON-DELINQUENTS IN PERIOD I		NON-DELINQUENTS IN PERIOD II		PROPORTIONAL INCREASE IN NON- DELINQUENCY
	Number	Per cent	Number	Per cent	
No change	58	41.7	97	53.9	1.3
Two or more changes	32	14.9	21	10.7	.7
Total	90	25.4	118	35.6	1.4

32. MOBILITY

	NON-DELINQUENTS IN PERIOD I		NON-DELINQUENTS IN PERIOD II		PROPORTIONAL INCREASE IN NON- DELINQUENCY
	Number	Per cent	Number	Per cent	
No mobility	73	42.0	96	50.8	1.2
Mobility	16	7.8	20	12.7	1.6
Total	89	23.5	116	33.4	1.4

33. NEIGHBORHOOD—TYPE

	NON-DELINQUENTS IN PERIOD I		NON-DELINQUENTS IN PERIOD II		PROPORTIONAL INCREASE IN NON- DELINQUENCY
	Number	Per cent	Number	Per cent	
Urban	68	23.4	89	33.2	1.4
Rural	15	57.7	19	57.6	1.0
Urban and rural	6	10.9	5	17.9	1.7
Total	89	23.7	113	34.3	1.4

34. NEIGHBORHOOD INFLUENCES

	NON-DELINQUENTS IN PERIOD I		NON-DELINQUENTS IN PERIOD II		PROPORTIONAL INCREASE IN NON- DELINQUENCY
	Number	Per cent	Number	Per cent	
Good	30	58.8	29	70.9	1.2
Fair	43	29.7	74	48.7	1.6
Poor	8	6.0	5	4.9	.8
Total	81	24.5	108	36.6	1.5

35. Home—physical

	NON-DELINQUENTS IN PERIOD I		NON-DELINQUENTS IN PERIOD II		PROPORTIONAL INCREASE IN NON-DELINQUENCY
	Number	Per cent	Number	Per cent	
Good	51	59.3	69	67.0	1.1
Fair	26	21.1	34	33.0	1.6
Poor	5	4.3	6	6.6	1.5
Total	82	25.2	109	36.7	1.5

Follow-up Period—Family Relationships

36. Marital status at end of period

	NON-DELINQUENTS IN PERIOD I		NON-DELINQUENTS IN PERIOD II		PROPORTIONAL INCREASE IN NON-DELINQUENCY
	Number	Per cent	Number	Per cent	
Single	15	8.6	19	14.8	1.7
Married, living with wife	69	44.2	91	56.5	1.3
Separated or divorced	4	8.0	7	12.5	1.6
Total	88	23.1	117	33.9	1.5

37. Relation to nearest relatives

	NON-DELINQUENTS IN PERIOD I		NON-DELINQUENTS IN PERIOD II		PROPORTIONAL INCREASE IN NON-DELINQUENCY
	Number	Per cent	Number	Per cent	
In touch with—friendly	75	40.0	99	53.8	1.3
In touch when in need	0	–	1	1.4	1.4
Rarely in touch	7	8.8	14	17.3	2.0
Total	82	23.6	114	33.9	1.4

38. Family relationships

	NON-DELINQUENTS IN PERIOD I		NON-DELINQUENTS IN PERIOD II		PROPORTIONAL INCREASE IN NON-DELINQUENCY
	Number	Per cent	Number	Per cent	
Succeed	86	46.2	109	62.6	1.4
Fail	3	1.7	8	4.7	2.8
Total	89	24.7	117	34.0	1.4

Follow-up Period—Economic Responsibility

39. ECONOMIC CONDITION

	NON-DELINQUENTS IN PERIOD I		NON-DELINQUENTS IN PERIOD II		PROPORTIONAL INCREASE IN NON-DELINQUENCY
	Number	Per cent	Number	Per cent	
At least marginal	87	26.4	109	40.3	1.5
Dependent	3	6.5	4	6.8	1.0
Total	90	24.0	113	34.3	1.4

40. DEPENDENTS

	NON-DELINQUENTS IN PERIOD I		NON-DELINQUENTS IN PERIOD II		PROPORTIONAL INCREASE IN NON-DELINQUENCY
	Number	Per cent	Number	Per cent	
No dependents	11	8.7	17	15.7	1.8
Dependents	79	30.6	100	41.7	1.4
Total	90	23.4	117	33.6	1.4

41. DISPOSITION OF EARNINGS

	NON-DELINQUENTS IN PERIOD I		NON-DELINQUENTS IN PERIOD II		PROPORTIONAL INCREASE IN NON-DELINQUENCY
	Number	Per cent	Number	Per cent	
Self mostly	13	6.6	20	11.1	1.7
Wife and/or children, has no dependent parents	65	49.6	89	61.8	1.2
Wife and/or children, and dependent parents	2	33.3	3	50.0	1.5
Dependent parents	7	28.0	4	40.0	1.4
Total	87	24.2	116	34.1	1.3

42. Social Services Rendered

	NON-DELINQUENTS IN PERIOD I		NON-DELINQUENTS IN PERIOD II		PROPORTIONAL INCREASE IN NON-DELINQUENCY
	Number	*Per cent*	*Number*	*Per cent*	
No	78	28.3	83	40.3	1.4
Yes	10	11.4	32	22.7	2.0
Total	*88*	*24.2*	*115*	*33.1*	*1.4*

43. Economic Responsibility

	NON-DELINQUENTS IN PERIOD I		NON-DELINQUENTS IN PERIOD II		PROPORTIONAL INCREASE IN NON-DELINQUENCY
	Number	*Per cent*	*Number*	*Per cent*	
Meets responsibility	84	35.4	105	50.4	1.6
Unable to meet responsibility	2	33.3	7	63.6	1.9
Fails to meet responsibility	4	4.8	5	4.2	.9
Total	*90*	*27.5*	*117*	*38.4*	*1.4*

Follow-up Period—Industrial History

44. Steadiness of Employment

	NON-DELINQUENTS IN PERIOD I		NON-DELINQUENTS IN PERIOD II		PROPORTIONAL INCREASE IN NON-DELINQUENCY
	Number	*Per cent*	*Number*	*Per cent*	
Regular	57	72.2	71	75.5	1.0
Fairly regular	25	21.0	37	32.7	1.6
Irregular	4	2.9	6	5.7	2.0
Total	*86*	*25.5*	*114*	*36.5*	*1.4*

45. Work habits

	NON-DELINQUENTS IN PERIOD I		NON-DELINQUENTS IN PERIOD II		PROPORTIONAL INCREASE IN NON-DELINQUENCY
	Number	Per cent	Number	Per cent	
Good	77	64.2	97	71.3	1.1
Fair	8	7.3	17	15.5	2.1
Poor	2	1.9	1	1.5	.8
Total	87	25.9	115	37.0	1.4

46. Skill

	NON-DELINQUENTS IN PERIOD I		NON-DELINQUENTS IN PERIOD II		PROPORTIONAL INCREASE IN NON-DELINQUENCY
	Number	Per cent	Number	Per cent	
Unskilled	16	11.7	20	16.8	1.4
Semi-skilled	53	29.6	71	42.5	1.4
Skilled	18	51.4	24	66.7	1.3
Total	87	24.8	115	35.7	1.4

47. Used massachusetts reformatory occupation

	NON-DELINQUENTS IN PERIOD I		NON-DELINQUENTS IN PERIOD II		PROPORTIONAL INCREASE IN NON-DELINQUENCY
	Number	Per cent	Number	Per cent	
No	70	23.6	93	33.6	1.4
Yes	15	23.8	21	42.0	1.8
Total	85	23.6	114	34.9	1.5

48. Longest period of time held job

	NON-DELINQUENTS IN PERIOD I		NON-DELINQUENTS IN PERIOD II		PROPORTIONAL INCREASE IN NON-DELINQUENCY
	Number	Per cent	Number	Per cent	
Less than 3 months	4	3.9	4	5.3	1.4
3–24 months	27	22.5	22	29.7	1.3
24 and more months	51	58.6	71	64.5	1.1
Total	82	26.5	97	37.3	1.4

49. Average period of time held job

	NON-DELINQUENTS IN PERIOD I		NON-DELINQUENTS IN PERIOD II		PROPORTIONAL INCREASE IN NON- DELINQUENCY
	Number	*Per cent*	*Number*	*Per cent*	
Less than 3 months	7	5.4	9	9.0	1.7
3–24 months	33	31.1	24	35.8	1.2
24 and more months	38	74.5	58	77.3	1.0
Total	*78*	*27.3*	*91*	*37.6*	*1.4*

50. Highest wage weekly

	NON-DELINQUENTS IN PERIOD I		NON-DELINQUENTS IN PERIOD II		PROPORTIONAL INCREASE IN NON- DELINQUENCY
	Number	*Per cent*	*Number*	*Per cent*	
Less than $25	10	11.6	25	29.1	2.5
$25–$35	31	31.3	31	42.5	1.4
$35 and more	40	42.6	53	51.5	1.2
Total	*81*	*29.0*	*109*	*41.6*	*1.4*

51. Average wage weekly

	NON-DELINQUENTS IN PERIOD I		NON-DELINQUENTS IN PERIOD II		PROPORTIONAL INCREASE IN NON- DELINQUENCY
	Number	*Per cent*	*Number*	*Per cent*	
Less than $25	27	27.3	43	38.1	1.4
$25 and more	50	47.2	56	53.3	1.1
Total	*77*	*37.6*	*99*	*45.2*	*1.2*

52. Usual reason for leaving work

	NON-DELINQUENTS IN PERIOD I		NON-DELINQUENTS IN PERIOD II		PROPORTIONAL INCREASE IN NON- DELINQUENCY
	Number	*Per cent*	*Number*	*Per cent*	
Steady worker, seldom changes	35	68.6	41	75.9	1.1
Not fault of worker, to better self	43	46.7	59	56.2	1.2
Fault of worker	7	4.1	10	7.8	1.9
Total	*85*	*27.2*	*110*	*38.2*	*1.4*

53. ILLEGITIMATE OCCUPATION

	NON-DELINQUENTS IN PERIOD I		NON-DELINQUENTS IN PERIOD II		PROPORTIONAL INCREASE IN NON-DELINQUENCY
	Number	*Per cent*	*Number*	*Per cent*	
None	89	36.0	116	50.2	1.4
Part of time	0	–	0	–	0
Throughout	0	–	0	–	0
Total	*89*	*27.9*	*116*	*38.2*	*1.4*

54. INDUSTRIAL HISTORY

	NON-DELINQUENTS IN PERIOD I		NON-DELINQUENTS IN PERIOD II		PROPORTIONAL INCREASE IN NON-DELINQUENCY
	Number	*Per cent*	*Number*	*Per cent*	
Success	59	76.6	68	82.9	1.1
Partial success	26	21.5	42	33.6	1.6
Failure	2	1.2	4	3.2	2.7
Total	*87*	*24.2*	*114*	*34.3*	*1.4*

Follow-up Period—Leisure and Habits

55. COMPANIONSHIPS

	NON-DELINQUENTS IN PERIOD I		NON-DELINQUENTS IN PERIOD II		PROPORTIONAL INCREASE IN NON-DELINQUENCY
	Number	*Per cent*	*Number*	*Per cent*	
Harmless	84	77.8	107	87.0	1.1
Harmful	2	.9	5	2.4	2.7
Total	*86*	*25.1*	*112*	*33.5*	*1.3*

56. HAUNTS

	NON-DELINQUENTS IN PERIOD I		NON-DELINQUENTS IN PERIOD II		PROPORTIONAL INCREASE IN NON-DELINQUENCY
	Number	*Per cent*	*Number*	*Per cent*	
Harmless	84	77.8	106	85.4	1.1
Harmful	2	.9	5	2.5	2.8
Total	*86*	*25.7*	*111*	*34.5*	*1.3*

57. Educational activities

	NON-DELINQUENTS IN PERIOD I		NON-DELINQUENTS IN PERIOD II		PROPORTIONAL INCREASE IN NON-DELINQUENCY
	Number	Per cent	Number	Per cent	
Yes	10	71.4	12	66.7	.9
No	69	20.5	86	28.8	1.4
Total	79	23.8	98	30.9	1.3

58. Society member

	NON-DELINQUENTS IN PERIOD I		NON-DELINQUENTS IN PERIOD II		PROPORTIONAL INCREASE IN NON-DELINQUENCY
	Number	Per cent	Number	Per cent	
Yes (wholesome)	9	64.3	11	73.3	1.1
Yes (not wholesome)	13	44.8	13	44.8	1.0
No	58	18.9	77	28.3	1.5
Total	80	22.9	101	32.0	1.4

59. Church attendance

	NON-DELINQUENTS IN PERIOD I		NON-DELINQUENTS IN PERIOD II		PROPORTIONAL INCREASE IN NON-DELINQUENCY
	Number	Per cent	Number	Per cent	
Yes	51	31.9	65	45.4	1.4
No	26	21.0	35	26.9	1.3
Total	77	27.1	100	36.6	1.4

60. Leisure and habits

	NON-DELINQUENTS IN PERIOD I		NON-DELINQUENTS IN PERIOD II		PROPORTIONAL INCREASE IN NON-DELINQUENCY
	Number	Per cent	Number	Per cent	
Harmless	84	76.3	108	90.8	1.2
Harmful	2	.8	5	2.2	2.8
Total	86	24.2	113	32.5	1.3

Follow-up Period—Mental Condition

61. Mental condition (disease or distortion)

	NON-DELINQUENTS IN PERIOD I		NON-DELINQUENTS IN PERIOD II		PROPORTIONAL INCREASE IN NON-DELINQUENCY
	Number	Per cent	Number	Per cent	
Mental abnormality	13	6.5	16	8.0	1.2
No mental abnormality	59	55.1	86	78.9	1.4
Total	*72*	*23.5*	*102*	*33.0*	*1.4*

62. Emotional stability

	NON-DELINQUENTS IN PERIOD I		NON-DELINQUENTS IN PERIOD II		PROPORTIONAL INCREASE IN NON-DELINQUENCY
	Number	Per cent	Number	Per cent	
Stable	58	65.9	80	90.9	1.4
Unstable	10	5.4	11	6.0	1.1
Total	*68*	*25.2*	*91*	*33.7*	*1.3*

Follow-up Period—Age

63. Age at beginning of period

	NON-DELINQUENTS IN PERIOD I		NON-DELINQUENTS IN PERIOD II		PROPORTIONAL INCREASE IN NON-DELINQUENCY
	Number	Per cent	Number	Per cent	
Under 21	11	23.4	0	–	0
21–25	40	23.7	12	25.5	1.1
26–30	29	30.2	59	34.9	1.2
31–35	5	14.7	34	34.3	2.3
36–40	3	21.4	8	23.5	1.1
41 and over	0	–	3	21.4	0
Total	*88*	*24.4*	*116*	*32.3*	*1.3*

INDEX

Accumulation of reformed offenders in certain age spans, 104–106

Adolescence, delayed, illustrated by case of Joseph, 145–148

Age of offenders:
at beginning of follow-up periods, 395
at end of second follow-up period, 20, 300
at first arrest, 4, 270
at first break in home, 3, 261
at first heterosexual experience, 264
at first known delinquency, 4, 232, 270, 383
at occurrence of reformation, 105–106
on entering Reformatory, 1, 275, 384
when began to work, 4, 267, 381
when first left home, 4, 232, 263, 381
when left school, 267

Age spans:
related to mental deviation, 127
significance of various, in reformation, 103–106

Aging, or maturation, as basic factor in reform, 103–106
accompaniments of, Chap. X

Alcoholism, chronic, as interference with maturation process, illustrated by case of Henry, 178–183

Aliases, use of, 75, 232, 291, 300, 345, 375

Arrests, 62–66, 241, 269, 271, 287, 288, 319, 321, 325, 326, 340, 368, 383. See also Criminal and delinquent conduct

Associates in crime, 75, 274, 321, 345, 385. See also Gangs

Attitude:
of community, 233, 326
of offender:
toward marital responsibility, 233, 307
toward children, 234, 309
toward investigation, 19, 234, 325
of relatives toward offender, 233, 306
of wives toward marital responsibility, 233, 308

Board of Probation, Massachusetts, 222

Breach with home, cause of first, 4, 263

Broken or inadequate homes, 3, 234, 261

Case analysis and coding, 228–230

Cases illustrating criminal careers, Chap. XIII

Causal relationships, question of, 87, 97

Children, number of:
among offenders, 33, 265, 295, 309, 332, 353
among parental families of offenders, 3, 262
legitimate, 308

Church attendance among offenders, 4, 58–59, 235, 266, 297, 317, 339, 366, 383, 394

Citizenship, 263

Climacterium period of renunciation, 204

Clubs, membership of offenders in, 4, 57–58, 254, 264, 298, 316, 339, 366, 394

Code-table index, 258 et seq.

Coding of cases, 228–230

Coefficient of contingency, significance of, 77

Color of offenders, 263

Community:
length of stay of offenders in, 24–26, 247, 286, 303, 330, 348
size of, in which offenders were resident, 265

Companionships, 4, 235, 264, 298, 317, 338, 365, 385, 393

Comparisons between various periods. See Follow-up periods

Complacent factors, 102

Conditions of parole, violations of, 6–7, 280

Conjugal relations of offenders, 34, 236, 265, 295, 307, 333, 354

Constitutional psychopathic personality:
definition of, 166–177 n
illustrations of, 166–178

Convictions, 9, 66–67, 241, 269, 271, 287, 288, 319, 320, 342, 370. See also Criminal and delinquent conduct

Date Due
